The Burning

Sheridan in the
Shenandoah Valley

John L. Heatwole

Rockbridge Publishing
an imprint of
Howell Press, Inc.
Charlottesville, Virginia

Published by

Rockbridge Publishing
an imprint of
Howell Press, Inc.
1713-2D Allied Street
Charlottesville, VA 22903
Telephone: 804-977-4006
http://www.howellpress.com

A *Katherine Tennery Book*

Cataloging in Publication Information

Heatwole, John L., 1948-
     The burning : Sheridan in the Shenandoah Valley / John L.
Heatwole. — 1st ed.
        p.   cm.
     Includes bibliographical references (p.   ) and index.
     ISBN 1-883522-18-8
     1. Shenandoah Valley Campaign, 1864 (August-November)
  2. Shenandoah Valley Campaign, 1864 (August-November)—Personal
narratives. 3. Sheridan, Philip Henry, 1831-1888. I. Title.
E477.33.H43 1998
979.7'37—dc21
                                 98-27464
                                 CIP

10 9 8 7 6 5 4 3 2 1
First Edition

 PRINTED IN CANADA

Table of Contents

For Miriam and David, my own ones,
and to the memory of Jay Monahan

"There may be lovlier country somewhere—
in the ISLAND VALE of AVALON, at a gamble—
but when the sunlight lies upon it
and the wind puts white clouds racing their shadows
the Shenandoah Valley is as good as anything America can show."
—Bruce Catton, *A Stillness at Appomattox*

INTRODUCTION

There was a chapter in my book *Shenandoah Voices: Folklore, Legends and Traditions of the Valley* that brought into print for the first time some stories of the war passed down through the generations in Valley families from parents, grandparents, or other family members who had experienced them firsthand. For people in the South, and in the Shenandoah Valley of Virginia in particular, "the war" means the American Civil War and no other, even to this day.

In order to corroborate these stories, I researched various records, including published and unpublished family genealogies. In many of the genealogies, which in most cases had been produced for a limited audience of individuals who had descended in the lines of that particular family, I noticed an interesting peculiarity: if there was but one detailed family story included amid the vital statistics, most often it told of the burning of the family farm in the fiery autumn of 1864. Whenever it was possible I interviewed the people who had compiled these family histories and thereby gained access to unpublished and underutilized memoirs, diaries, and letters of the very people who had been caught up in the maelstrom. Many of the stories describe the events in minute detail, their words an indictment or an approbation of those who were sent to perpetrate the deeds.

As more and more material came to light in the course of my research, I became convinced that here was a story that deserved to be told. The events in these stories were an important part of the fabric of the existence of the Shenandoah Valley civilians who suffered through the turmoil of the fall of 1864; their descendants have kept their stories alive—a legacy of the time when a great conflict of armies, governments, and philosophies broke over their ordered lives and changed their perception of the world forever. Ironically, the resentment and bitter feelings expressed were most often directed toward those in command positions, not the enlisted Union men who set the fires and drove off the livestock. Even today the mention of Philip Sheridan and George Armstrong Custer will elicit cold stares of contempt in certain communities.

The days when the spectacle of autumn in the Valley was overshadowed by the destructiveness of man have come to be remembered collectively as 'The Burning,' although at the time the destruction was reported in such a manner that people not directly involved in the event viewed it as a minor episode in the armed confrontations between the forces under Sheridan and the Confederate troops of Gen. Jubal Early. It is interesting to note that published histories of the 1864 Valley Campaign barely mention the destruction that occurred there *between* the battles other than to recount Sheridan's bloodless report in the official records that his forces destroyed "2,000 barns filled with grain and implements, not to mention other outbuildings, 70 mills filled with wheat and flour," and "numerous head of livestock driven off and killed."

In scores of books that contain sections covering the campaign, and even in works devoted solely to it, invariably less than a page is devoted to the Burning. It is as if there was an unconscious effort from the beginning to remove the face of civilian suffering from the picture as a whole. This amazing event has, for the most part, been under-studied by historians. The fact is that Grant's order to cripple the ability of the Shenandoah Valley to supply the Confederate government with the crops and forage it needed to sustain its armies at a critical juncture of the war contributed significantly to the demise of Southern aspirations for an independent country. Further, the civilian population of the Valley was affected to a greater extent than was the populace in any other region during the war, including those in the path of Sherman's infamous march to the sea in Georgia.

Surgeon Alexander Neil of the Twelfth West Virginia Infantry wrote to his parents of the action and its effect: "We are burning and destroying everything in this valley, such as wheat stacks, hay stacks, barns, houses. Indeed, there will be nothing but heaps of ashes and ruins. . . . [The Southerners are] heartily tired of the war and now fully realize that Secession has been a dear thing to them."

• • •

As Jeffry Wert so aptly put it when reflecting on the Burning in his book *From Winchester to Cedar Creek*, "Americans had never before seen such demolition, executed with this skill and thoroughness." Stephen Starr, in his three-volume study *The Union Cavalry in the Civil War*, summed up the Burning perfectly when he wrote, "The deliberate, planned devastation of the Shenandoah Valley has deservedly ranked as one of the grimmest episodes of a sufficiently grim war. Unlike the haphazard destruction caused by [Gen. William T.] Sherman's bummers in Georgia, it was committed systematically, and by order."

The destruction of private dwellings by Union forces in Georgia has been greatly exaggerated. Lee Kennett based *Marching through Georgia* on exhaustive research that made it clear that the main targets of Sherman's columns were the railroads, telegraph lines, cotton gins, and mills. Rarely mentioned is the destruction of barns or farm structures, yet the opportunities were there, as livestock were driven away or destroyed on the spot.

Most reports have not considered that citizens in front of Sherman's advance were urged to destroy all buildings, bridges, roads, and crops that could be of use to the Federals, and that those calling for the destruction were the governor of Georgia, Confederate general P.G.T. Beauregard, and the Georgia delegation in the Confederate Congress. James Bonner's study of the often-told story of the burning of Milledgeville has found that the destruction of private dwellings was "rare indeed, either in the town or along the route of march."

Sherman's own report of the destruction in Georgia points to a concentration on targets other than structures used in the day-to-day business of private farming, which would include occupied homes. From this data it becomes apparent that even though the destruction caused by Sherman's men in Georgia was greater than that in the Shenandoah Valley when compared in dollars, the human impact was much more concentrated—and thus far more intense—in the Valley, which is a contained region with mountain and river boundaries and strong family connections from one end to the other. The trampled civilians caught up in the whirlwind of Sherman's operations, Atlanta aside, were but small knots in long, narrow strings; their memories were, for the most part, singular, not part of the collective consciousness as in the Valley. Sherman cut a path to the sea, moving along railroad lines and concentrating on hard military support targets; Sheridan burned a swath in the Valley that had no peer in any other area of civilian population during the war.

• • •

Some of the oral history passed down by Shenandoah Valley civilians most properly belongs in the realm of folklore because of embellishments that may have been added through the years, yet it is included here because it retains the echoes of the original emotions experienced by those who first related it. I suggest that oral history has its place in this setting, since there are few contemporary or first-person accounts in existence from the civilians who were burned out; their attentions were understandably elsewhere at the time. To rely too heavily on the dusty tomes that have been used traditionally as references for accounts of this campaign would have resulted in another book told mainly from the point of view of the military.

This is not to say that I do not recognize that the action of the military provides the framework upon which the story of the plight of the civilians must be built. To that end I have made an effort to uncover the recollections of the soldiers of this period also. Happily, I was able to locate several unpublished letters and diaries that reflect the thoughts and attitudes of Northern soldiers about one another and the civilians they came into contact with during this phase of the campaign. These sources relate interesting and at times surprising perceptions of what the invaders thought it was all about.

Nevertheless, this is primarily the story of the civilians of every political and ethical stripe who were caught up in some of the most devastating days in American history. Rockingham County has the most complete lists and records of losses suffered by its citizens of the four counties caught up in the Burning, aside from the Southern Claims Commission papers in the National Archives. This is not to say that Augusta, Shenandoah, and Page counties were not acutely aware of the trauma in their jurisdictions. In the aftermath of the Burning, considerations other than record-keeping were more pressing.

The Civil War has rightly been called the defining moment in the life of the nation; the Burning was the defining moment in the life of the Valley.

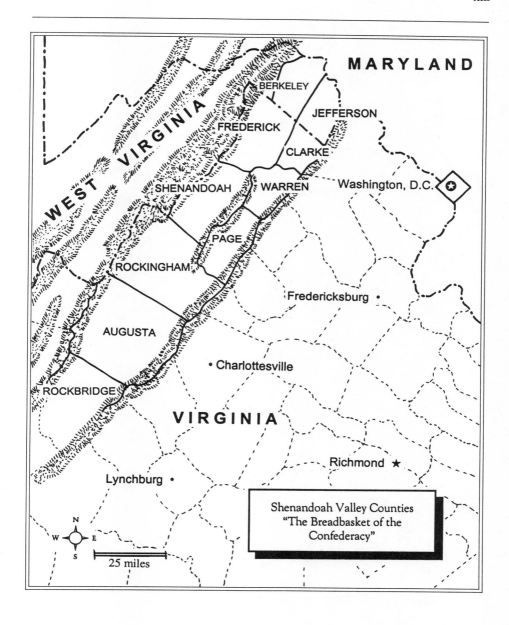

MARYLAND

WEST VIRGINIA

BERKELEY

JEFFERSON

FREDERICK

CLARKE

SHENANDOAH   WARREN

Washington, D.C. ◈

PAGE

ROCKINGHAM

Fredericksburg •

AUGUSTA

• Charlottesville

ROCKBRIDGE

VIRGINIA

Richmond ★

Lynchburg •

N
W ✦ E
S

25 miles

Shenandoah Valley Counties
"The Breadbasket of the
Confederacy"

Chapter One

COMMUNITIES AT THE CROSSROADS

The Shenandoah Valley is the northern portion of the more extensive Great Valley of Virginia. It is bounded on the east by the Blue Ridge Mountains and on the west by the first risings of the Alleghenies, known generally as the Shenandoah Mountains. Its 125-mile length angles northeastward from the northern part of Rockbridge County in the south to the Potomac River in the north. At its widest it is twenty-five miles.

The Upper Valley comprises the southern counties of Shenandoah, Page, Rockingham, and Augusta; the Lower Valley comprises the northern counties of Frederick, Warren, and Clarke in Virginia, plus Jefferson and Berkeley in West Virginia. The twin forks of the Shenandoah River flow generally in a northerly direction, coming together north of Front Royal and flowing as one stream to Harper's Ferry, where its waters enter the Potomac.[1]

Because the river flows northward, a person traveling in that direction is heading downriver and so is said to be going *down* the Valley. Conversely, to go south is said to be going *up* the Valley. This is the traditional and correct way to frame directions in this unique region.

The land comprises every type of terrain imaginable, from lush river bottoms to high, rolling grazing land to rocky wastes and dark, hidden ravines. The mountains, both comforting and brooding, have always given Valley residents a sense of aloofness from regions to the east and west.

---

1.   (Staunton *Spectator*, November 12, 1872)

The Massanutten range, stretching about forty miles from Peaked Mountain in Rockingham County northward to Signal Knob above the town of Strasburg, separates the main valley from the smaller Page Valley to the east; despite its isolation, Page County is a part of the Shenandoah Valley proper.

In 1864 the Shenandoah Valley was already noted far and wide for its vast wheat harvests, with the production of corn and livestock running a close second. Progressive farmers in the first half of the nineteenth century belonged to agricultural societies and subscribed to journals in which the latest methods and theories of farming and husbandry were discussed at length. They tapped into the even greater potential of their holdings with new techniques and equipment. New breeds of livestock were imported; some stockmen were well known beyond Virginia for the successes of their breeding experiments. Orchardists and nurserymen adapted trees and plants to the varied landscapes of the Valley and shipped hardy plants, fruit, and vegetables to distant places.

Virtually every livelihood in the Valley was to one degree or another tied to the amazing productivity of the region. Barrels of flour produced in the multitude of mills along the rivers and streams west of the Blue Ridge had lined the docks of Alexandria and Baltimore before the war. Mechanics in the villages and towns modified reapers, binders, and grain drills acquired from various manufacturers outside of Virginia and invented new equipment to make work in the fields even more efficient. For the most part, even the smallest holdings were productive enough to support their inhabitants and have a little left over for trade. Early on in the war the Valley became known as the Breadbasket of the Confederacy.

The farm-boys-turned-soldier from the North were impressed by what they saw, and many letters home commented on the order and bounty of Valley farms. One infantryman later recalled that "the wheatfields were large, well fenced with rails, and worked with modern machinery. . . . In the rich pasture-fields were large herds of cattle, hogs, and sheep." Col. George Wells, commanding one of Gen. George Crook's Army of West Virginia brigades, called the Shenandoah "the loveliest valley in the world."[2] Even soldiers who had grown up in the Valley were in awe of the richness of their homeland. During the summer of 1864, John Apperson of the Fourth Virginia Infantry wrote in his diary that he thought that year's wheat crop was the finest he had ever seen.[3] It was the very productivity of the Valley that eventually led to its burnt landscape.

2. (Hanaburgh 1894, 132)
3. (Greenwood 1993, 5-7)

Prior to the war very few counties in the Valley relied heavily on slave labor, with the exception of Clarke, Jefferson, and Frederick in the Lower Valley, which were settled by members of the plantation society from tidewater Virginia. Slave populations in the Upper Valley were never high compared to most of the counties east of the Blue Ridge; while Upper Valley counties registered slave numbers at around ten percent of their total populations, most eastern counties counted fifty percent or more.[4] Most Upper and Middle Valley farms relied on family members or the help of a hired man or two to keep things running smoothly; some individuals hired slaves for seasonal labor. At harvest time it was traditional for neighbors to make the rounds from farm to farm to help one another.

The pacifist Mennonites and Dunkards, both of German-Swiss ancestry, were also known as anabaptists because of their belief in adult baptism. They and others strongly opposed to slavery made up a considerable portion of the populations of Rockingham, Shenandoah, and Page counties. They arrived in the Valley in the earliest years of settlement, with a major migration from Pennsylvania occurring after the Revolution.[5] The Dunkards were formally called the German Baptist Brethren. They were nicknamed Dunkers or Dunkards because they practiced total immersion in their baptismal ceremonies. By contrast, the Lutherans and those of German-Swiss ancestry who had joined denominations that were looked upon by anabaptists as being more secular in their dealings with the world felt no reluctance to owning slaves or bearing arms if the situation warranted.[6]

In the prewar militia system, which dated back to before the Revolution, all able-bodied men were carried on county muster rolls and served at the discretion of the governor. They were required to attend periodic meetings to drill and had to be ready to serve at a moment's notice in case of emergency. Non-attendance at the musters resulted in the levy of a small fine that Mennonites and Dunkards were more than willing to pay. Company captains knew that to avoid doing something that was against their churches' teachings, these peace-loving people would always take this path; in fact, they expected them to do so as a matter of course.

When Virginia joined the Confederacy, however, the militia units became the nucleus of the force that the Commonwealth contributed to the cause. The paying of muster fines was not acceptable during this time of first crisis; pacifists

4. (Greenwood 1993, 5-7)
5. (Heatwole 1970, 19)
6. (U. S. Agricultural Report for 1864, 30)

found themselves being marched off to training camps along with everyone else. Those who refused to go, or who tried to escape and were captured, were held under guard while elders of their church and sympathetic friends worked behind the scenes to secure their freedom and safety.

Men like Thomas Jonathan ("Stonewall") Jackson and Virginia House of Delegates member John T. Harris recognized the sincerity and loyalty of the pacifists even if others did not. Jackson offered them noncombatant positions as clerks, cooks, and teamsters, while Harris worked in Richmond to legislate relief. On March 29, 1862, Virginia passed an exemption act stating that anyone who did not wish to serve in the army because of religious convictions could be excused upon the payment of five hundred dollars plus two percent of the assessed value of their property. This applied only to those who could prove membership in one of the pacifist churches prior to the passage of the act. In the fall of 1862 the Confederate Congress passed a similar bill permitting a person to provide a substitute to take his place in lieu of the fee.[7]

Some individuals felt that by paying the fee or by furnishing a substitute they would still be supporting the war and the killing of fellow human beings. Rather than submit to something that they thought morally wrong, these men became fugitives. Young men who had not formally joined a church prior to the exemptions had to go into hiding or try to reach the North, where they could sit out the war. Male members of Mennonite and Dunkard families who reached military age during the war were also at the mercy of the Confederate conscription officers because they could not claim membership in churches they had not been old enough to join before the acts were put into place. They, too, had to flee or keep constant vigil so as not to be taken up by the provost marshal squads.[8]

Of the other ethnic groups who had settled the Upper Valley, the Scots-Irish were the next largest. They were a staunchly independent, high-spirited people who had left Northern Ireland in droves to seek better lives in the New World. Like the English, Germans, and Swiss who had come before, many of them were drawn to the colony of Pennsylvania with its promise of religious freedom. They found that most of the rich farmland in the eastern part of the colony had already been taken up, however, and they were compelled to move westward into more rugged country, where they became a buffer on the frontier between the unpredictable American Indians and the populous eastern counties. Their precarious situation made them self-reliant and inured to hardship, which in

7.   (Horst 1967, 65-70, 80)
8.   (Zigler 1914, 87-88)

turn made them ideal people to settle new lands.

Shortly after the Shenandoah Valley was opened to settlement in the early eighteenth century, some of these hardy pioneers came south to settle in the Upper Valley; some continued farther south into the regions of the Great Valley of Virginia drained by the James, Jackson, and Roanoke rivers. Other Scots-Irish settlers came to the Valley directly from the British Isles at the invitation of land speculators. The speculators earned title to a certain number of acres of land for every family they placed on parcels within the huge royal grants issued to proprietors such as William Beverley and Benjamin Borden.[9]

The sons and daughters of these settlers were instrumental in populating Tennessee, Kentucky, what is now the state of West Virginia, and other new territories. By the time of the war, men born into Valley Scots-Irish communities had already made a significant impact on the nation as a whole. Sam Houston was one of the principal figures responsible for bringing Texas into the Union, and Cyrus McCormick opened the plains to cultivation. The blood of their race was nourished by the produce of Valley fields, well watered by winding rivers shaded by willow and oak and beech. Their neighbors in Rockingham, Shenandoah, and Page were just as deeply touched and formed by their surroundings, and some of them put their ties to the land above all else.[10]

The people of the Valley were well aware of the importance of their area to both belligerent factions. It was a significant supply base and a natural back door for invasions of the North. Ulysses S. Grant, general-in-chief of the armies of the United States, knew he had to close this door firmly in order to empty the Confederate supply lines, weaken Southern resolve, and curtail the interference in military matters of politicians who feared that the Confederates would turn up in Washington itself.

9.   (Waddell 1972, 28-33)
10.   (Tompkins 1952, 64)

Chapter Two

A Change of Seasons

The Shenandoah Valley was the scene of high drama during Stonewall Jackson's campaign in 1862. Jackson's 'foot cavalry' had run rings around several Union forces and made him a legend in both the North and the South. Now Grant was in charge of the federal war effort, and he was determined to keep pressure on the Confederates on all fronts.

Early in May 1864 Union general Franz Sigel was charged with clearing out the Valley, but his efforts proved to be ineffective. Sigel's goal was to reach Staunton in Augusta County and destroy the supply base there, then to move eastward, tearing up the tracks of the Virginia Central Railroad to Charlottesville, and destroy that distribution center. With this accomplished, he was then to come to the aid of the Army of the Potomac as it grappled with Robert E. Lee in the Wilderness and at Spotsylvania Courthouse.

Sigel moved at a snail's pace, however, and events did not go as planned. On May 15 he was defeated by a Confederate force under Maj. Gen. John C. Breckinridge at New Market, and on May 19 he was replaced by Gen. David Hunter, who moved southward with virtually the same orders as his hapless predecessor. Lt. John Rodgers Meigs, the chief engineer officer on Sigel's staff, was retained in that position by Hunter. The lieutenant was vigilant and took note of the road systems, landmarks, river and stream crossings, and general terrain features.

Under Hunter's leadership the forces of the Union penetrated farther into the Valley than ever before, defeating Gen. W. E. Jones's Confederate troops at the battle of Piedmont on June 5 and moving on to Staunton without further opposition. The Northerners finally entered Staunton on June 6. Some of them destroyed government warehouses and supplies while others began tearing up the railroad tracks. The Confederates rallied under the command of Brig. Gen. John C. Vaughan and fortified the mountain gaps above Waynesboro, effectively blocking the Federals from advancing on Charlottesville, so Hunter moved on to another objective: Lynchburg. The town was a major warehouse supply center with railroad and canal distribution capabilities.

On the way to Lynchburg Hunter slowed long enough to wreak havoc in Lexington, the seat of Rockbridge County. His men burned buildings of the Virginia Military Institute and the home of former Virginia governor John Letcher. Lieutenant Meigs, availing himself of the opportunity, helped himself to a fine set of mathematical instruments before the institute's buildings were set ablaze.[1]

Two days of burning and looting in Rockbridge occupied Hunter long enough for Lee to anticipate the Union general's next target and hurry Breckinridge to Lynchburg. Breckinridge, through some energetic and imaginative movements of his small force, gulled Hunter into timidity, delaying his attack until Jubal Early and the Second Corps arrived by train from Richmond. The combined Confederate force drove Hunter across the Great Valley into the mountains of West Virginia.

With Hunter gone from the Valley, Early claimed the open Valley Pike as his high road to Washington. His troops reached Fort Stevens, on the outskirts of Washington City, on July 13, whereupon the Union VI Corps was detached from Grant's army and sent to protect the capital. Grant knew that the Confederate forces could continue to use the Valley to threaten Washington and thus weaken his force contending with Lee. He wired the army's chief of staff Henry Halleck on July 14, stating that a force should be assembled "to eat out Virginia clear and clean . . . so that crows flying over it for the balance of this season will have to carry their provender with them." The very next day he told Halleck that "Hunter . . . should make all of the Valley south of the B&O road a desert as high as possible. I do not mean that houses should be burned, but all provisions and stock should be removed, and the people notified to move out."[2]

After his brush with destiny and the Union VI Corps at Fort Stevens, General Early was closely followed by federal troops as he withdrew to Virginia. On July

1.   (Sheridan 1888, 503)
2.   (OR, Series I, Vol. XLIII, Pt. 2, 366; Pt. 1, 719)

18 he fought a bloody little battle at Cool Spring Farm in Clarke County, where he defeated Gen. George Crook, who was commanding Hunter's much smaller Army of West Virginia, and drove the Federals back to the east side of the Shenandoah River.[3] Another success for Early against forces under Crook's command at the second battle of Kernstown on July 24 caused greater concern and consternation among the federal hierarchy because lines of the Baltimore & Ohio Railroad now seemed to be at the mercy of the Confederates.

That mercy was not on Early's mind at this point in time was demonstrated clearly when he sent Gen. John McCausland's cavalry on a swift and destructive raid into Pennsylvania. McCausland's burning of Chambersburg in retaliation for Hunter's destruction in Lexington brought July to an unsettled and volatile close.

Lt. Gen. Jubal Early. (USAMHI)

Hunter finally arrived back at Harper's Ferry, having followed a circuitous route through West Virginia. He had shown a degree of agressiveness in his first drive into the Shenandoah but had failed to keep Early south of the Potomac.

Upon his return to the Lower Valley he refitted his command, received reinforcements, searched for Early in vain, and began to terrorize the immediate area. The destruction he wrought on the south bank of the Shenandoah seemed to stem more from pique and his own personal need for vengeance than from a rational plan of attack. Near Shepherdstown, West Virginia, he had several private residences burned to the ground, including the home of a distant cousin. Henrietta Lee, another victim of Hunter's wrath, wrote to the general after her home was destroyed: "Your office is not to lead like a brave man and soldier, your men to fight in the ranks of war, but your work has been to separate yourself from all danger, and with your incendiary band steal unawares upon helpless women and children, to insult and destroy."[4] Hunter's own artillery chief, Henry

3.   (Meaney 1980, 42)
4.   (Rable 1989, 170)

Maj. Gen. Philip H. Sheridan.
(*Richard C. Swanson*)

DuPont, wrote that his commander was "dominated by prejudices and antipathies so intense and so violent as to render him at times quite incapable of taking a fair and unbiased view of many military and political situations."[5]

Realizing that changes in the command of the forces in the Valley were imminent, Hunter resigned his command of the Army of West Virginia, and General Crook was named to replace him.

During July and August Early and his men had relieved some of the pressure on Lee at Petersburg and had demonstrated in the North by their burning of Chambersburg that an "eye for an eye" policy was in effect. It was not immediately apparent to the Southerners that Grant's reaction sealed the fate of the Valley and its people and opened the door to some of the most desperate acts of war ever targeted against civilians.[6]

• • •

When Grant was given free rein by the Lincoln administration to conduct the war in the field as he saw fit, few realized that a new and exciting corner had been turned. The game of musical generals, which the Union had been playing with such disasterous results, had ended. Grant understood the strength and depth of the resources of the Northern states and recognized the ability of the population to sustain and replace his losses in both men and matériel as he moved forward with his plan to keep unrelenting pressure on the armies of the Confederacy. To this end, he was committed to keeping all of the forces of the United States active and aggressive.

It was obvious to Grant that Hunter was not the man to keep his plan on track in the Valley. He needed someone who could combine aggressiveness with superb leadership ability. Some months earlier, as the spring campaign of 1864

5.   (DuPont 1925, 37)
6.   (*Battles and Leaders of the Civil War* [1887] 1956, Vol. IV, 522)

progressed, Gen. George Meade, commander of the Army of the Potomac, had spoken to Grant about a personal feud he was having with cavalry leader Gen. Philip Sheridan. Sheridan had complained that if Meade would stop interfering with the cavalry, he could accomplish much more. He even boasted that were he given free rein, he could defeat Gen. J. E. B. ("Jeb") Stuart's vaunted Southern horsemen. "Well," Grant had told Meade, "he generally knows what he's talking about. Let him start right out and do it." Now, three months later, Grant recognized in Sheridan the man who could neutralize the Valley. He knew that Sheridan would fight, and he respected his intelligence and capacity to adapt to unforseen circumstances.

Sheridan had started out in the war as a captain of the Thirteenth United States Infantry and served as quartermaster and commissary officer for his regiment. Before long he was appointed quartermaster for Maj. Gen. Henry Halleck, then the commander of the Department of the Missouri, and held that position during the campaign for Corinth, Mississippi. He was recognized for the efficient performance of his office, but in reality he chafed at staff duty and was remembered as not being very pleasant. In fact, Sheridan seemed to be at odds with almost everyone, including Brig. Gen. Samuel R. Curtis, who commanded in Southwest Missouri. Their run-in stemmed from some shady dealings in the procurement of horses to replace cavalry mounts lost in operations in February of 1862. Men in the quartermaster's unit had stolen animals from local farmers and sold them to the army in order to line their own pockets. Having discovered this practice, Sheridan refused to pay the thieves, declaring that the mounts were captured property and thus not subject to payment. Curtis, not under-standing all that had taken place, ordered Sheridan to release payment for the horses. Sheridan refused to obey the order and responded with some rather hastily chosen words, whereupon he was placed under arrest and sent to St. Louis to face a court-martial. Fortunately for Sheridan, Halleck intervened and ordered him to Tennessee before the court-martial board could be seated.[7]

Sheridan at last obtained his wish for front-line action when he was given command of the Second Michigan Cavalry. Although he exhibited almost immediately a natural talent for leading fighting men, the temperamental colonel, whose first instinct was always to strike, experienced some difficulties as he learned to refine that ability. By the fall of 1863 he had risen to the rank of major general of volunteers and in that capacity commanded the XX Corps of infantry at Chickamauga and Chattanooga.[8]

7.   (Shea and Hess 1992, 276)

Sheridan's obvious confidence in his own abilities, together with his aggressive nature, made him stand out among the commanders in the West. When Grant was elevated to lieutenant general and commander of all Union military forces in March 1864, he named Sheridan to direct the cavalry corps of the Army of the Potomac, making him one of only three combat-tested general officers chosen to accompany Grant to the Eastern theater of the war.

• • •

On Sunday, August 7, 1864, the light was quickly fading in the lobby of a dingy hotel in Harper's Ferry, West Virginia, as a crowd of officers waited to see the new commander of the United States troops in the Shenandoah Valley and West Virginia. From December 1859, when Robert E. Lee, in command of a company of U.S. Marines, captured the abolitionist John Brown and regained control of the U.S. Armory, until this hot day in August five years later, the little town had served as a way station, target, and staging ground in the unfolding drama of the American Civil War. Three-and-a-half years of almost continuous occupation by one side or the other had rendered it a dreary and seemingly godforsaken place. Thousands of troops had denuded the surrounding hills of trees to feed their endless campfires, and the town itself, with most of its shabby buildings commandeered for military use, offered little sense of welcome or security despite its location at the northern end of the verdant Shenandoah Valley. It had come to resemble a medieval seige camp.

Sheridan had arrived by special train from Washington a little earlier in the day. His presence in the Valley, and the orders under which he operated, were a manifestation of Grant's commitment to stopping the enemy in the field. Sheridan understood his mission. He would lose no time in learning the composition of his forces and the disposition of the enemy. It was his need to know the terrain that prompted him to call young Lt. John Meigs to headquarters. Meigs was not nervous as he waited to see the general; he had served almost exclusively as an engineer officer with United States forces west of the Blue Ridge Mountains for the past year. He knew the territory.[9]

8.   (Morris 1992, 86)
9.   (Faust 1986, 485)

Chapter Three

ADVANCE AND RETREAT

When Lt. John Meigs, fair-haired and every inch the image of a hero, was led into Sheridan's presence, he found a stockily built man with a decidedly odd-shaped head and hard, serious eyes. Sheridan was reading orders that were soon to be dispatched, and as he signed them he glanced up at the young officer, taking his measure. Sheridan, at age thirty-three, was eleven years older than Meigs, and their backgrounds could not have been more different. Sheridan was born somewhere along his immigrant parents' route from Ireland to Ohio. Meigs came from a family of prominence—his father was Montgomery C. Meigs, the quartermaster general of the Union army. Sheridan ranked thirty-fourth out of forty-nine in the West Point class of 1853; Meigs ranked first in his class ten years later. Sheridan was known for his volatile temper, Meigs for his self-control and even disposition.[1]

The two pored over maps of the Valley, with Sheridan undoubtedly questioning distances, condition of roads, fords, and bridges, the location of high ground, and the state of crops and forage. As they conferred, it became apparent that the two were opposites in all but one department, the one most important to them as military officers. Both were men of keen intellect who could organize their thoughts quickly when facing difficult situations. Sheridan posed his questions to the younger man and considered the responses, recognizing a strength and energy that he wanted to keep near him in the coming campaign.

1.   (Faust 1986, 485, 679)

Two days later Meigs was assigned as chief engineer with Crook's Army of West Virginia, which would serve as a corps in Sheridan's own Army of the Shenandoah.[2]

Less than a week later, on August 15, as Sheridan pondered how to proceed, he brought Meigs onto his own staff as aide-de-camp. Officially Meigs retained his position with the Army of West Virginia, which made him, at age twenty-two, the chief engineer of all of the forces under Sheridan's direction. From that day on, Meigs was never far from Sheridan's side. Years later, when Sheridan penned his memoirs, he wrote: "I found that, with the aid of Meigs, who was most intelligent in his profession, the region in which I was to operate would soon be well fixed in my mind. Meigs was familiar with every important road and stream, and with all points worthy of note west of the Blue Ridge, and was particularly well equipped with knowledge regarding the Shenandoah Valley."[3]

• • •

Sheridan was a clear-thinking planner as well as an opportunistic combatant. He shared Grant's understanding that the setbacks suffered by the federal forces in the east necessitated a change in the basic rules by which American warfare was waged. It was no longer enough simply to come to grips with the enemy. To bring a satisfactory conclusion before the country lost heart, the institutions that allowed the enemy army to live and move and fight had to be destroyed. This complex change took much planning and preparation, and weeks passed with only a scattering of actions taking place in the Lower Valley after Sheridan's arrival.

While Sheridan made ready to bring Early to battle, the politicians began to second-guess his appointment. When Grant had first proposed Sheridan for the appointment, President Lincoln; Edwin Stanton, the secretary of war; and Henry Halleck, the army's chief of staff (who had been a Sheridan partisan) had been hesitant to endorse the choice, the thinking being that he was too young to exercise such a responsibility.[4] Many were of the opinion that Sheridan was reluctant to engage Early, and the newspapers questioned why he was not moving in force against the Confederates. One writer for the New York *Sun* blamed rising gold prices on Sheridan's perceived inactivity, while others named

2.   (OR, Series I, Vol. XLIII, Pt. 1, 739) Under Sheridan, the Army of West Virginia would be
      known as the VIII Corps.
3.   (Sheridan 1888, Vol. I, 503)
4.   (Wert 1987, 12)

him and his static position as a cause of the general instability of the markets. Such critics did not understand the conditions that Sheridan was facing.[5] To give the Southern commander his due, Early was not acting as if he were outnumbered by a ratio of more than three to one, and his almost constant movement kept his opponent wondering in which neighborhood the gray columns would show up next.

The men in the ranks also waited anxiously for the campaign against Early to gain momentum. One Union cavalryman wrote from an area close to Winchester on August 23, almost a month before the first significant meeting of the two armies: "This is a rich valley we have plenty to eat you need not be disappointed if you do not get letters as oft as comon till this fight is over."[6] Everyone knew a confrontation was inevitable, but the question was: when?

Besides skirmishing with elements of Early's army almost daily in August and on into September, Sheridan had to contend with raids on his camps, supply trains, and lines of communication by irritating, though nonetheless deadly, guerrilla bands.

In mid-August, in direct response to the guerrilla activity and acting on instructions from Grant, Sheridan ordered his cavalry chief, Alfred Torbert, to destroy wheat and hay in Clarke and Frederick counties south of a line running from Millwood to Winchester and Petticoat Gap. A commander of one of Sheridan's cavalry divisions noted on August 20 that "the guerrillas have murdered ten or twelve of our men in this neighborhood already." Torbert and his troops were to seize "all mules, horses, and cattle that may be useful to our army. Loyal citizens can bring in their claims against the Government for this necessary destruction. No houses will be burned, and officers in charge of this delicate, but necessary, duty must inform the people that the object is to make this Valley untenable for the raiding parties of the rebel army." This action was contained and not general, as it was meant to be a warning to the residents not to support or harbor raiders.[7]

Reports regarding Early's strength and dispositions were received frequently, but those based on observations by civilians could not be relied upon without corroborating evidence. The most valuable intelligence was provided by those who risked their life to obtain it. One such informant, a young man from Illinois serving as a secret service scout, arrived at Union headquarters at Charles Town, West Virginia, late one evening. He had ridden among Early's camps disguised

5.   (Hanaburgh 1894, 142-43)
6.   (USAMHI, Martin Papers)
7.   (OR, Series I, Vol. XLIII, Pt. 1, 43, 864)

as a Confederate cavalryman at terrible risk and had discovered that Early expected to receive reinforcements soon. The scout came away with the impression that "as soon as rations could be gotten he [Early] would again appear, as the only hope of dislodging Grant from before Richmond was the fear of losing Washington."[8]

Grant, concerned that the politicians would again cry for troops to be dispatched to protect the capital, met with Sheridan on September 16 at Charles Town. His subordinate was confident in his preparations, and Grant came away satisfied that the hammer was ready to fall on Early.

As he had promised, within days of their meeting Sheridan advanced with almost three corps of infantry and three divisions of cavalry. The season of sparring had come to an end—the time had come to test mettle. On September 19 the opponents fought the ferocious third battle of Winchester. What had looked like anybody's fight early on was decidedly a Union victory by nightfall. While numbers were an important factor, Sheridan pulled a page from Lee's book of tactics and accomplished the unexpected when he sent his cavalry against the wavering Southern infantry, causing the collapse of the Confederate left flank. In the end, although Sheridan sustained the greater number of casualties, he was able to push ahead, having superior numbers and the ability to replace losses—privileges that Early did not enjoy.[9]

When Sheridan entered Winchester, he wrote a brief report to inform Grant of the outcome of his first major clash with Early and issued orders for the troops to be up and moving by 5 A.M. on the 20th. If Early thought to stop and turn to fight, then Sheridan wanted to be on him before he had time to reorganize.

On September 22 Sheridan and Early met outside the town of Strasburg, in the shadow of the northern terminus of the Massanutten range. For the battle of Fisher's Hill Early selected a defensive position on heights that he felt might narrow the odds for his badly bruised troops. Unfortunately his cavalry missed the flanking march by Crook's VIII Corps. Crook came in hard on the Confederate left with little warning and in cooperation with the general Union assault against the front of the battle line. It was more than the Southerners could withstand; the gray units gave way and were soon streaming up the Valley Pike.

Earlier in the day Sheridan had ordered Torbert to move part of the cavalry force around the northern end of the Massanutten and into the Page Valley. From there he was to proceed southward and cross the Massanutten at New

8.   (WLU, Dodge Papers)
9.   (Kennedy 1990, 243-46)

Market Gap to cut off the expected retreat of Early's force in the main Valley. Torbert broke off further action, however, when he met resistance while approaching the gap, and Sheridan's fervent desire to corral the Confederates while they were most vulnerable was not accomplished. From then on Sheridan had little confidence in Torbert.

Brig. Gen. William Averell's cavalry division also failed to meet Sheridan's expectation that it press the Confederate's withdrawal on the Valley Pike from the rear. Before the day ended, Sheridan had removed Averell from command of the Second Division of Cavalry and replaced him with a Welsh-born colonel, William Henry Powell.[10]

The following day, near the town of Front Royal, a contingent of Col. John Singleton Mosby's Confederate partisan rangers, under the command of Capt. Samuel Chapman, attacked what was thought to be a lightly guarded federal supply train. It was, in fact, the rear of Torbert's column, and the rangers soon found themselves embroiled in a fight with Col. Charles Russell Lowell's reserve brigade of Wesley Merritt's First Division. In the confusion that followed, a Union lieutenant was killed. Word spread that he had been shot down after having surrendered. Eight of Mosby's men were captured. Six of them were paraded through the town, and four of them were shot, including a local seventeen-year-old who had borrowed a neighbor's horse and attached himself to the command that morning. The remaining two prisoners were interrogated, but when they refused to give information, they were hanged from a walnut tree in a wagon yard. For the rest of the campaign there would be no quarter asked and none given when federal cavalry and Confederate rangers clashed.[11]

Grant, on receiving word of the victories at Winchester and Fisher's Hill, ordered one-hundred-gun salutes before Richmond and Petersburg with live ammunition to celebrate the occasions. The news of the two victories was gratefully received by the Lincoln administration, which was facing an upcoming election of which the outcome was much in doubt.[12]

Sheridan continued in pursuit of the Confederates. He thought he had delivered a mortal blow, but one way or another he wanted to be sure. Early did his best to regroup his scattered forces and move them quickly to a strong defensive position in Brown's Gap in southeastern Rockingham County. There he could assess his situation, rest his men, and wait for some who had escaped into the mountains to rejoin the command. He also awaited reinforcements,

10. (OR, Series I, Vol. XLIII, Pt. 2, 638)
11. (Wert 1987, 152-53)
12. (Jaquette 1937, 152)

which he expected Lee to send from the army at Petersburg. His twice-beaten force was badly battered and in sore need of help, yet Sheridan had surmised correctly—like a wounded rattlesnake, it could still be deadly.

The Confederate presence in the immediate vicinity of Sheridan's army after the battle of Fisher's Hill comprised understrength elements from John Imboden's, John McCausland's, and Williams C. Wickham's cavalry brigades. Partisan ranger bands operated on all sides of the moving horde. The most effective—and consequently the most vexing—were those led by Mosby and Capt. John Hanson ("Hanse") McNeill. Also active were Maryland partisans under the commands of majors Harry Gilmor and T. Sturgis Davis, and some western Virginians rode with Capt. George Stump, whose company was carried on Imboden's rolls but usually operated in a semi-independent manner. Another group, led by a Missourian, Capt. Charles ("Buck") Woodson, contained men from Missouri, Louisiana, Maryland, Mississippi, the Shenandoah Valley, and one from Indiana. Besides the recognized units, there were also numerous bushwhackers who took advantage of the opportunity to pick off stragglers, men who ventured too far from camp, and lightly defended wagon trains.[13]

The hit-and-run raids became so intense on all sides that Sheridan ordered guerrillas and bushwhackers to be put to death when captured. He also said that anyone in civilian clothes caught with a weapon in his hands was to be shot, thus making no distinction between duly sanctioned Confederate partisans and the freebooting individuals who were not much better than outlaws.[14]

As the Union forces led by cavalry moved up the Valley from Fisher's Hill, they encountered increased sniping from the surrounding woods and hills. Tensions ran high. Near Woodstock, the seat of Shenandoah County, some troopers from Gen. George Custer's Michigan brigade captured a civilian with a rifle in a body of woods. The man was brought before the general, who declared

13.   (Hulvey Collection, Good Letter; *Memorials of Edward Herndon Scott, M.D.*, 11, 18) Charles ("Buck") Woodson is mentioned three times in the ORs, specifically in Series I, Vol. XLIII, Part 1. In these records he is confused with Maj. Blake Woodson, a Virginian and an infantry officer. Charles Woodson was a Missourian active in western Virginia as a leader of mounted rangers under orders from Confederate authorities in Richmond.

14.   (Jones [1944] 1972, 223) The retaliatory measures taken by Mosby later in November, when he had some Union prisoners executed as a warning that he would not tolerate a repeat of the episode at Front Royal, finally ended this policy, at least toward the recognized partisan rangers. Sheridan and the federal high command were forced to reconsider their position when Mosby's action was approved by Lee and Confederate secretary of war James Seddon. It would have been better had both sides been able to come to an agreement to end this mode of vindictive warfare earlier, but the summary executions, exacerbated by anger and fear, continued unofficially on both sides during this period.

him to be a bushwhacker. The unfortunate person was Davy Getz, a 39-year-old man with the mind of a child. He told his captors that he was out hunting squirrels, although it hardly seems credible that his aged parents would have sent him out to hunt with thousands of soldiers moving through the countryside.

When Joseph Heller, an Austrian-born merchant of Woodstock, learned that Custer was going to have a local man shot and found out who it was, he was shocked. Heller sought out the young general and pleaded with him for Getz's life, saying that he was harmless. In fact, Getz had been terrified earlier when it had been suggested by some of the local wits that he enter Confederate service. Getz had a younger brother serving in the Confederate cavalry with Thomas Rosser's command. He may have looked upon this brother as a hero and tried to emulate him with disastrous results.

In any event, Custer would hear none of it. Getz was roped to the back of a wagon and made to march up the Valley with the brigade. That he was not executed on the spot seems to indicate that Custer wanted him to be a warning to all they passed against entertaining similar ideas. According to local legend, Heller and several other elderly men from Woodstock followed the column for a distance and continued to plead with Custer to change his mind. When they realized that their pleas would not be heeded, Heller told Custer: "You will have to sleep in a bloody grave for this."[15]

15. (Wayland 1927, 509-10; 1860 Census Records for Shenandoah County) Wayland incorrectly gives David Getz's age as thirty.

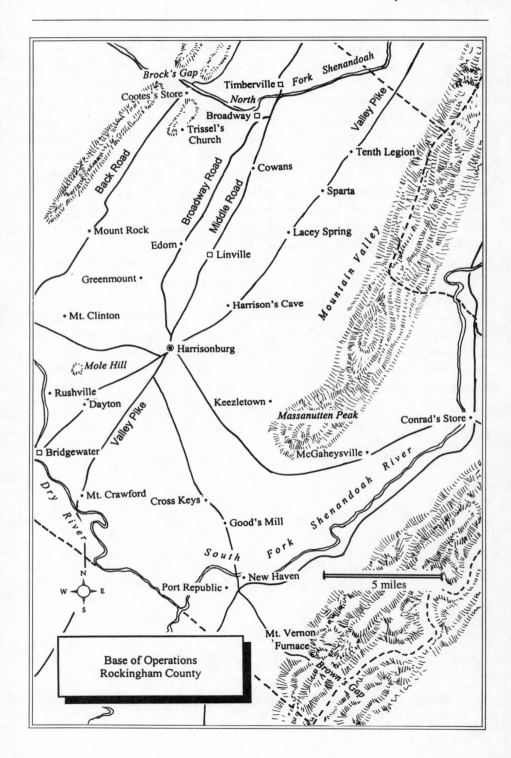

Brock's Gap
Fork Shenandoah
Timberville □
Cootes's Store •
North
Broadway □
• Trissel's
Church
Valley Pike
• Tenth Legion
Back Road
Broadway Road
• Cowans
Middle Road
• Sparta
• Mount Rock
Edom •
□ Linville
• Lacey Spring
Greenmount •
Mountain Valley
• Harrison's Cave
• Mt. Clinton
◉ Harrisonburg
Mole Hill
• Rushville
• Dayton
Keezletown •
Massanutten Peak
Conrad's Store •
Valley Pike
□ Bridgewater
McGaheysville •
Shenandoah River
• Mt. Crawford
Cross Keys •
Dry River
• Good's Mill
South   *Fork*
5 miles
N
W   E
S
Port Republic •
• New Haven
Mt. Vernon
Furnace
Brown's Gap

**Base of Operations
Rockingham County**

Chapter Four

BASE OF OPERATIONS

The citizens of Harrisonburg, the Rockingham County seat, knew what was coming—they saw it on the drawn faces of Early's walking wounded as they shuffled and limped up the Valley Pike, the main street of the town, toward the Confederate hospital on the south side. They were aware of the imminent occupation of their town by Union forces, and they knew that resistance was out of the question.

Without knowing the full impact of what was to come, the residents prepared as best they could. Capt. Abraham S. Byrd, the Confederate provost marshal, saw no reason to sacrifice his small contingent of scouts. He told them to disburse and go to their homes to see to their families' safety. Scout Ben Mowbray hurried to his farm and removed the hay from his barn, hiding it in the attic of his house in an effort to keep it from being hauled off by the federal forage masters. All over town people gathered up personal items and foodstuffs and secreted them between false walls. Others buried money and silverware in their gardens.

In the house known as the Byrd Manse, the family took steps to hide foodstuffs before Union foragers made an appearance. In the attic, the boards above the walls were pried up and the space between the walls was filled with wheat.[1]

On the morning of September 25, the advance cavalry units swept into town. A cavalry band followed and played national airs as it passed through the streets.

---

1. (HRCHS, Stoneleigh House File) Later, when the Northerners left the area, holes were drilled at the base of the walls; most of the grain was retrieved and ground into flour for bread.

Lt. Charles Veil of the First U.S. Cavalry found a relative in the South. (USAMHI)

One Union soldier noticed that the town was full of "sick and wounded Johnnies" who could go no farther. In every town visited by Sheridan's troops as they pursued Early, they found Confederates who had been wounded in the recently concluded battles and others from the second battle of Kernstown back in July. They rounded up the demoralized stragglers and herded them north to prison camps, where most would sit out the rest of the war.

The Hartman family, whose farm was near the north end of Harrisonburg, noted that even before the first federal soldiers were seen, all of the dogs in the neighborhood set to barking.[2] Peter Hartman, the 17-year-old son of the family, reported that after the Union cavalrymen passed, the infantry came in close behind and shot their livestock. "We had thirty fat hogs, and they were all killed," he wrote. They also "shot the chickens and about thirty or forty sheep."[3]

As the First Cavalry Division passed through Harrisonburg on the morning of the 25th, Lt. Charles Veil of the First U.S. Cavalry, who was on the staff of Charles Russell Lowell, the brigade commander, noticed a woman in a doorway waving a handkerchief at the passing federal horsemen. This was unusual, as very seldom had they been accorded anything but hostile stares or insults as they moved through the Southern towns and villages. Most often the streets were nearly deserted and the houses closed tight, as if the residents felt that by taking no public notice of the enemy they might disappear. Many times the only humans to be seen were boys darting between buildings.

On this particular morning, at least for Lieutenant Veil, there were forces at work beyond explanation. As he passed the woman and glanced at her face, he was reminded of his mother. He was carried along with the flow of moving horses and men, yet the woman in the doorway remained in his thoughts. His mother

2.   (*Rockingham Recorder* 1959, 192-94; Morgan and Michaelson 1994, 178)
3.   (HRCHS, Stoneleigh House File; Hartman, 24)

had told him of her only sister, who had married before Veil was born and moved south with her husband. Decades ago the sisters had lost track of one another. Veil began to think it singular that the sight of this woman's face should affect him so, and it nagged at him so strongly that he requested permission to ride back to speak with her. He found her standing in the same place, still waving her handkerchief. He dismounted and walked up to her, begging her pardon for the intrusion. "You look so much like my mother that I could not pass without calling and inquiring," he said. He was about to relate his story when the woman broke in and exclaimed, "You are not Mary's boy, are you?"

The woman was indeed Charles Veil's Aunt Patty. He was persuaded to stay and meet her family. Over a hastily put-together meal he chatted with his aunt and related news of his mother. Eventually, with great reluctance, he had to take his leave and catch up with Lowell's staff, but he carried the memory of the unlikely reunion with him for the rest of his life.[4]

Another resident of the town was also touched by the hand of fate that day in an amazing manner, but the outcome was far less pleasant. Frances Campbell volunteered her free time as a nurse at the Lutheran Church Hospital on North Main Street, and in recent days she had been very busy seeing to the needs of a roomful of wounded Confederates. With the casualties had come word that Early's army had been severely mauled at Winchester and Fisher's Hill and warning that Federals in force would be arriving soon. That morning the Union cavalry had arrived as promised, and that afternoon Campbell stood on the steps of the church watching thousands of infantrymen pass through the town. Suddenly her attention was riveted on a soldier who carried a knapsack that she thought she recognized. She waded into the crowd, pushing her way through until she caught the man by the arm. With a shaking voice she asked him how he had come by the knapsack. His answer was something that she had dreaded to hear—he had taken it from the body of a dead Southern officer.

In this manner she learned that her husband, Charles Campbell, a captain in the Tenth Virginia Infantry, had been killed on September 19 during the third battle of Winchester. She had made the knapsack and most of the things in it when the regiment was formed in 1861. Of all the knapsacks and parcels in a veritable sea of Federals that filled the street, she had somehow spotted the one that had been made with love by her own hands.

The widow Campbell asked the soldier for the return of the knapsack and its contents. He did not object, but in turn asked if he might keep the underwear,

4.   (USAMHI, Veil Memoir)

*1885 photograph of Harrisonburg looking to the west from Red Hill in the vicinity of
Sheridan's headquarters. (USAMHI)*

as winter would be coming on soon. This she allowed. The soldier told her that
her husband had been buried by a whitewashed stone wall and that his name
had been scrawled on it with charcoal, then he took leave of her and went on
his way. Back in the church she opened the knapsack and found among her
husband's effects a shirt she had made for him. It was stained with his blood, but
the discoloration did not obscure his name, company, and regiment where she
had printed it on the waist.[5]

•   •   •

Sheridan established his headquarters in the house of Provost Marshal Byrd
on Red Hill, which was crossed by East Market Street coming out of Harrisonburg. When the first Union cavalrymen had arrived in the vicinity that morning,
they found some abandoned Confederate caissons in the street in front of the
house. These were quickly taken away to a federal artillery park. An open

5.   (Interview: Nellie Cline) The information about the wall enabled the widow to retrieve her
       husband's body later and bring it home for burial.

scaffold made of three poles and standing about fifteen feet high was erected outside and a red-and-blue lantern was suspended from the crossbar. This marked the commanding officer's headquarters so it could be easily located after dark.[6]

Several young local boys went about sizing up everything and storing away what they observed. They saw guards posted and walking back and forth in front of the Byrd home after Sheridan's arrival. One saw a 17-year-old prisoner, Charles Bush, a Southern cavalryman from the county, taken before Sheridan for interrogation. Afterward Bush was sent off to a Northern prison.[7]

As Sheridan settled into headquarters, his infantry camps spread over the hills surrounding the town, from which they made daily forays into the countryside to gather livestock. Some units bivouacked along the Valley Pike for several miles south of town, while others went into camps to the west and south, along the Warm Springs Turnpike. A Vermont soldier wrote to his local newspaper: "We are lying quietly here near the village of Harrisonburg—a pretty place once, containing some fifteen hundred inhabitants, but now, like almost all of these Southern cities and villages, bearing abundant evidence of the paralyzing effect of war. The camps are spread out on both sides of the city, enlarging its borders and making it tenfold more populous for the tented suburbs annexed."[8]

When the Union troops were not contemplating future engagements, they wandered to nearby homes and farms and "requisitioned" whatever tempted their palates. Not far from Sheridan's headquarters on Red Hill was the small holding of a family named Mullins. The Red Hill area had a rough reputation, and Mrs. Mullins fit right in. While she was known for being "the best cook you've ever seen and the best thing with the kids," she was also known to have a temper and would, every once in a while, imbibe rather copious amounts of whiskey. Where her husband was at the time is not known.

Young soldiers overran her place and helped themselves to whatever they liked. This was plain theft, yet they only shoved her aside and laughed at her complaints. With arms loaded, they walked back to camp to enjoy their booty. Mrs. Mullins fumed, but she managed to keep her temper. Even when more soldiers came by and raided her smokehouse, she kept herself in check. But when they put a rope on the family cow and took her with them, Mrs. Mullins had had enough. She went into her house, grabbed her shotgun from its hiding place, loaded it, and with a determined set to her jaw went off to the camps to retrieve

6. (Frank Leslie's Illustrated Newspaper)
7. (HRCHS, Kaylor, 1-2; Armstrong 1989, 127)
8. (Rosenblatt and Rosenblatt 1983, 260-61)

her stolen cow. She spotted it in time to save it from the cooking spit, and as she approached she leveled the shotgun at the thieves.

"You gimme my cow," she demanded, "or I'll kill every one of ya! I gotta have her to feed my children or they'll starve!" It is not known whether the soldiers were moved by her concern for the well-being of the Mullins offspring or the conviction in her voice that she was willing to shed some blood to have her way, but they promptly gave in to her persuasive authority. The Mullins property was carefully avoided from that moment on.

The men of the XIX and VI Corps settled into camps in south central Rockingham County, mostly around the town of Mount Crawford. The houses of the town hugged both sides of the Valley Pike, the western side of the settlement framed by a bend of the North River. To the south and east were small farmsteads scattered among rolling hills.

On the Pifer farm a small girl played under a large walnut tree, heavy with nuts, in a field within sight of an encampment on a nearby hill. Some of the boys in blue decided to have a little fun at the girl's expense by shooting their rifles into the branches high above her, which caused walnuts to rain down on the child's head. No doubt this amused the tormentors greatly, but the girl was furious as she retreated toward home. She met her mother along the way, who could do no more than tell her to stay indoors until the hooligans left the neighborhood.[1]

Back near Harrisonburg, on the outskirts of the southern end of town, hard by the Warm Springs Turnpike, was Kyle's Meadows, the plantation occupied by Captain Byrd's recently widowed daughter, Mary Kyle. She and her 6-year-old brother William, who was then staying with her, were cared for by about a dozen slaves. When Union troops began to set up camps on her property, Mary feared looting and went to her father's home, now Sheridan's headquarters, to request a guard. Sheridan received her cordially—he had met Mary at a dance at West Point in prewar times—and promised her that a guard would be assigned. By the time she returned home, one had taken up his post in the hall.

Like most of her neighbors, the widow Kyle had endeavored to get her livestock out of harm's way and had sent about seventy-five hogs to a wooded area where she thought they would not be found easily. Somehow the soldiers learned of their whereabouts and slaughtered all of them. Only about twenty were cooked on spits and eaten by the troops; the majority had spikes driven

9.   (Interview: Nell Baugher)
10.   (Interview: Gray Pifer)

into their foreheads. For some reason the soldiers thought the spikes tainted the meat and caused it to become unfit for consumption by the enemy.[11]

The guard at the house did his duty and turned out fellow soldiers looking for food or loot. One day during the occupation Mrs. Kyle was in the dining room watching William play when a Union cavalryman burst in, followed closely by the guard. She jumped to her feet and asked him what business he had there. He told her he had been informed by one of the slaves that she was keeping a fine McClellan saddle for her father in an upstairs room, and he had come to get it.

He moved toward the staircase, which was in that room. The guard told him to halt, but the man still moved purposefully toward the stairs. He was called upon to halt a second time, and when his foot touched the first tread, the guard fired. The cavalryman fell backward and died on the spot.[12]

At the Strayer sisters' townhouse on South Main Street, Clara Strayer kept an eye on the occupying forces. She remembered: "We were repeatedly robbed . . . by the Federals during Sheridan's encampment around town. We had to do our cooking after dark, as the smoke from the chimney was an invitation for the enemy to raid our kitchen and larders." The Strayers' house girl, a slave named Fanny, found a way to supplement the family's food supply. When the Federals brought their rations to Fanny and asked her to cook them, she demanded a portion of the food as payment. This they gladly gave her. She also saved the broth from the cooking and carried it to the nearby hospital for the wounded Confederates.[13]

• • •

At his headquarters on Red Hill, Sheridan assessed his position. He thought he had dealt Early's army a crippling blow at Fisher's Hill, but because Early had caused so much consternation in July and August, Sheridan was not ready to count him out completely. He told Grant that he thought the destruction of the bounty of the Shenandoah Valley should be the end of this campaign and that it would be best to withdraw back down the Valley, systematically burning and

11.   (Interview: Paul V. Heatwole)
12.   (HRCHS, Churchman and Kyle's Meadows/Homeland Files) After the war Mary Kyle married the Reverend L. S. Reed and became stepmother to his son, who would grow up to be Walter Reed, M.D. When Lee surrendered at Appomattox, Mary Kyle's father, Capt. Abraham S. Byrd, still had seventy-five cents in U.S. coin; he exchanged it with one of his men for Confederate script, saying, "Ben, while I am blowing up I want to do a good job of it."
13.   (RCLP, Kemper)

gathering livestock as he moved toward Strasburg. Grant would have preferred that Sheridan advance on Charlottesville and Lee's flank, but he deferred to his lieutenant's judgment, telling him only that upon his arrival in Strasburg he would be expected to dispatch part of his army back to the Army of the Potomac.[14]

The operation that Sheridan had in mind required a coordination of far-flung elements of his command. It was imperative that any movements of the enemy be reported as soon as discovered so that appropriate notice could be sent out to the units most likely to be affected. The undulating landscape of the Valley afforded many opportunities for concealed troop movements.

One of his first actions upon arrival in Harrisonburg, most likely at the suggestion of Lieutenant Meigs, was to send his headquarters signal corpsmen with an escort of two companies of the Second West Virginia Cavalry to the peak of Massanutten Mountain, six miles to the east. The signalmen established their station on a spur that had an almost unobstructed view for miles in three directions. From the top of the peak, which they quickly cleared, signal fires were kept burning. Messages were sent by torch signal.

The escorting men, who had to carry water and provisions the two miles to the summit, camped near the base of the mountain. As a reward for their efforts, the signal officers allowed them to look out over the Valley with their "powerful field glasses." The cavalrymen were there for a week and a half and made the most of their stay, helping themselves to sweet potatoes from a nearby patch and exchanging flour with the locals for "butter, eggs and honey," which they could not readily acquire from commissary stores. Some of the veterans were quick to recognize by the way some of their comrades guarded their canteens that they had discovered a source for applejack brandy.[15]

Early sallied out from Brown's Gap several times to contend with the probes of the federal cavalry near Port Republic. His cavalry was small compared with the number of men Sheridan was able to keep in the saddle, so for a time he had to use his infantry to support the Southern horsemen. Sheridan heard rumors of reinforcements being sent to Early, but he was not able to convince himself that the rumors were anything more than mere speculation. Soon the signal station sent word to Sheridan's headquarters that Confederate cavalrymen were passing through eastern Rockingham from Page County to join Early's forces at Brown's Gap. The size of the unit was not ascertained, yet its presence con-

14. (OR, Series I, Vol. XLIII, Pt. 2, 266)
15. (Sutton 1892, 163-64)

firmed—to Sheridan's satisfaction, at least—that the Confederates were not ready to quit the Valley. In fact, Lee had sent Maj. Gen. Joseph Kershaw's infantry division and Fitzhugh Lee's cavalry division, commanded by Thomas Rosser, to Early's support.

In Harrisonburg Union private William Fisk took the measure of the town and its inhabitants. He observed that many of the citizens "are heartily praying for peace, let it come in what way it will. They have tasted the bitter fruit of secession, and have had enough of it. They find that it does not satisfy, that it was a poor remedy for their imaginary grievances. They see the grim determination of the North and they begin to feel that to hold out longer is to fight against inevitable destiny."[16] It is highly doubtful that Private Fisk had his finger on the pulse of the whole community, but the coming firestorm would plant the seed of eventual defeat in the mind of even some of the most steadfast supporters of the Confederacy.

16. (Fisk 1983, 260-62)

Chapter Five

THE FIRE DEMON REIGNS

On August 26, 1864, Grant had set the tenor of the current campaign when he ordered Sheridan to:

> Give the enemy no rest, and if it is possible to follow the Virginia Central [rail]road, follow that far [to Charlottesville]. Do all the damage to railroads and crops you can. Carry off stock of all descriptions, and negroes, so as to prevent further planting. If the war is to last another year, we want the Shenandoah Valley to remain a barren waste.[1]

Sheridan's current instructions from Grant were to press on from his success at Fisher's Hill, push Early's crippled force out of the way, cross the Blue Ridge and destroy the rail center at Charlottesville, then go even farther if he could and wreck the James River Canal at Lynchburg.[2]

Sheridan had dispatched most of his cavalry to the south and east by the end of his second day in Harrisonburg in an effort to determine Early's location and condition. All of the information that had come in so far told him that there were Confederates in a mountain pass east of Port Republic, but there also were rumors that Early had retreated as far as Charlottesville.

1.   (OR, Series 1, Vol. XLIII, Pt. 1, 916)
2.   (Ibid., 202)

Gen. Alfred Torbert, Sheridan's cavalry commander. (Library of Congress)

General Torbert, with James Wilson's Third Division of Cavalry and Lowell's reserve brigade of Merritt's First Division of Cavalry, went up the Valley Pike to Staunton to destroy the supply base there. Torbert's orders from Sheridan were then to move eastward from Staunton, destroying the tracks of the Virginia Central Railroad. Upon his arrival at Waynesboro he was to eliminate a key railroad bridge over the South River and blow up the railroad tunnel that pierced the heart of the mountain. The latter strike was designed to force the Confederates to display what strength they had left in the area. Torbert's force was also to begin the destruction of crops, barns, mills, and businesses that would be of use to the Confederates.[3]

Infantryman John Rowe wrote to his brother from Mount Crawford: "General Sheridan sent the cavalry out 8 miles farther with instructions to burn all barns and mills on their route, which was done."

September 26 presented a fine, clear early fall day, with more leaves still green than had turned. The First New Hampshire Cavalry Band, which served as General Torbert's escort, played the Star Spangled Banner as the troops passed out of Harrisonburg that morning, moving south. On the day before, Pvt. George Sargent, a bugler who described himself as "one of the blowers in the band," had received his first square meal in three days, and it is probable that he was also issued rations at that time for the next day's movement.[4]

With the weather so beautiful and the surroundings equally so, many of the soldiers may have found it difficult to think about the war. A few miles north of Staunton, just before reaching Middle River, Sargent was brought back to reality. There, deep in the enemy's territory, his mount played out and had to be shot. This was an act difficult for a cavalryman in either service, but orders had been given to destroy horses that could not go on so they would not be of

3.   (Elliott Private Collection, Rowe Letter)
4.   (Morgan and Michaelson 1994, 111)

service to the enemy later. Sargent was lucky—a friend had captured another horse on the road that day. He transferred his gear and rode on with the band.[5]

Torbert wanted to get to Staunton as quickly as possible to assess the situation and to dispatch his regiments on their various assignments of destruction. Even so, the need for sustenance got the better of him, and he called a halt at the home of Samuel Cline, which overlooked the Middle River where the pike crossed it. Below the house and within sight of it, Cline's grist mill stood on the river bank.

Cline and his young son Cyrus were out in the yard watching the Union troopers pass when Torbert rode up and asked, "Can you give a hungry man a bite to eat?" Cline invited the general in and said he was willing to feed anyone, no matter the uniform, so long as the food lasted. It was fortunate that Cline felt that way, since the general's hungry staff followed him into the house. Cline's wife and daughters prepared a meal, for which the Northerners were most appreciative. As they took their leave, the staff officers thanked the ladies for the repast. One commented, "We would not mind soldiering if we could get a dinner like that every day." Before making his own exit, Torbert asked for a piece of paper, upon which he wrote, "Mr. Cline's property is to be protected." He signed the slip, gave it to his host, and rejoined his men moving up the pike.

From a hill to the rear of their house, Cline and his family watched as the smoke from burning barns and mills began to rise in the surrounding area. In the late afternoon another detachment of Union cavalry reined up in front of their home. Cline, with little Cyrus still trailing behind him, asked the officer in charge, "Why [are you] burning up our property in this manner?" The officer replied, "You rebels burnt Chambersburg." He ordered his men to apply the torch to Mr. Cline's mill, and they started off immediately. Cline protested that he had a written protection for his property. He pulled Torbert's safety order from his pocket and handed it up to the officer. Upon reading it, the officer told an orderly to "go over there—don't let them burn that mill."

The officer, having satisfied himself that Cline's property was not to be interfered with, then turned his attention to a farm on the south bank of the river. He ordered his men to cross and burn the substantial barn there. Cline spoke up again, saying, "I would not burn that barn if I were in your place. The owner's not there. He's in the brush with his negroes and horses. He's a non-combatant, taking no part in this fight. Two lone women are there and you'll scare them to death. For mercy's sake, don't do it." In defiance of all logic,

5.   (Ibid.)

Cline's words somehow reached the officer, who ordered his men to fall in. They rode off, leaving the neighbor's property unmolested.[6]

At the approach of Torbert's cavalry, many citizens fled. A newspaper story based on word "from reliable citizens of Staunton . . . [reported] that a small body of Sheridan's cavalry entered the town at 6 o'clock on Monday evening. There was a mighty stampede, and the roads from Waynesboro, and even further east, were crowded with men, women, carts and ambulances, carriages and buggies, horses and mules, niggers and beeves, all fleeing from the wrath of the invader."[7]

Sargent described Staunton as "a large and handsome town containing many large, pretty, and substantial public buildings such as the Deaf and Dumb and Insane asylums, young ladies seminary, etc. It is a kind of headquarters or base of supplies for the Reb army operating in the Valley." A government bakery was operating full blast, and the aroma of baking bread must have attracted hungry Federals like flies. As the bread came out of the ovens it was immediately consumed; those who got none demanded that more be made. Sargent's description of the scene is colorful:

The Knights of the Dough looked on with open mouths, considering whether it was best to remonstrate or not. No doubt they had worked hard for it and kneaded it much for their army, but we considered it as one of the trophies of war and confiscated it as such.[8]

The next day, the 27th, Sargent witnessed the raid on the Confederate government warehouses and the loading of the cavalry's supply wagons. His account of what was destroyed also takes in what was happening on the road and railroad leading east, toward Waynesboro.

Millions-worth of property was destroyed—arms, ammunition, clothing, rations, saddles, horse equipage, and government goods of every description; the railroad was torn up, sleepers burnt, rails twisted, bridges burnt, telegraph wires cut, and poles chopped down. The fire demon reigned supreme during the rest of the day.[9]

6.   (Paul Kline 1971, 9; Fechtmann Private Collection, Cline Memoir) To this day in the
       Shenandoah Valley the noon meal is called dinner.
7.   (Richmond *Dispatch*, September 29, 1864)
8.   (Morgan and Michaelson 1994, 178-79)
9.   (Ibid.)

It was reported that a large number of wounded and convalescent prisoners were captured along with quantities of rebel hard bread and flour, wall tents, and tobacco. The soldiers were allowed to take anything that was left. Goods not carried away were piled up and burned.[10] Local slaves were rounded up. Maj. Jedediah Hotchkiss, who had been Stonewall Jackson's topographical engineer in the 1862 Valley Campaign, now served General Early in the same capacity. He noted that "the northerners impressed all negro men into their service, and took them down the railroad to destroy the track and bridges. The colored people were very indignant, and did much less damage to the railroad than they could have done."[11] Perhaps they held back because they realized from past experience that once the men in blue were gone, they would be put to work rebuilding the tracks by the Confederates.

Lt. Charles Veil, with a portion of the First U.S. Cavalry, was sent out along the railroad with orders to push on to Waynesboro. Some units were to tear up track, while Veil's men, and other units like his, were to concentrate on specific targets. Veil later recalled that "during the forenoon I had instructions to destroy a large tannery and contents of a flour mill in town. The mill had probably five hundred barrels of flour and, after the command had all they could use and I had distributed all the negroes could carry away, I had the balance rolled out and the heads of the barrels knocked in, and scattered over the ground." He had just seen the task completed when Southern horsemen came riding down on them from out of the foothills in enough force to drive them out of town, "faster than we had come."[12]

Lieutenant Veil was called upon to exercise his staff duties while in Waynesboro, and in that role he ordered a regiment of the reserve brigade to scout ahead for signs of the enemy. As Veil retreated from Waynesboro he met General Torbert in the road.

Custer, temporarily in command of the Second Cavalry Division, was about ten miles north, near the hamlet of Piedmont. He had sent word that he thought Early was about to try to cut Torbert off from the main army at Harrisonburg. Based on this information, which proved to be true, Torbert asked Veil if the other regiment had been called in. When the lieutenant answered that it had not, Torbert told him to "go out yourself and find the regiment. If you cannot get back here, cut across to the Staunton Road. I'm going back by that."[13]

10.   (OR, Series I, Vol. XLIII, Pt. 1, 99)
11.   (WPL, Hotchkiss)
12.   (USAMHI, Veil Memoir)
13.   (OR, Series I, Vol. XLIII, Pt.1, 429)

Torbert turned the rest of his force toward the west, slowing only to destroy some crops and barns as he raced to the pike. A local man noted in his journal, "this afternoon the Yankees burned all the hay near the C[entral] R[ail] Road."[14]

Veil backtracked with two orderlies, but it was not long before they ran almost headlong into a force of Confederate cavalry. Shots were fired as they turned and spurred away, and the orderlies were never seen again. Veil, however, soon came upon the regiment they had been seeking. They had thrown out a skirmish line when they heard the firing. Under cover of the timber and darkness, the regiment managed to get back to the main force.[15]

Veil's opponents that day had been Wickham's cavalry brigade, sent forward by Early under the command of Col. Thomas Munford, along with artillery, to counter federal designs on the railroad tunnel and bridge. Trooper Beverly Whittle of the Second Virginia Cavalry wrote to his sister a few days later, "Started from Brown's Gap through the mountains . . . to the tunnel at Rockfish Gap & surprised two divisions of Yankee cavalry, who were after blowing up the tunnel. We charged and routed them & ran them ten miles when night came on & we stopped. . . . All will be right yet, although things look dark now."[16] The Richmond *Examiner* of October 5 reported that "there was a fight between the Mountain Top and Waynesboro on Wednesday, in which our cavalry whipped the enemy's cavalry and drove them several miles through Waynes-boro."

The bridge over the South River was an iron one, and Union troopers had been in the act of dismantling it piece by piece when Munford's men charged. Without the right tools, they had done only minimal damage before having to retire under fire. Even as the federal horsemen fled, Confederate engineers were at work repairing the span. Nevertheless, Sheridan, with only sketchy informa-tion, reported to Grant on September 29 that his cavalry had destroyed the iron bridge over the South Branch of the Shenandoah [South River], seven miles of track, the depot buildings, a government tannery, and a large amount of leather, flour, and stores in the vicinity of Waynesboro. Unfortunately for the Confed-erates, most of what he reported was all too accurate. From that point onward, there would be little need for the bridge, as there would be no significant amount of grain left in the Valley in need of transport to Lee's beleaguered army. Sheridan ended his report by vowing, "I will go on and clean out the Valley."[17]

14.   (Hildebrand 1996, 52)
15.   (USAMHI, Veil Memoir)
16.   (UVAL, Whittle Papers)
17.   (OR, Series I, Vol. XLIII, Pt.1, 29)

To that end, burning parties were made up and set about their grim task. The leader of each detail was issued a whistle with which to call in his men when it was time to move on to the next farm. The shrill sound of the whistles would be heard far too often in the coming days.

As the Northern horsemen moved out across Augusta County, the warm weather began to change with the falling of a light, cool rain that must have brought dread to the civilians in the area.[18] Those living along South River had seen Early's veterans limping into the defensive works in Brown's Gap a few days earlier; they did not look as if they had much fight left in them. Guards had been posted at the river crossings along the South Fork of the Shenandoah and on South River to watch for the Federals, but they could be driven away easily. There had been a few sharp actions after Fisher's Hill, but now, west of South River, it looked as if the only enemy the Federals had to contend with were some partisan rangers and a few bushwhackers, although, aside from Hanse McNeill's rangers, none were very active at this time.

Torbert ordered his men to move fast, destroy everything that could be of use to the enemy, then move on quickly to new targets. They were instructed to spare empty barns, outbuildings, and mills, and to refrain from looting. The farms of widows were to be left strictly alone. While the majority of officers and enlisted men tried to follow the orders to the letter, some broke away from any ethical or moral grounding they may have once possessed.

Farmers living east of South River, in the area just north of Waynesboro, suspected trouble beyond the usual fighting when they saw columns of smoke rising from the town and along the path of the railroad toward Staunton. Each feared it was only a matter of time before his own farm would become a target. As soon as word reached them that Union troopers had entered Waynesboro, they loaded valuables on wagons and in buggies started off into the mountains on a seldom used road, which they hoped would be overlooked by the raiding parties. Their goal was to get beyond Early's lines before federal horsemen could pick up their trail.

Thirteen-year-old William Patrick had assumed the responsibilities of man of the family when his father, Maj. William Patrick Sr., was killed in 1862 at the second battle of Manassas, and tremendous responsibilities they were. The Patrick holdings along South River were extensive; the major had left his family very well off with the farming and milling interests he had developed over the

18.   (Hildebrand 1996, 52)

years. Undoubtedly young William would have traded it all away to have his
father at his side once again, but with the help of his mother, Hettie, and his
two younger sisters, he loaded a farm wagon with valuables that probably
included silver, family papers, heirlooms, hard cash, and maybe a few hams.

He made his way up over the hill from the river and joined the line of wagons
as it wound onto the shelf land and into the foothills. The train had hardly
reached the hard pull when William felt something shift unnaturally under the
wagon. A few more yards and a sickening splintering sound reached his ears—a
wheel had come apart, crippling the wagon. He had neither an extra wheel nor
the tools to change it if he had. None of his neighbors were willing to help; they
imagined the enemy horsemen galloping into their rear. The only aid he received
was a hand in getting his wagon off to the side of the road so that the conveyances
behind could pass on toward the gap.

Soon he was alone, and the realization of his failure to get his family's goods
to safety crashed in on him. Expecting blue marauders to swoop down on him
at any moment, he sat beside the path and cried. The youth's luck was proven,
however, when a mile or two farther up the road a squad of Union cavalrymen
cut off those who had left him behind and captured every wagon but his.[19]

A little farther west, across South River and near the hamlet of Hermitage,
the Weade family farmed a large tract that was planted mostly in wheat and
corn. They must have heard that a raiding party in their area was burning houses
as well as barns and mills, as they hastily moved furniture and other valuables
out of their home and hid them in a field of standing corn. As the Weades had
feared, their house was burned to the ground, although the barn and slave
quarters were spared.[20]

A few miles west of the Weade property, along a stream known as Meadow
Run, was Long Meadows, the home of David and Susan Coiner. Coiner, a
Confederate soldier, had been captured and sent to the prisoner-of-war camp
at Point Lookout, Maryland. His wife was on the farm with their two small sons,
an infant daughter, and her younger sister, Rebecca, who was visiting from her
boarding school in Staunton. In 1860 there had been eight slaves at Long
Meadows; by the fall of 1864 all but two had left. Both the large barn and the
granary were full from a successful harvest just gathered in.

On the 27th, as evening drew on, the sisters stood on the portico watching
the smoke rise from their neighbors' farms. They counted at least seven barn

19.   (Interview: Dr. James Patrick; 1860 Census for Augusta County, Virginia)
20.   (Interview: Louis Wood)

fires brightening the darkening sky to the east, and with mounting fear they expected it would soon be their turn. Mrs. Coiner's thoughts turned to the fine flock of sheep, her husband's pride. The flock was lodged in the barn, which was down the lane, near where it entered the public road. "Beck, we must go and let the sheep out of the barn, as ours may be next," she said. Rebecca cautioned that there might already be men skulking around the barn that they could not see because of night falling and said she thought they should look to securing the house. Her elder sister was not to be dissuaded. "Come on, Beck," she said. "The Lord will take care of us." Rebecca replied, "You go on, Sue. I'll watch for you. And besides, He will find it easier to take care of one than two."

The next day Union cavalrymen came pounding up the lane, an officer in the lead. Mrs. Coiner had prepared for this moment. Whenever she sold anything during the war she tried to get payment in coin, which she hoarded with the realization that if the Confederacy were to fail, its paper money would be worthless. Her nest egg was well hidden in a small chamois-skin bag that hung on a nail under a floorboard in the attic, yet she was ready to part with it if its loss would keep the farm buildings intact.

Despite her resolve, and much to her relief, it soon became apparent that this group was more interested in food and forage than in burning barns. The officer told his men to look for fodder for the mounts but not to break any locks while doing so. It seemed as if he would not condone looting, but he did demand food and entered the house to find it. The sisters followed him inside. A mulatto slave boy named June burst into the room and exclaimed to his mistress that some of the soldiers had broken the lock on the springhouse door. The officer headed there immediately, with the sisters and June close on his heels. There they found the troopers drinking milk directly from the large stoneware crocks. The officer was enraged that his orders had been disobeyed and had the rest of the milk poured out on the ground.

As the men mounted up, the officer noticed a riding mare grazing in a nearby paddock with her colt. He ordered the mare bridled, and as she was led away the colt naturally followed. Mrs. Coiner begged that the colt be left behind as it was too young to be of any use to them. The officer seemed to listen, yet in the next moment he coldly ordered one of his men to shoot it. The trooper did so without hesitation as the sisters and the slave watched in horror. The detachment rode away as the three standing over the body of the slain colt huddled together and wept.[21]

---

21. (Culpepper 1982, 304-6; 1860 Augusta County Slave Schedules)

Even farther down Meadow Run some of the parties came into an area where a group of prosperous Dunkards had settled among the Scots-Irish and established a small community of neat farms centered around their own mill, which the Federals promptly burned.[22]

As night began to fall on the 28th, some of Torbert's force drew together near the Valley Pike and went into bivouac on the farm of the widow Mary Shover, who, with her daughter Sarah, lived in a small frame house with a one-story porch and two brick chimneys. It was a modest, yet comfortable, home. After the soldiers pitched their camp in a nearby woods, some of them came down to the house and either demanded food or simply helped themselves to whatever they could find. Whatever the case, Mrs. Shover found them a nuisance and trudged up through the woods to the camp. There she located the commanding officer, made a complaint against his men, and asked for protection. Remembering the orders concerning the farms of widowed women, and realizing she was at their mercy, he detailed three men to guard her property and person.

The next morning, as his men broke camp and saddled their horses, the officer rode down to the farm to make sure that his orders had been followed. Being satisfied with what he found there, he was observed by mother and daughter as he helped himself to a drink of milk from the springhouse. He then remounted his horse and rode off to lead his men toward their assigned camps near Bridgewater.[23]

All of the Third Division Cavalry units crossed the Valley Pike north of Staunton on the evening of the 28th or on the morning of the 29th and turned to the northwest. They hoped to reach their strong bivouac positions before having any more contact with Confederate cavalry, which had proven to be extremely determined in the actions near Waynesboro.

The country the Northern horsemen traversed was broken, with numerous meandering streams winding through dark ravines and around thickly wooded hills. Here and there they encountered broad stretches of bottomland that opened to reveal prosperous farms tended by the descendants of Scots-Irish pioneers.[24] Their orders were to move in haste and pick up livestock along their lines of march, but the people of this region had been alerted. Horses, cattle, and sheep, along with those hogs that could be driven, had been removed to hidden places into which Union boys would be wary of venturing.

22.   (Kauffman 1940, 657)
23.   (VSL, WPA Inventories, Augusta and Bath Counties)
24.   (Hotchkiss and Waddell 1885, 65)

Close by the Greenville road, three miles west of the Valley Pike on a tributary of Bell Creek, was the rich Old Burnt Cabin Farm of Alexander Anderson and his family. Anderson, who was close to sixty, was away with the county reserves in the Blue Ridge. In the first months of the war his three eldest sons had enlisted in Confederate cavalry units; by 1864 two were in the ground.[25] It fell to his wife Sarah, age fifty, who was described by family members as a small woman with immense character and will, to stand to the coming emergency. She had sent 13-year-old James away with the horses, yet for some reason had left her own riding mare hitched to a fence post by the house.

When a Yankee captain and several cavalrymen rode into the Anderson yard, the feisty lady of the house faced them defiantly, her hands clasped behind her and concealed by a fold of her dress. The officer looked around suspiciously and asked the whereabouts of her menfolk. Looking directly into his eyes, she snapped back, "Off fighting you all."

The captain turned his attention to a small structure to one side of the main house that looked to be closed up tight. "What's in the cabin over there?" he asked. "Why don't you go see?" she challenged. The cabin contained only bacon, hams, and other cured meat, but her response had planted a seed of doubt in the young officer's mind. He decided prudence was the better part of valor, no doubt fearing that the building harbored death for his small group.

The captain ordered his men to move along and directed one to bring Mrs. Anderson's mare. The enlisted man leaned from his saddle and unhitched the reins from the post, but as he turned away with the mare in tow, her owner sprang forward. Her sudden movement and the sight of the big butcher knife that appeared from the folds of her skirt must have startled the horsemen. With the smooth flash of the blade she slashed the reins, and the animal ran free.

When the captain recovered from his surprise at the onslaught, he laughed. "Let her have her horse if she's got that much spunk," he declared. With that they rode away, leaving Mrs. Anderson in full possession of the Old Burnt Cabin Farm, its only casualty a length of leather.[26]

On September 29 Major Hotchkiss of Early's staff noted in his journal that part of the Union cavalry force "had cut across country from the pike toward Mossy Creek and Bridgewater," and that "they made the night light with burning barns, hay stacks, etc." The next day he noted, "the Yankees went to Bridgewater yesterday and a great deal of burning was going on to-night toward Rocking-

25.   (Driver 1988, 97)
26.   (Interview: Kathleen Roller)

ham."[27] At the same time a Union infantryman in a camp near Dayton wrote in his diary, "This evening there was a great light toward Staunton."[28]

The wake of burning that Hotchkiss witnessed on the 29th was the passage of James H. Wilson's Third Cavalry Division. They also destroyed a mill and some of the buildings at the Mossy Creek Iron Works before moving on down the Warm Springs Turnpike, all the while burning barns as they went.

Just short of their destination they came to the Miller family farm with its large, well-kept barn. The Millers, having seen the shafts of smoke coming their way, had gathered in all of the horses, put them in their stalls, closed the great door, and locked it. When the Northerners found the iron lock too stout to force, they called for the key. They could hear the animals inside nickering to their own mounts, and they were anxious to take them away. When told the key was lost and could not be found, the cavalrymen could not bring themselves to sacrifice the horses. The Millers' gamble had been a risky one, but it had paid off. The Federals left, sparing the barn and its living contents.[29]

Torbert reported that the damage he had done in Augusta County amounted to $3,270,650.00.[30]

27.   (McDonald 1973, 234)
28.   (Wildes 1884, 188-89)
29.   (Hess 1976, 302-3)
30.   (Staunton *Spectator*, November 5, 1872)

Chapter Six

"MY SOUL FILLED WITH HORROR"

With General Torbert in Augusta County and out of close communication with the rest of his corps, Brig. Gen. Wesley Merritt was the senior cavalry officer in Rockingham County, in charge of the horsemen in his own First Cavalry Division and General Custer's temporary command, the Second Division. General Merritt maneuvered his own two brigades in the Cross Keys and Port Republic areas during the last week in September. Virtually every day one unit or another under his command was involved in some sharp action with the Confederates.

Cpl. Augustus Hanly of Battery K, First U.S. Artillery, was attached to the First Cavalry Division. He kept a daily diary of his movements and contacts with enemy soldiers and civilians, noting that on September 27 they had "attacked Rebels again at Port Republic" and fallen back toward Harrisonburg, abandoning some of their supply wagons to Early's men. The next day, somewhere between Port Republic and Harrisonburg, Hanly and his companions satisfied a basic need when they "killed a pig and boiled it" to supplement their rations.

On September 28, General Custer took part of the Second Division cavalrymen and moved south from Port Republic to the village of New Hope in Augusta County before turning toward Mount Crawford. The men of his brigades fanned out across the land as they burned barns, mills, and standing crops and drove off as much livestock as they could manage.

On the 29th artilleryman Hanly was again on the move as his unit retraced their steps toward the Blue Ridge. Things were gearing up as the soldiers moved through Port Republic and "burned part of the town." Leaving the Second Division in the area to continue the work of destruction, the First Division brigades and batteries turned again toward the west and Harrisonburg and carried out orders to "burn everything that was [of] use to the Rebels . . . [then] fell back . . . through Mount Crawford."[1]

• • •

Cornelius Shaver's home place, near the village of Piedmont, had served as General Hunter's headquarters during the battle fought there on June 5. When the armies moved away after that signal Union victory, the countryside was littered with debris from the conflict. Shaver had gathered a wagonload of discarded military equipment from the house yard and dumped it in a nearby swamp. His young sons, George, age ten, and John, age six, had gathered their own cache of relics as their father strove to get the farm back into production after the traumatic interruption to their daily lives.

The boys pulled their little wagon out into the fields to harvest remnants of the battle, which included several unexploded artillery shells. Using a broken sword, they unscrewed the fuses and emptied the black powder into small sacks. They did not know exactly what they might do with the powder, but they thought to put it safely away until a need arose.

Their barn, like most in the Valley, had an earthen ramp that led to the upper floor, where the hay, grain, and farming implements were stored; the animals were kept on the ground floor. To prevent the wooden wall of the lower portion of the barn from rotting from contact with the damp earth of the ramp, a narrow walkway faced with stone was left between the ramp and the barn wall; a short wooden bridge connected the ramp to the upper floor of the barn. The boys found some loose stones in the ramp's retaining wall and hollowed out a space behind them. Into this chamber they loosely packed their sacks of powder and then replaced the stones.

Four months later a squad of Union cavalry clattered up the Shaver's lane. Thomas Hoy's mill over by the river was already engulfed in flames, and one of the Shaver girls counted at least a dozen ropey columns of smoke rising in the immediate neighborhood.

The cavalrymen set their fires in and around the Shaver's barn, with its full complement of hay and grain, and then watched to make sure that it caught

1.   (USAMHI, Hanly Diary)

well and was not interfered with. When part of the fire reached the boys' hoard of black powder, there occurred an "awesome bang" that startled the horsemen, who jumped to their saddles and "took off" running over the hill and out of sight. The destruction from the blast was minimal as the powder had not been packed tightly, but the explosion and subsequent retreat of the Northerners gave the Shavers time to enter the structure and remove wheat by the bushelful before the building was totally consumed. They ran the wheat to the house, where they dumped it in the parlor, and in this way saved enough of the grain to survive the coming winter.[2]

Gen. George Custer. (Library of Congress)

The next day Custer was ordered to move his troops quickly—first to Mount Crawford, then back into Augusta County as far south as Mount Sidney and Fort Defiance. Once he reached those areas, he was to turn around, throw out his forces on either side of the pike, and move northward, burning as he came. The troopers entered the pike near the village of Mount Crawford, passed through the infantry camps in a light drizzling rain with something colder behind it, and reached Fort Defiance after a hard ride of twelve miles. There they faced about and began their work.

A trooper in the Twenty-second Pennsylvania Cavalry wrote in his diary of this mission: "coming back burned all barns of grain and all hay, and drove in stock. It was an unpleasant duty, but we had to obey orders. The scheme is to consume all forage and subsistance in the Valley to cut off the Rebel supplies and thus prevent their coming down again."[3]

William Beach of the First New York Lincoln Cavalry remembered, "Orders were to leave nothing in this fertile Valley on which a hostile army could subsist. Detachments were sent on every road, with orders to set fire to all mills, grain, and hay." It seems as if some men had already had enough and were willing to

2. (Interview: William H. Sipe; ACL, Whitesel, 3)
3. (Farrar 1911, 394)

The McCue home, Belvidere, from a photograph taken shortly after the war. (Susan
Winters McCue)

risk court-martial rather than continue to be agents in the destruction of civilian
property, for in his memoirs Beach stated, "Men who never flinched in the
hottest fight declared they would have no hand in this burning."[4]

One of the first places encountered by the Second Division as it turned back
to the north was Belvidere, the home of Thomas McCue. McCue was away with
the Augusta Reserves, who were helping to hold the passes in the Blue Ridge so
that Sheridan would think twice about trying to move on Charlottesville. He
and his comrades from the northeastern part of the county had no idea that by
doing so they had contributed to the decision by Grant to let Sheridan have his
way with the Valley. As McCue watched the mounting evidence of federal
intentions from his remote perch in the mountains, horsemen in blue descended
on his own holding.

Belvidere was a substantial concern with a fine brick manor house and
well-kept outbuildings and fields. A work force of fourteen slaves and a capable
overseer and his family had kept the plantation in an excellent state of repair
and production. Perhaps it was because it was such a prosperous place, with

4.   (Beach 1902, 438)

Elizabeth McCue, from a prewar
portrait on porcelain. (Susan Winters
McCue)

Bettie McCue in a photograph taken
at age 25. (Elizabeth Barry Thrift Brown)

more than the usual number of slaves for an Upper Valley farm, that the unit of spoilers decided to make an example of it.

Nine members of the McCue family were at home. Four-year-old Edward McCue was playing near a downstairs fireplace when some of the soldiers entered the room, startling him with their loud, booted footsteps and clanking scabbards. He jumped to his feet but was knocked over by accident as one of the cavalrymen brushed past him to light torches from the fire in the hearth. Leaving Edward in bewilderment, they proceeded from room to room setting fires. The house slaves followed at a discrete distance and extinguished the fires before they could get fairly caught.

As they moved through the house some of the soldiers helped themselves to whatever appealed. The silver, however, had been buried in a carefully camouflaged spot in the yard, and a number of hams had been hidden in a secret attic room that could be entered only through a well-concealed trap door. The soldiers failed to notice the telltale grease marks on the ceiling of the room just below.

Outside, the commanding officer's order to burn the barn was heard by
Elizabeth McCue, Thomas's wife. She pleaded not to have the order carried out,
but when she sensed her entreaties were falling on deaf ears, she asked the officer
how much money he would take to spare the structure. The officer accepted the
three hundred dollars in gold that she had hidden away in one of her slippers
for just such an emergency and called his men off.

Before leaving, he asked the location of Clemmen's Mill. Mrs. McCue told
him she did not know, although she suspected he meant Samuel Cline's mill,
which was on Middle River just a couple of miles below her house.

As the soldiers mounted up, one of the cavalrymen noticed a fine brooch that
seventeen-year-old Bettie McCue was wearing at her neck, and he demanded
that she hand it over to him. Bettie, who was known for being fiesty, removed
the piece of jewelry, but as the soldier reached for it, she stuck him in the finger
with the pin back as hard as she could. He grabbed the brooch with the other
hand and jumped back, sucking on the wounded finger between howls of pain.
No doubt the delight of his onlooking comrades helped save brave Bettie from
serious retaliation. The robber mounted his horse, told the young lady that he
admired her spunk, and then rode off with the prize.[5]

The McCues were fortunate, having suffered only the loss of the livestock
driven off by the Yankees. Some of the burning units who extorted money to
spare property would ride off, leaving the family to savor a few minutes of relief,
only to have another group appear and burn the place to the ground. The second
party, their work completed, would then meet up with the first party to split the
loot.[6]

As Custer's force neared the Rockingham County line again, the troopers
took special care to clean out the area around the busy little village of Burke's
Mill. The settlement straddled the pike where it crossed Naked Creek, which
enters the North River only a short distance to the east. This region, a center
for farm trade, had been settled by particularly industrious individuals and
boasted several types of businesses along the banks of the creek.

The blacksmith shop overseen by old Capt. Thomas Burke was one of the
first buildings to be swallowed by flames. David VanPelt, who had taken over
Burke's major commercial enterprises before the war, suffered a tremendous loss.
The Union cavalrymen torched his merchant mill, sawmill, shingle mill, the
miller's house, and the cooper's shop, which held enough wood for a thousand

5.   (VSL, WPA Inventories, Augusta and Bath Counties; Interview: Sarah Winters McCue; 1860
      Census Records for Augusta County)
6.   (SHSP 1904, Vol. XXXII, 93)

barrels. At B. F. Spicer's they found another blacksmith shop and set it ablaze before moving a few hundred yards down the road to Benjamin Switzer's farm. There they burned the large barn, corn house, cider press, and farming implements as Mary Switzer and her four young children looked on in horror. Within sight of the Switzers' smoke- and flame-wreathed buildings, the Linn farm suffered in a like manner as a squad of blue-clad cavalrymen drove off the livestock and then burned the barn. On both the VanPelt and Linn farms the soldiers took special care to make sure the threshing machines were destroyed.

Perhaps the worst calamity to befall the community was the destruction of Samuel Funkhouser's woolen factory east of the village on North River. The factory had been set up to make cloth for the Confederate army at the onset of hostilities; such a direct association with the enemy ensured that the place would be given particular attention. The Federals who were given the task of destroying the operation went at the machinery with sledgehammers before firing the building. Funkhouser and his family could do no more than look on in disbelief. Having taken much more time to destroy the factory than they would have taken with a barn, the soldiers moved on, leaving the house and the rest of the Funkhouser property intact.[7]

Just to the west of Burke's Mill, in a region known as the Hills of Judea, the burning continued in the hollows and vales. The Federals were still under orders not to molest the property of widows, and the oral record confirms that most of them obeyed the order scrupulously. The widows, though, did not know such a directive had been issued, and advantage was sometimes taken of them. One squad of burners told a widow who owned a farm in a remote area that they would spare her barn if she would cook a meal for them. They enjoyed this respite from their grim chores and after eating their fill thanked the lady and rode away.[8]

7. (*Rockingham Register*, November 25, 1864; Funkhouser 1902, 72) Funkhouser, age forty-one, was not one to sit and wring his hands while waiting for someone to deliver him from ruin. A few weeks later, when he was confident that the Union forces had withdrawn from the area and Confederates were once again in control of the neighborhood, he made an effort to get his factory up and running. He made sure, as best he could under the circumstances, that his family was provisioned so they would not want in his absence, and set out for Pendleton County, just to the west and over Shenandoah Mountain. He knew of some machinery for sale in that area. Back in the mountains he ran into a band of pro-Union guerrillas known as the Swamp Dragons. Perhaps trying to safeguard his funds, he fled when called upon to stand and was shot and mortally wounded. The loss was greatly lamented in the Burke's Mill area, as Funkhouser was considered to have been a man of "high moral standing" with an "industrious disposition"; a man who "constantly devoted his time to the interests of his business." He died of his wounds on October 31.

8. (Interview: Glenn Wine)

On a nearby farm a mother who had seen the smoke and flames approaching feared for her meager supply of food; she quickly gathered it together and hid it under some loose floorboards in her home. She cautioned her small children not to speak of the food no matter what happened or she would whip them. After a bit she again warned them not to answer any questions that the "Yankees" might put to them or they would risk a beating. As time passed her fear of the dire consequences that would arise should their provisions be discovered and carried off prompted her again to admonish her children not to speak of the hidden supplies. Finally the distraught woman told them, "Come to think of it, I'll whip you anyway, just so you'll get the point!"[9]

As the burners of the Second Division moved over the hill north of Burke's Mill and left Augusta County for Rockingham County, they left fifty barns, seven flour mills, five sawmills, and Samuel Funkhouser's woolen factory burning in their wake.[10] All along the Valley Pike the smoke rising sluggishly from damp barns and crops burning in the fields caused a murky, low-hanging ceiling to spread out over the land. In addition to the unnatural fog, the acrid, dank smell of char assaulted the eyes, noses, and lungs of everyone who was a party to or a victim of the destruction.

• • •

The Second Division crossed into Rockingham County on the Valley Pike and bore down on Grassy Dale, the home of Justice Peter Roller, a strong secessionist and the most powerful man in that part of the county. In 1861 Justice Roller had overseen the voting on the Secession Ordinance at Mount Crawford. All of the votes but one had favored secession. The squire determined who had cast the negative vote and sent some of his supporters to bring him back. Roller made the man change his vote so that the decision would be unanimous in his magisterial district. Other citizens in the area had not voted at all because they disagreed with Justice Roller and feared his heavy hand. They would have been more than happy now to see him taken up by federal authorities, but it was not to be.

As the Federals spread out over the property, Justice Roller was nowhere to be found. A week earlier, at the first approach of the Union forces, he had gone into the hills, fearing that should he be taken, he would be arrested and held in confinement. He took his horses with him so that his son John, a Confederate

9.   (Ibid.)
10.   (*Rockingham Register*, November 25, 1864)

cavalryman, would have a remount if he needed one. During the time that he was in hiding, the squire crept back to his home several times under the cover of darkness. The home was searched at random, and he barely eluded capture on more than one occasion. The house at Grassy Dale remained unscathed except for some looting, but the barns, stables, and other support buildings, along with farming implements of every kind, were consumed by flames. Tons of hay and bushels of wheat and corn also went up in smoke. Of Justice Roller's six slaves, at least one, called Bill, went off with Sheridan's army.[11]

Less than a mile beyond Grassy Dale, on the east side of the pike, one of the oldest estates in Rockingham County was beautifully situated on a high shelf of land in a gentle curve of the North River. Contentment, built in the late 1700s to replace an even earlier residence, was the home of Mrs. Elizabeth Grattan and her daughter Lucy. The peace had been broken at the Grattan home place when Sheridan sent infantry brigades to Mount Crawford on the 26th. A few of the units had crossed North River and were encamped on the south side of the stream in order to keep that avenue open for elements of the cavalry as they returned from their strikes into Augusta County.

When the horsemen returned on the evening of September 29, they rode over the place preparing to do some damage, but Mrs. Grattan's status as a widow saved the farm structures from being reduced to ashes. Had the Union officers known that her two sons, Charles and George, were Confederate officers, the tune played might have been different. Indeed, Charles had served on the staff of the Union cavalry's mortal enemy, Gen. J. E. B. Stuart. And the Grattan daughter, fair Lucy, was engaged to Confederate captain George Chrisman of the Third Battalion Virginia Reserves.

Sherman's Mill, which once belonged to the Grattan family, also escaped destruction this day as the Union infantry used it to grind flour for its own use.[12]

The New York *Herald* told its subscribers, "All day of the 29th both Custer and Merritt were engaged in destroying the crops, mills, and all property of use to the rebel army. The scene presented on this occasion was indeed a very saddening but still a very necessary one. In the course of the day we destroyed enough wheat to subsist the whole rebel army for a year to come. On Friday, the 30th, the destruction and collection operations were continued."[13]

An Ohio infantryman in camp near Mount Crawford wrote to his wife on September 30, "I cannot witness the burning of barns + mills without thinking

11. (May 1976, 432-33; 1860 Rockingham County Slave Schedules, RPLGR)
12. (May 1976, 433; Crute 1982, 188; CSR Maj. George Grattan, NA)
13. (Richmond *Examiner*, October 10, 1864)

of the great suffering that will be brought upon the poor people of this country, who had no part or voice in bringing on this most cruel war."[14] A young schoolteacher wintering on the fringe of the burned out area of Augusta County wrote in her diary on November 20, "hundreds have been made desolate [by] the midnight torch of the fiendish incendiary. How my soul filled with horror as I was compelled to stand and witness (without the power of arresting) one building after another consumed to ashes. Barns, Mills, Foundrys, with their lurid glare sent many a pang of hopelessness to houseless citizens. Truely the great? general, Sheridan has achieved a wonderful victory over the helpless women and children of the Valley of Virginia."[15]

By laying waste to the northeastern section of Augusta County, Sheridan had apparently weakened his ability to follow Grant's order to force the gaps in the Blue Ridge and descend on Charlottesville. To do so he would have had to cross the area just burned and barren of supplies, then fight Early somewhere in the passage. But perhaps he acted by design, for on the night of September 28, prior to the burning of that section, he had written to Grant: "It will be exceedingly difficult for me to carry the infantry column over the mountains and strike at the Central road. I cannot accumulate sufficient rations to do so, and think best to take some position near Front Royal. . . . I will however stay here for a few days."[16] On October 1 Sheridan sent a dispatch to Henry Halleck in the capital: "All the crops, mills, etc., have been destroyed from Staunton to Mount Crawford, which is my present front."

14.   (Greenwood 1993, 21)
15.   (Madison 1949)
16.   (Pond 1881, 193)

Chapter Seven

TOWNS AMONG THE CAMPS

While Custer was burning along the turnpike on September 29 he was ordered to turn over command of the Second Cavalry Division to Colonel Powell and to assume command of the Third Cavalry Division from General Wilson, who had been ordered to Sherman's army in the west. Custer, accompanied by his escort, splashed across the North River at the old ford sometime on the afternoon of September 30 and rode down the main street of Bridgewater with his one-star pennant flying. Where once Stonewall Jackson was honored by cheering, handkerchief-waving ladies, children, and old people, only silent houses greeted Custer.

The town of Bridgewater in south central Rockingham County dates from colonial times, when a village took root at the river crossing known as Magill's Ford. Two enterprising brothers by the name of Dinkle arrived a little later; one took a Magill woman as his wife, bought land along the river, and laid out a town known for a few years as Dinkletown. In the early nineteenth century a span was built across the river, and the community came to be called Bridgeport. Flatboats built there were launched down the river laden with produce, iron, hemp, and hides, which eventually wound up in the major trade centers at Georgetown, Alexandria, and Baltimore. By 1830 the town was called Bridgewater.

When the war came, Bridgewater was the scene of much activity due to its location on the Harrisonburg–Warm Springs Turnpike and the presence of the mills that lined the river banks above and below the town. Businesses flourished,

Main Street (the Valley Turnpike) in Bridgewater in the late nineteenth century. Less than half a mile long, it was lined with well-kept houses of brick, frame, and log; two alleys paralled it. (Town of Bridgewater)

as did several churches and a playhouse. The taverns of the town welcomed and rested travelers like Andrew Jackson and Henry Clay.[1] A Confederate soldier passing through the town in May of 1862, during Jackson's Valley Campaign, wrote, "We reached Bridgewater about 4 P.M. It was a place of which I had never heard, and a beautiful village it proved to be, buried in trees and flowers."[2]

The bridge had burned in 1862 and would not be rebuilt until after the war, however the ford was passable except in cases of extreme flooding. Produce still came into Bridgewater in great abundance, but no longer was it shipped to commercial markets. Confederate authorities established a commissary post there to take in supplies levied from citizens as tax-in-kind in lieu of money to support the Southern war effort. An eight-room log house that stood on the east side of Main Street at the town's northern limits, opposite the Methodist Episcopal Church, was used as the government storehouse for south central Rockingham and north central Augusta County. Produce, grain, and preserved

1.   (Wayland 1912, 199)
2.   (Moore 1988, 52)

View overlooking Bridgewater toward the east, with Massanutten Peak in the distance. (David L. Blevins)

meats were hauled to this building, inventoried, and then sent on to main distribution centers. A Confederate remount station was also located there.

After Early's defeat at Fisher's Hill, the Union forces had come on so swiftly that the Confederate commissary officer in Bridgewater had neither the time nor the wherewithal to get his provisions loaded and moved out of harm's way. He called in the town's residents and told them to take what they wanted, but he cautioned them to hide whatever they took as the voracious Northerners would surely search their homes. The citizens carried away as much as they could, and what was left was brought out into the yard and burned so it would not fall into enemy hands. Perhaps the agent hoped that by emptying the building it might possibly escape destruction.[3]

Custer, now permanently in command of the Third Division, joined a portion of his unit in the flat fields just north of town; another part of the division was to the east, camped on the rise of the nearly level plateau between Bridgwater

3.   (VSL, WPA Inventories, Rockingham and Scott counties)

and Mount Crawford on the Valley Turnpike. The main body of the division had established its camps the day before the arrival of its new commander and had been assigned to picket all of the crossings of the North River between Mount Crawford and Spring Creek, just above Bridgewater.[4]

Capt. John Phillips of the Eighteenth Pennsylvania Cavalry in the First Brigade had been involved more in the skirmishing around Rockfish Gap east of Waynesboro in the preceding days than in the destruction of barns and mills. He and his men were now in camp north of town, "unsaddled" and taking a breather. After he saw his company settled, Phillips went down into Bridgewater and sought out some of the townspeople, who were keeping a generally low profile. Being of an affable disposition, he was soon speaking freely with some of the inhabitants and softening their distrust. Before too long he received an invitation to supper, which he gratefully accepted. Perhaps he dined on a little Confederate tax-in-kind ham.

Phillips noted, "The boys are taking tobacco in town." Whether he meant they were stolling along the street while enjoying a pipeful of the soothing weed or they were in the act of looting private homes was not made clear.

A couple of days later Phillips's regiment and another were ordered to move their camp from the fields to the wooded hills just to the north. The Confederates, watching from across the North River, thought it was a withdrawal, and two regiments of Wickham's brigade crossed the river, driving in the federal pickets. The Eighteenth Pennsylvania and the Second New York Cavalry were ordered to charge the Confederates, who were by then clearing the town and entering the fields of the just-vacated Union cavalry camp. A sharp yet brief fight ensued, and the Southerners were driven back across the river. The casualties were light on both sides, but men were killed in the melee.[5]

At about the same time, farther up the river near Spring Creek, members of the Eighteenth Virginia Cavalry of Imboden's command were exchanging tobacco for coffee with the federal cavalrymen across the river. Their officers swapped Southern newspapers for Northern ones.

Custer set up his headquarters in the charming little town of Dayton, a few miles north along the Warm Springs Turnpike, about halfway between Bridgewater and Harrisonburg. It is one of the oldest towns in Rockingham County. An Anglican chapel was established there prior to the Revolution. A stone house built by one of the Harrisons in the late 1740s was fortified and used by

4.   (OR, Series I, Vol. XLIII, Pt. 1, 99)
5.   (Phillips 1954, 116)

Town of Dayton at the beginning of the twentieth century. (Joseph H. Meyerhoeffer)

neighboring farmers as a refuge during times of Indian unrest. Fort Harrison, as it was called, was on the north side of meandering Cook's Creek; before long a settlement grew on the southern bank.[6]

In time Dayton became the primary trading center for a large community of Mennonites and Dunkards whose farms were mostly to the west and north. On the eve of the Civil War a majority of them still spoke the Pennsylvania-German dialect often erroneously referred to as 'Dutch.' Many also spoke English, and the question of whether English should be substituted for Pennsylvania-German in religious services had caused irreparable rifts in several congregations.

Rockingham County was a part of the Middle District of the Mennonite Church in the Valley. In 1860 Bishop Martin Burkholder of the district passed away, and Samuel Coffman was selected to take his place. Coffman's family, artisans and yeoman farmers, had come into the Valley in 1760, exactly one hundred years prior to Lincoln's election as president of the United States. The new bishop's home was a substantial brick structure a few miles north of Dayton on the Rawley Springs Turnpike.

6.   (Wayland 1912, 198)

Bishop Samuel Coffman. (Minnie Carr)

In those days it was the custom to let the Lord select new deacons, ministers, and bishops. This was accomplished by placing a slip of paper into a prayer book and mixing the book with others, one for each candidate. Each man selected a book, and the one who found the slip of paper inside became the new church official. It was in this manner that thirty-year-old Samuel Coffman had been ordained to preach the gospel in the church in 1852. Once, when Coffman was having doubts about the effectiveness of his ministry, Bishop Burkholder said to him, "My brother, you do not know anything yet of the weight of responsibilities. Should it ever be your lot to bear the burden I have on me, then you might have some reason to complain."

To young Coffman fell that lot. He drew another book to become bishop on May 11, 1861. He had again been chosen by the Lord, but this time to shepherd a much larger flock in its greatest time of trial. The war was already on, and even Martin Burkholder could never have imagined the serious responsibilities that would fall on the younger man's shoulders.[7]

The bishop's brief tenure had thus far been a difficult one. In June 1861, prior to the passing of the Exemption Act of 1862, a Confederate captain attended a service at Weaver's Mennonite Church, where he announced to the congregation that all men between the ages of eighteen and forty-five were to report the next day for military service. Everyone in attendance that day was moved to tears.[8]

Many men fled to the mountains to the west in an attempt to get to Union-held territory. Some of them were intercepted and sent to Richmond, where they were imprisoned for a time. The men who did report to the army took a "no shoot" pledge before they left home, and in skirmishes and battles stood in the line and discharged their guns into the air. After a particular battle,

7.   (Brunk 1959, 336)
8.   (Ibid., 157)

The home of Bishop Coffman and his wife Frances on the Rawley Springs Turnpike west of Harrisonburg. (Nancy Hess)

an officer asked one of the Mennonites if he had fired his weapon. The man said he had not seen anything to shoot at. The officer was incredulous. "Why, didn't you see all those Yankees over there?" The Mennonite answered, "They're people. We don't shoot people."[9]

When the Confederate goverment issued the Conscription Act in April 1862, Bishop Coffman decried it from the pulpit. He sent out word to his congregation that anyone who responded would be disqualified from membership in the church. Because of his firm and uncompromising stance against participation in the war, threats made against his life were considered serious enough to take him out of the area until passions cooled. He spent the rest of 1862 and part of 1863 in Maryland, returning home only when he was sure that the Exemption Act was genuine.[10]

The bishop spent his time trying to care for those of his people who were most affected by the war and keeping peace with his neighbors. He would not,

9.   (Horst 1967, 33)
10.   (Brunk 1959, 164)

however, back away from his conviction that war is evil. When asked to call for a day of prayer in his churches to mark a celebration of thanksgiving across the South in late January 1863, he refused, despite the urging of Jacob Hildebrand of Augusta County, the older bishop of the Southern District of the Virginia Mennonite Conference. Coffman did not think there was any cause for thanksgiving so long as the war lasted, and he refused to take any part in an observance that could be misconstrued in any way or to any degree as approval of the war effort.[11]

When the Federals came to Harrisonburg on September 25, details had been sent out to gather forage and livestock. Companies were directed to visit the farms to the west, along the Rawley Springs Turnpike, as far as the village of Dale Enterprise, which was sited on a hill overlooking the Coffman farm. The bishop and his wife were sitting on the porch watching their younger children at play on the lawn and their eldest son, John, age sixteen, was lying under a tree reading a book when a detachment of cavalry turned into their lane. Mrs. Coffman rounded up the smallest children and took them inside. The bishop and his sons John and Jacob walked to the yard gate.

The soldiers bypassed the yard and rode directly to the barn and pasture field beyond the house. Soon there was heard the sharp crack of revolver and carbine as the pigs were killed in the barnyard. The Coffmans saw a young heifer topple over in the pasture. John pleaded with his father to do something to stop the slaughter as he watched the sheep being gunned down, but his father shook his head and said something to the effect that the soldiers had obviously come on a mission, and the best the family could do was pray for a little mercy. Jacob observed that if the killing continued, the family would have nothing left. His father responded gravely that that was his concern, too. As the cavalrymen came back toward the house leading Judy and Prince, the family's best team of horses, the bishop remarked quietly, "At least they didn't shoot them." John, looking beyond, groaned audibly when he saw the soldiers also leading away Nell, their best saddle horse.

As the soldiers passed the yard gate, the bishop called out to them as he would to a neighbor, wishing the officer in charge a good day and remarking to the lieutenant that they had a good team in their charge. The men stopped, and while stroking Judy's neck the lieutenant observed that the horses had obviously been well cared for. The bishop admonished the young man to "just see that they still are," and then asked him what the raid was all about. The officer replied

11.   (Ibid., 59; *Shenandoah Mennonite Historian*, 1-3; EMU, Church Records)

Mennonite and Dunkard youths applying to Sheridan for passes. These people were known as "broad brims" because of the style of hat they wore. (Author's collection)

that they had orders not to leave anything behind that would be of use to their enemies, and that was all he knew about it. "Or anything that might feed innocent women and children?" the bishop asked. The officer could think of no suitable reply, so he rode on, leading Judy, while one of his men followed on Nell and leading Prince.

When the soldiers had gone, the bishop and his sons walked back to the barn, pens, and pasture to survey the damage. Dead animals lay everywhere, yet a few pigs and sheep had been nimble enough to escape, along with a couple of milch cows and a few chickens that began to emerge from their hiding places. Jacob remarked that the soldiers must have run out of bullets or they would have killed these few survivors as well. What animals were left were driven to safety on nearby Mole Hill.

The bishop felt that he had a duty to his church members to stay, but he discussed with his wife the possibility that she and the children should go north with other refugee families. She would not even consider it. They would be all right, she told her husband, and as far as food to see them through the winter, "God will take care of us."[12]

Young John Coffman was among the group of men affected when the Confederate Congress nullified the 1862 Exemption Act in September 1864 because of the dire shortage of manpower.[13] He was afraid that when the Northerners withdrew he would be forced into the depleted ranks of Early's army. On October 3 he, his friend Peter Hartman (who had also witnessed the slaughter of his family's hogs, chickens, and sheep when the Northerners first arrived), and four other young Mennonite and Dunkard men solicited Sheridan for help. Hartman later described Sheridan as "the most savage looking man I ever saw." But that day the general listened to them and then declared that all single men who wished to do so could go to the army's horse herd and pick out a mount to carry them away from the grasp of Confederate authorities. Both Coffman and Hartman took advantage of the offer; Hartman walked home for a saddle before choosing his horse.

Sheridan understood that to create damage sufficient to prevent the Valley from being of further value to the South, the barns and mills of friends and enemies would have to be destroyed. He sent out word that anyone—whether Northern or Southern sympathizer—not wishing to be stranded in the midst of the desolation could apply for guarded passage with his wagon trains as they withdrew to the North. He promised to see that everyone who made that decision would be supplied with a wagon and a team of horses to carry his belongings.

Bishop Coffman harbored no doubts that it was imperative that his son leave while he had the opportunity to do so, and he made sure the boy was provisioned to make his escape. He decided that he and the rest of the family, however, would stay where they were so he could look after the people of his district.[14]

A couple of hundred yards south of Dayton was the home of Joseph Coffman, a Lutheran whose family had settled in Page County a hundred years earlier, and his wife Abigail. The Lutheran Coffmans were not related to the Mennonite Coffmans. Their wealth and education separated them from the Dunkards and Mennonites socially. From early on and through the years Joseph Coffman's forebears had mixed easily with the prominent English settlers, and by the time of the war they were almost completely anglicized in speech and custom. Joseph had come to Rockingham County before 1820 and, because of his wealth and social prominence, had married into one of the leading local families. His house

12.   (Coffman 1964, 47-49)
13.   (Hess 1979, 133)
14.   (Hartman 1964, 24-25)

and Samuel Coffman's were very similar, although Joseph's had been built with the help of slave labor, and the bishop's had not.[15] The Lutheran Coffmans, like the Mennonite Coffmans, decided to remain in the Valley, come what may.

The Lutheran Coffmans' eighteen-year-old granddaughter, Lizzie, took note of the civilian exodus in a letter to her cousin, Lt. Julian Pratt of Imboden's cavalry, less than a week after the Northerners withdrew. She wrote that a "great many families here [have] gone North. The villains tried to force us to go, too, and I believe had they staid two weeks longer, they would have forced everyone to leave. I told them if they did burn us out I intended staying with my home to the last, but they said, 'you will starve.' I replied, 'I glory in starving for my crumbs.' "[16]

. . .

There had been no time during the operations in Augusta County to settle the fate of the hapless Davy Getz, who must have been left near Harrisonburg with the Michigan brigade's supply wagons while Custer went dashing about during the last week in September. Now, at his headquarters in Dayton, the young brigadier convened a drumhead court and condemned the bewildered young man to be shot as a bushwhacker. He was led through Joseph Coffman's orchard to a small rise of ground, where he was made to dig his own grave before being summarily shot.[17]

After Getz was executed his body lay uncovered, at least overnight. Zume Brown, a local fourteen-year-old lad, tempted his fourteen-year-old friend Andy Thompson to go with him to the grave. "Andy, that fellow the Yankees shot had on a dandy pair of new boots, and they haven't buried him yet. Let's go get 'em." Andy agreed, and the two crept into the orchard. As they tugged on the boots the head lolled, and a gurgling sound emanated from the corpse's throat. The boys ran back to Dayton "in high gear," fearing the man was not really dead.

15.   (Wayland 1912, 198)
16.   (Leigh Private Collection, Coffman Letter)
17.   (Wayland 1927, 386-87; Interviews: John A. Getz and Bennie Getz) Shortly after the close of
      the war, seventy-six-year-old Andrew Getz succumbed to his grief over the death of his son
      David and committed suicide. In an undated manuscript in the Shenandoah Valley Civil War
      Round Table Collection John W. Wayland writes of having interviewed people who witnessed
      the events around Dayton in 1864. He states that Getz was executed "a day or two" before
      John Rodgers Meigs was killed (October 3, 1864); In her letter, Lizzie Coffman mentions that
      "one of our men" had been executed in her grandfather's orchard. This may have been Davy
      Getz; it is interesting that she makes no mention of the man having been an innocent. The
      death of Davy Getz has not been forgotten in Dayton nor in the Valley to this day.

The next morning Zume went by Andy's house to show him the boots. "I went back again and he was dead all right[,] so I got 'em," he reported.[18]

The presence of the Northern soldiers aggravated the citizens of Dayton and the surrounding area. On the whole, the members of the 116th Ohio Infantry, who had charge of the town, were remembered in a favorable light as having behaved like gentlemen while going about their duties; the cavalry was another story altogether. Orders forbidding looting had been issued to the occupying troops, yet they were seldom enforced. And theft was not limited to the enlisted men—officers, too, occasionally helped themselves to items that caught their fancy. Capt. John DeForest of the Twelfth Connecticut Infantry remembered the stay in Rockingham County as a time for "devastating crops and devouring cattle." Others did not limit their acts to those carried out in pursuance of orders.[19]

While the military situation developed in the minds of the commanders, the soldiers rested from the recent hard marching and fighting. Blistered feet were treated and given a little time to heal. A good number of men had worn out their shoe leather, and they no doubt made repairs or looked for replacements.

Issued rations had been consumed long ago, so foraging parties were sent out as soon as the camps were established. The leaders of the gathering parties were instructed to give the citizens receipts to be redeemed after the war. The 116th Ohio Infantry sent its quartermaster-sergeant into the region surrounding Dayton to secure supplies. Sgt. Ezra Walker, who was accompanied by an orderly named Webster, noted in his diary on September 27 that:

> [We] got among Dunkards to-day. They universally seemed scared to death when they saw us coming. One woman begged us not to take her cow or sheep. After we promised her time and again that we would pay her for everything we got she would still say: "Yes take everything you want, but leave some for the others, or they will be mad and threaten to shoot us." Webster and I each got three large loaves of bread, two heads of cabbage, beets, tomatoes, onions, etc.[20]

18.   (SVCWRT, Wayland undated) In 1876, the year Custer was killed at Little Big Horn, Zume Brown, then twenty-six, attended the Baldwin District Fair in Staunton with his wife. They were viewing the exhibits when a trustee of the Western State Lunatic Hospital walked up to Zume and shot and killed him for no apparent reason.
19.   (Wayland 1987, 81-82; Interview: Joseph H. Meyerhoeffer)
20.   (Wildes 1884, 188-89)

With what Walker and others were bringing into the camps, the men were able to cook some pretty substantial meals. A few days after his first expedition to the full larders of the "Dutch," he went out again, this time with the brigade forage train. He recorded that after an early start he returned to camp at "about 1 P.M. with a bucketfull of honey, one of apple butter, bread, sweet potatoes, cabbage, chickens, a pretty good haul for one day."[21]

Lizzie Coffman wrote to Lieutenant Pratt of the foraging. "The Yanks camped in Grandpa's orchard & nursery (both sides of the land) burning the fences of course and destroying the fruit. . . . Took everything we had to eat, stole the beans and all the vegetables." Although the Yankees had cleaned out the larder, Lizzie assured Pratt that she had kept safe the extra uniform she was storing for him, having gone so far as to wear one of his hats to protect it from theft, although there were men abroad in the land who would not have thought twice about plucking it from her head or giving her the back of a hand had she protested.[22]

While the Third Cavalry encamped southwest of Harrisonburg, Sheridan sent General Merritt with the First Cavalry to take care of business near Port Republic and the South Fork of the Shenandoah River in southeastern Rockingham County. This area of rich, rolling farmland, well watered by several streams, lay about twelve miles east of Harrisonburg. It was not in the planned path of the coordinated thrust of destruction that Sheridan was planning, yet it was territory that could not be left untouched.[23]

21. (Ibid.)
22. (Leigh Private Collection, Coffman Letter)
23. (Wert 1987, 133)

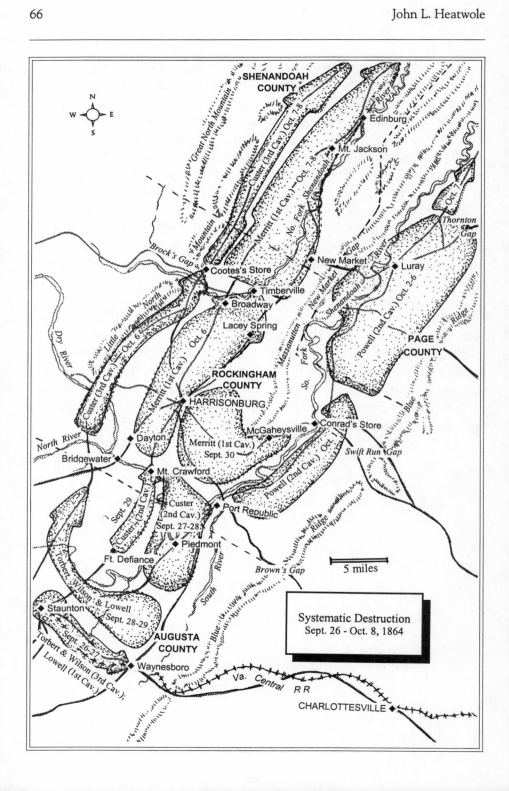

SHENANDOAH COUNTY

N
W   E
S

Great North Mountain

Custer (3rd Cav.) Oct. 7-8

Merritt (1st Cav.) — Oct. 7-8

No. Fork Shenandoah River

Edinburg

Mt. Jackson

Oct. 7

Thornton Gap

Brock's Gap

Cootes's Store

Timberville

Broadway

Lacey Spring

New Market Gap

New Market

Luray

Shenandoah River

Gap

Powell (2nd Cav.) Oct. 2-6

PAGE COUNTY

Massanutten

So. Fork

Dry River

Little North Mountain

Custer (3rd Cav.) — Oct. 6

Merritt (1st Cav.) — Oct. 6

ROCKINGHAM COUNTY

HARRISONBURG

McGaheysville

Conrad's Store

Blue

Merritt (1st Cav.) Sept. 30

Swift Run Gap

North River

Dayton

Bridgewater

Mt. Crawford

Sept. 29

Custer (2nd Cav.)

Custer (2nd Cav.) Sept. 27-28

Port Republic

Powell (2nd Cav.) Oct.

Ridge

Piedmont

Ft. Defiance

South River

Brown's Gap

5 miles

Torbert, Wilson & Lowell Sept. 28-29

Staunton

Blue

Sept. 26-27

Torbert & Wilson Lowell (1st Cav.)

AUGUSTA COUNTY

Waynesboro

Va. Central R R

Systematic Destruction
Sept. 26 - Oct. 8, 1864

CHARLOTTESVILLE

Chapter Eight

THE BURNING OF SOUTHEASTERN ROCKINGHAM COUNTY

Brig. Gen. Wesley Merritt was a no-nonsense cavalryman who, when on campaign, would brook no deviation from orders. An 1860 graduate of the U.S. Military Academy at West Point, he was older than most of his classmates and now, at thirty years of age, was one of the cavalry's rising stars and the senior division commander in Sheridan's cavalry force. When he was elevated to brigadier general on June 29, 1863, during the opening rounds of the Gettysburg Campaign, he was a captain in the Second U.S. Cavalry. Custer was promoted on the same day to the same rank, but he was jumped from second lieutenant and so was ranked by Merritt. There was an unspoken but very visible rivalry between the two young commanders that led each of them to bold, decisive actions.[1]

While Torbert was making his well-planned and direct incursion to the south, Merritt commanded all of the horsemen operating in Rockingham and upper Augusta counties—the First Division (shy the brigade that was with Torbert) and the Second Division. He was responsible for the activities of all of the cavalry detachments assigned to the rear guard, picket duty along the nearby rivers, gap watching, stock herding, scouting, and destruction of materials that might be of benefit to the enemy. He was a very organized individual, and indeed had to be to keep everything that was expected of him in balance.

As Sheridan sorted things out in Harrisonburg and made the argument to

---

1.   (Warner 1964, 321)

Grant about how the campaign should end, Merritt moved the forces under his direction all over south eastern Rockingham and north eastern Augusta counties. Near Port Republic, which is at the head of the South Fork of the Shenandoah and very near Brown's Gap, his men had been in action several times with Confederate cavalry and infantry. During those last few days in September Merritt, as senior division commander, ordered Custer and the Second Division to go out east of Port Republic in an attempt to distract whatever Confederates were still in Brown's Gap from taking notice of Torbert's raid. The portion of the First Division under Merritt's command ranged freely to the west, almost as far as Harrisonburg, burning, driving stock, and carting away anything that could be of use to the Confederates.[2]

The farm of Alexander Kyger was located in the Mill Creek community, a couple of miles east of the Cross Keys battlefield on the Port Republic Road. The majority of the farms and businesses there were owned by Dunkards. The Kyger family was, for the most part, affiliated with that church.

Kyger was a very successful farmer and blacksmith, and his substantial stone house was a landmark in the area. Before his wife died in 1855 she had instilled in their then eleven-year-old son, Jacob, an abhorrence of slavery and predicted that a war would be fought over that issue. As Jacob grew older he was not shy about voicing his sentiments about the wrongness of holding fellow human beings in bondage, yet in his extended family there were those who owned slaves and who were not pleased to be told the institution was morally reprehensible. His uncle, Chris Kyger, when passing the house of his brother and nephew would yell out, "Hell and damnation to all the damned Abolitionists!"

As the war drew closer the younger Kyger made a decision that was in keeping with his feelings toward slavery and his love of the Union forged by the patriots of the Revolution. In late April of 1861, at the age of sixteen, he left the fledgling Confederacy and journeyed to the home of an aunt in Ohio. He shared the news from Virginia, then took his leave for Iowa, where a former neighbor had established himself. There he did a little more soul-searching and eventually joined the Thirty-fifth Iowa Infantry.[3]

Back on the Stone House Farm, his father had to contend with armies passing over his property that trampled fields and confiscated whatever was desired, ownership aside. Merritt's men arrived on September 30 to burn the fine, big Pennsylvania standard barn that had been constructed in 1852. Kyger surely

2.   (Pond 1892, 190)
3.   (Interview: Dr. Ellsworth Kyger)

told them he had a son in the Union army, but people were making all sorts of insupportable claims in an effort to save their property from the flames, and his words did not have the desired effect. In a last ditch effort, he told them that if they would spare the barn he would disclose the burial spot of a barrel of brandy. The soldiers readily accepted the offer, and the barn was left unmolested.[4]

West of the Cross Keys battlefield, about five miles east of Harrisonburg, one Union cavalryman, away from his company and out for booty, approached a large frame house adjacent to the Port Republic Road. At home at the time were Eliza Hedrick, her daughters Minnie, age seven, and Lizzie, age five. Her husband had taken their horses to a place of safety, never thinking that his wife and children might be in physical danger. The soldier pushed his way into the house and demanded to know where the gold and silver were hidden. Mrs. Hedrick insisted they had none, but

Minnie Hedrick. As a young girl, she saw her mother kill a Northern marauder with a crock of apple butter. (Cheryl Lyon)

the man ransacked the downstairs, throwing drawers to the floor and moving rugs and furniture in his search for trapdoors and loose floorboards.

In the previous three years the family had been visited many times by foragers from both sides who usually sought only a bit of food. This soldier was different—he seemed like a mad animal bent on tearing the Hedricks apart, and mother and children were badly frightened. With him between them and the door, their only avenue of escape was blocked. They climbed the stairs to the second floor and from there climbed a ladder into the attic.

As they crouched in the dim light under the eaves, they could heard the soldier cursing and crashing their belongings to the floor down below. When he had fully searched the first level, he pounded up the stairs to the second floor, where he turned over the beds, ripped open the ticks and pillows, and roared

4.   (HRCHS, Kyger Family and Lynwood Farm Files)

that he would "make them" tell where the plunder was hidden. Soon he started up the ladder to the attic, swearing and threatening them in no uncertain terms.

Mrs. Hedrick, desperate for a weapon, fixed on a row of one-gallon crocks filled with apple butter. When the ruffian was halfway up the ladder, she raised a heavy crock high and threw it down as hard as she could onto the top of their tormentor's head. When he hit the floor at the base of the ladder, his head and shoulders covered in blood and apple butter, he was dead.

Once they were sure the intruder would not get up, mother and daughters descended from their refuge. With a herculean effort, Mrs. Hedrick and Minnie maneuvered the body out of the house and into a nearby sinkhole. There they hid it as well as they could and covered the spot with brush. Mrs. Hedrick shooed the man's horse away and then hurried back to the house to clean up the gruesome mess.

A few hours later more horsemen in blue arrived and inquired after the missing man. Mrs. Hedrick pointed down the road in the direction the horse had taken when she had run it off and told them that the man had passed by earlier in the day but had not returned. As they were in a hurry, they accepted her story and rode on.[5]

A few miles to the south of the Hedrick place, and a little to the east along the North River, was a group of farms owned by Dunkards of the Mill Creek Church. On Peter Showalter's farm the family stood on a hill and watched its neighbors' barns and crops going up in smoke. As each new plume climbed to the sooty cloud cover, one member of the family or another called out in horror the name of the owner of the farm then under attack. All too soon the Showalters witnessed the destruction of their own farm structures.

Very near Showalter's place was the farm of Mathias Diehl. When the burners arrived on this property one dismounted and entered the house to get some fire with which to destroy the barn. He was followed by Diehl's twenty-year-old daughter, Mary, and her five-year-old brother, Jacob. The cavalryman pulled a burning piece of wood from the fireplace and turned to get on with his work. Mary confronted him in the middle of the room and defiantly wrenched the

5.   (Interviews: Jon Ritenour, Ruby Thacker, and Cheryl Lyon) Two years prior to this incident,
      some Southern horsemen had halted in the road in front of the house. Standing in the road
      and looking up at one of the men, Minnie said, "You'd better not go down that road; it's
      awfully muddy down there." The man smiled and said, "Little girl, I'm used to mud. Now, you
      shouldn't be out here among all of these horses and men. You'd better go back to your yard."
      The soldiers rode off a few minutes later. Minnie asked one of the last to leave to whom it was
      that she had spoken. The man replied, "Why, little lady, that was Stonewall Jackson."

brand from his hand. She "threw it back into the fireplace" and, standing resolutely, told him, "You cannot burn our barn!" She then sought out the officer in charge of the detail and showed him letters that proved her brothers Amos and Josiah had gone into Northern-held territory, refusing to bear arms against the United States. The officer told his men to desist, and they rode away.[6]

During this period another one of the free-ranging parties passed through the village of McGaheysville, which was on the road leading from Harrisonburg eastward toward Conrad's Store at the western base of the Blue Ridge. At the eastern edge of the settlement the soldiers came upon Bonny Brook, the beautiful McGahey family estate. Just below the house was a workshop where swords had been made for state troops in the Mexican War. In the years just prior to the Civil War it had been used

When she was a young woman, Mary Diehl saved the family farm from destruction. (I.W. Diehl)

to make piano parts, but in the early fervor of this war Warren and James McGahey had set to manufacturing swords once again, and also percussion caps, for the South. This was a find of significant importance; the shop was quickly broken up and set afire. Burning timbers crashed around the broad grindstone that had been used to put an edge on the swords.[7]

A few miles north and west of McGaheysville was the village of Keezletown. Just north of the village was the home of Joseph Funkhouser, a fifty-three-year-old Methodist circuit rider. In the late afternoon of September 30, as he watched the smudges of smoke rising to the south and east, he knew what was coming. Funkhouser feared that the house would be ransacked, yet there was possibly an oasis of safety. His wife, Christina, who had been ill for some time, was bedridden. He hoped that the soldiers would respect the privacy of her room. He hid one of their prized possessions, a set of china bearing transfers of scenes

6.   (Interview: I.W. Diehl; Diehl 1990, 34-35)
7.   (Harrisonburg *Daily News-Record*, September 16, 1960; HRCHS, Civil War Files)

from *The Courtship of Miles Standish* that they had bought early in their marriage, beneath her bed. He may also have placed one of his personally prized possessions there, an old bible with one column of each page printed in English and one in German, a reminder of his former membership in the United Brethren, the so-called German Methodists, before he changed his church affiliation.

Funkhouser waited in the yard for the cavalrymen, who eventually arrived. He was not surprised when the officer in charge said, "We've come to burn your barn." He answered simply, "I have put the barn in the hands of the Lord." The officer said something to one of his men that the minister could not hear, and then all but that man rode away. The man dismounted and made himself and his horse comfortable beneath an apple tree at the edge of the orchard, where he remained the rest of the day. At dusk the trooper, who had been left behind to warn off other detachments that might come by, rode away, leaving the Funkhouser's holdings intact.[8]

Col. James Kidd, commanding Custer's old Michigan brigade, had been given the task of picketing the fords on the South Fork of the Shenandoah River from Port Republic to Conrad's Store, a distance of about twenty miles. Colonel Kidd had quite a few millers in his command, and he put them to work in the mills along his line, grinding flour for the use of the regiments.

The work had only been going on for a couple of hours when Merritt himself arrived on the scene. He was furious that the mills were still functional and ordered that they be destroyed without delay. Kidd later recalled that "the wheels were not stopped but the torch was applied and the crackling of flames intermingled with the rumbling of the stones made a mournful requiem as the old mill went up in smoke." He may have sensed the rivalry between Merritt and Custer at work; he suspected that Merritt was concerned that Custer would garner more credit than he by carrying out Sheridan's orders more promptly.[9]

In Port Republic itself, the imminent firing of the mill prompted some of the women to plead with the soldiers that they be allowed a few moments to collect a little flour to feed their children before the destruction took place. Time, though, had become a valuable commodity now that Merritt seemed to be looking over everyone's shoulder, and the emotional appeals were largely ignored.

The supervising officers were warned by Colonel Kidd to take care lest the flames from the mill spread to the nearby private dwellings, yet despite their

8.   (Interview: Mary Elizabeth Kite)
9.   (Kidd 1969, 397-99)

precautions, the fire jumped. Kidd "ordered every man to fall in and assist in preventing the further spread of the flames." Crying women stood watching, their babes in arms and frightened children at their sides. They all feared the loss of their homes. The soldiers quickly put out the fires in the houses and brought the mill fire under control.

Not far away William Downs's government tannery also succumbed to the torch.[10]

Across North River from the village was an area on the bluffs called New Haven, named in anticipation of development in the early part of the century. The town never materialized, but several substantial houses with commanding views of the surrounding countryside had been built. One of these homes belonged to Harrison Bateman, whose family was involved in the prewar river trade that saw products from the Valley shipped downriver to Harper's Ferry in flatboats known locally as gondolas or 'gundalows.' His granddaughter, nine-year-old Alice Bateman, "a pretty little blonde

Col. James Kidd commanded the Michigan cavalry brigade, Custer's former unit in Merritt's Division.
(Personal Recollections of a Cavalryman)

girl," saw the columns of smoke rising. She knew what was happening and was anxious for the safety of her grandfather's barn.

It so happened that a Union officer sat on the porch of the Bateman home at that very moment. He, too, was taking in the scene across the river. The "young Yankee Colonel was tough," but he had been kind to Alice since his arrival at the house, and her desperation moved her to approach him. She sat on his lap and sweetly voiced a plea that her grandfather's barn be spared. How could the officer not be moved? He lifted her to her feet, then walked to the edge of the porch, where he called to his men to fall in before him. Once they had complied, he drew his revolver out of its holster and told them that he would "shoot in the head" any man who dared to set fire to the Bateman barn. This enemy officer, whose name she did not know, became a hero who Alice would never forget.[11]

10. (SPRP, Kaylor Letter)

*John F. Lewis, superintendent of the
Mount Vernon Furnace. (Estate of
John W. Wayland)*

By 1864 the Lewis family had owned estates and property in and around Port Republic for more than a hundred years. The founder of the family in Rockingham County was Thomas Lewis, a brother of Gen. Andrew Lewis of the Revolutionary Army. Thomas's descendants had been men of mark in the county throughout its history, and a major portion of the battle of Port Republic had been fought over Lewis property in 1862.

John F. Lewis, Thomas's great-grandson, was a leader in eastern Rockingham society. He had been opposed to the war from the start, and his neighbors and other residents of the county thought enough of him and his opinions to have elected him their representative at the Secession Convention held in Richmond in April 1861. On April 17 Lewis voted with the minority against the secession ordinance that sent the decision to a public referendum; the vote that took place on May 23 officially severed Virginia from the Union. Lewis was the only delegate east of the Alleghenies who refused to sign the document. Unlike those who had been opposed to breaking the ties that had been forged in the Revolution but who now felt they must support Virginia as a state of the Confederacy, Lewis steadfastly declared himself a Union man.

When the Northern troops first came into the Port Republic area during the present campaign, Lewis was warned that barns and mills would be destroyed, but those found empty would be spared. As the superintendent of Mount Vernon Furnace at the foot of Brown's Gap, Lewis sent the furnace wagons to his father's mill about a mile and a half below the town and emptied it. Loads of grain were hauled to safety near Weyer's Cave on the South River. When the troopers came to the mill, there was nothing left in it. Someone suggested it be burned anyway, but the decision was made to spare it as the homes of the millers and their families were built so close to the structure that they would surely be

11.   (Wayland 1912, 421; SPRP, Heidenreich Statement; Interview: Anita Cummins)

consumed if the milling operation were set ablaze.[12]

Lewis's furnace, also known by the diminutive "Margaret Jane," was not as fortunate as his father's mill. Its owner's pro-Northern feelings aside, the Union officers felt the enterprise, which produced iron for Confederate munitions, had to go. The soldiers were ordered to damage the operation beyond repair.[13]

A neighbor expressed an opinion held by some in the community regarding the loss: "John F. Lewis manufactured iron for the Southern Confederacy, who in turn converted it into cannons and shells to kill and cripple Yankee soldiers, and when occasion demanded he would declare himself a loyal citizen of the United States. Such loyalty smacks of opportunism."[14] It is interesting to note that Lewis was not averse to having soldiers from Confederate infantry units detailed to work at the furnace when production demands warranted extra laborers.[15]

Some of Early's infantry, seeing the smoke from the burning ironworks, came out from their fortifications in the gap only to observe the burning party withdrawing out of range and the works too far gone to be salvaged. When Merritt was recalled to Harrisonburg, Lewis sent his fifteen-year-old son, Samuel, along to keep him out of reach of the Confederate conscription officers.[16]

With Merritt ordered to the Valley Pike, Colonel Powell and the Second Cavalry Division were sent to Port Republic immediately upon their return from burning along the pike in Augusta County. They had orders to move at daybreak the next morning, October 1, and to destroy everything of military value from Port Republic to Luray in Page Valley. There Powell was to wait until Sheridan and the infantry came abreast of him across the Massanutten at New Market by the end of the following week. He was also to scout for any Confederate force that might have designs on flanking Sheridan's army from the east while Early pitched into it from the south.

12.   (HRCHS, Fisher, 35)
13.   (Cheney 1901, 225-26)
14.   (JMUSC, May, 173-74) In 1865 John F. Lewis ran for Congress as a Union candidate and was defeated. Four years later he was elected lieutenant governor of Virginia and in the same year was appointed Virginia's U.S. senator. During that term he was mentioned as a possible vice-presidential running mate for Grant. In 1881 he was again elected lieutenant governor of Virginia, obviously having regained the respect of some who had once regretted his pro-Union leanings.
15.   (Swanson Private Collection, Confederate Special Order)
16.   (Cheney 1901, 226)

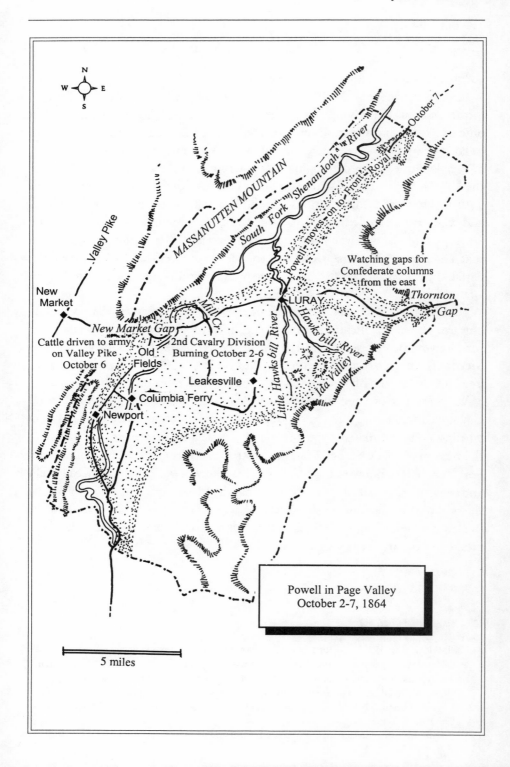

Powell in Page Valley
October 2-7, 1864

Chapter Nine

POWELL IN ROCKINGHAM AND PAGE COUNTIES

On October 1 Sheridan wrote to General Halleck, who had to hold the politicians' hands in Washington, "I strongly advise General Grant to terminate this campaign by the destruction of the crops in the Valley and the means of planting, and then transfer the VI and XIX Corps to his army at Richmond. . . . What we have destroyed and can destroy in this Valley is worth millions of dollars to the rebel government."[1]

Grant telegraphed Secretary of War Stanton on October 3 that he agreed to Sheridan's plan and expected the two corps mentioned in Sheridan's dispatch to Halleck to be sent to him by rail from Front Royal at the conclusion of the Burning. On the same day Grant communicated to Sheridan: "You may take up such position in the Valley as you think can and ought to be held and send all forces not required for this immediately here. Leave nothing for the subsistence of an army on any ground you abandon to the enemy."[2]

On October 1, Sheridan started Col. William Henry Powell with the Second Division of Cavalry north from Port Republic by way of Conrad's Store into the Page Valley. Powell was to begin the systematic destruction of the eastern third of the Valley.

Colonel Powell was the right man for the job. On September 23, after the battle of Fisher's Hill, Sheridan had replaced Averell with Powell as commander

1. (Kellogg 1903, 109-10, 209)
2. (Pond 1892, 195)

Col. William Powell, commander of Sheridan's Second Division of Cavalry. (National Archives)

of the Second Cavalry Division. Powell performed well in pursuing Early's retreating cavalry, and he had effectively brushed aside Confederate resistance at Forestville on the Middle Road on the 24th. Two days later Custer assumed temporary command of the division, but, just a few days later, when Wilson was sent to Sherman and the command of the Third Division opened up, Custer was reassigned. Powell reassumed his role as leader of the Second Division on the 29th.

He was immediately assigned two important tasks: clean out the eastern portion of the Valley and protect the Army of the Shenandoah's flank against any attack that Lee might send from east of the Blue Ridge.

Powell, who was Welsh by birth, had been brought to the United States by his parents when he was five. The family entered by way of New York and eventually settled in Ohio. He became an engineer in the iron industry and was managing an operation in Ironton, Ohio, at the commencement of hostilities. At age thirty-six he recruited a company of cavalry from the ironworking districts in the area that would become part of the new state of West Virginia in 1863. Powell was accustomed to dealing with rough and strong-willed individuals at the furnaces and rolling mills and soon had his charges disciplined in the routines and intricacies of cavalry service. In the Second (West) Virginia Cavalry, Powell rose from company commander to regimental major, lieutenant colonel, and colonel. Now he led the division.[3]

The Second Division began its movement toward Luray on the morning of October 1; this was not considered a withdrawal since the unit was not being driven from the land behind them. As the cavalrymen moved, they referred to their rear as their front. From the vicinity of Port Republic they were to move northward between the South Fork of the Shenandoah River and the Blue Ridge

3.   (Sifakis 1988, 520)

Eastern Rockingham County. The South Fork of the Shenandoah River is in mid-picture. (Estate of John W. Wayland)

Mountains toward Conrad's Store and the Page Valley. Their orders were to burn all the barns and mills in their path and, on their arrival in Luray, drive the livestock they had gathered over the Massanutten to New Market. There the herders were to meet the main column, which would be moving along the Valley Pike. Once Sheridan's force on the west side of the Massanutten Range had moved well beyond New Market, Powell was to resume his course down the Page Valley and cross into Warren County to secure the railroad at Front Royal.

Patches of fall color on the mountains served as a backdrop for the dozens of smoke pillars that rose silently to the sky as the burning parties moved steadily northward. The main portion of the Second Division, broken up into scores of small raiding parties delegated to the burning and herding, moved very quickly. A few regiments were left behind at Port Republic in case any of Early's men should appear. A unit was also sent through Swift Run Gap as far as Stannardsville in Greene County to ascertain whether any Confederate flanking movements were being contemplated from that quarter.

Hard by the South Fork, down from Port Republic, on the vast and rich river bottom fields, were several large plantations. Smaller holdings lay in the foothills of the Blue Ridge. Burning squads stretched from the road that ran along the riverbank to the line of woods at the base of the mountains, a swath nearly a mile wide, as they progressed toward Page County, seventeen miles ahead.

At Locust Dale plantation, the home of Robert and Frances Gibbons, the officer in charge of the detachment noticed a Masonic symbol over the door of the house. Upon inquiry as to the identity of the owner and his whereabouts, Mrs. Gibbons said that her husband was with the Confederate army. The officer then asked where he could find water for his men, who were parched from hot work, and she directed him to the well. As the group trotted in that direction, the officer told his men, "We will not burn this barn as it belongs to a Mason."[4]

Less than two miles downriver from Locust Dale the ground rises suddenly for a short distance. The river road still hugged the bank and stayed level, but well above it stood Hill Top, the home of the Teel family. Lucy Teel, her three teenaged daughters, young son Louis, his friend George Sipe, and a black housemaid were at the home when a burning party galloped up the lane and into the yard. The troops swiftly dismounted and fanned out to do their work. Everything happened very fast—in no time the barn, stables, and all the other dependencies were ablaze in an arc around the east side of the house. Soldiers went through the house, taking whatever they wanted. Amid the chaos the maid ran into the house, screaming that she was being pursued by one of "the soldier brutes." It took a few moments for Lucy to get her settled down.

A cavalryman ran up the side porch stairway and entered the bedroom of one of the girls, where a fire burned in the hearth against the early autumn chill. He lifted a log from the andirons, and, ignoring the pleas of the girls who stood in the open doorway to the porch, he flung the burning fagot on the bed before departing. Soon smoke rolled through the doorway, and the girls stepped back, crying and wringing their hands in despair. Just then a Union officer rode into the yard below. He realized the situation, leapt from his horse, and ran up the stairs. Heedless of the smoke, he entered the room, and with his sword he impaled the burning wood, carried it to the porch, and flung it into the yard. He then returned to the room, gathered up the smoldering bed ticking, and pitched it over the railing as well. The house was saved.

4.   (Interviews: Dr. George Hedrick and William H. Sipe; Yancey 1977, 156) There are many
        stories from the Civil War in which an affiliation with the Masons helped one party or another
        in time of need, yet such support was not universal. Once, when the Confederate partisan
        ranger leader John Singleton Mosby was informed that a Union officer had been given special
        treatment by one of his men because it was found that he was a member of the Masons, Mosby
        was said to have exclaimed that he was not running a lodge.

The officer then called the men together and ordered them to move on; no doubt he felt they had inflicted enough damage at this location.

The Teel family, though in great distress as they stood in the cold viewing the ruins of their farm structures, had trouble trying to think of words worthy enough to praise the actions of the officer who had saved their home. One of the girls, named Lucy after her mother, still had tears running down her cheeks as she asserted that she would "love that Yankee" as long as she lived.[5]

When the officer and troopers departed, fourteen-year-old George Sipe decided to take his leave. Several farms in the area were spared but for the loss of livestock; apparently some of the units were following the directive that empty barns and the buildings of widows were to be passed unmolested. But as George hotfooted it to his home near the foothills, there were enough farms in flames behind him to inspire his limbs to greater speed.

As a boy, George Sipe was an eyewitness to the burning along the South Fork on October 1, 1864. (I.W. Diehl)

At home George's mother, Mary Sipe, was aware something terrible was coming their way. It would not be unrealistic to assume she had already sent the slaves into the mountains with some of the livestock by the time George came panting into the yard and reported what had transpired at the Teel place. George's father was away with Jubal Early's force, serving in the senior reserves of the county. His mother decided that she would stay to meet the troopers, but he, as the man of the family, must take the horses to safety in the mountains. The boy gathered the horses and started up the slopes in great haste.

Soon thereafter Union cavalrymen rode up the lane. Mrs. Sipe's pleadings did not dissuade them from carrying out their orders. The Sipe's bank barn was large and fine, and while some of the Northern farm boys might have admired the

5.   (Interview: Sue H. Yancey; 1860 Census Records for Orange, Page, and Patrick counties)

Brig. Gen. John D. Imboden. His brother George's Eighteenth Virginia Cavalry was a part of Imboden's brigade. (USAMHI)

structure, it was soon on fire. The family had one of the few tobacco houses in the region. It, too, was put to the torch, but not before the soldiers stuffed their saddlebags with the highly prized Southern leaf. A smaller barn, in which cattle had been locked, was not ignited because the men were in a hurry to move on. Much to Mrs. Sipe's relief, the house was not threatened. George, who was safe in the mountains with his stock, looked down into the Valley, where he saw "barns burning everywhere."[6]

The burners were acutely aware of their vulnerability to guerrilla attack as they spread out into the countryside and were not prone to linger too long at any one place. Maj. Henry Neff's farm, in the foothills near Swift Run Gap east of Conrad's Store, was an exception. Henry Neff, once the sheriff of Rockingham County, had established a good farm over the years. He and his wife, Elenora, had passed away early in the war, and at the time of the great Burning their three sons were absent because of the war. Only a few of their daughters remained on the property.

The Federals told the girls to stay out of their way. They would brook no interference. Fires were kindled and encouraged in the barn and in all of the farm's outbuildings. This was all done very quickly, yet instead of riding away from the scene of its arson, the party retired to an apple tree on a nearby hill and settled in comfortably. There the soldiers sat, eating ripe, stolen fruit as they watched the buildings that had been devoted to the family's agricultural endeavors reduced to blackened, crumbling ruins. From that time forward, as long as the tree survived, it was known as the "Yankee Apple Tree."[7]

6.   (Yancey 1977, 164; Interview: William H. Sipe) The winter following the Burning saw many outlaws prowling the countryside in eastern Rockingham County. When these men were captured by Confederate authorities they were dealt with summarily. The execution of one of these outlaws occurred very near to the Sipe farm.

7.   (Smith 1967, 53)

In the country close to Conrad's Store the Federals burned a large flour mill and as many barns as they could reach, plus William Kite's tannery a mile to the east. By nightfall on that Saturday, October 1, most of the Second Division was encamped north of Conrad's Store, awaiting first light to resume their march.[8]

The next day the cavalrymen crossed the swiftly flowing Naked Creek on the Rockingham-Page county line, where Ambrose Huffman ran a large milling operation—a combination mill that ground flour and feed and a water-powered sawmill—and a store. A good many of the extended Huffman family lived on adjacent properties.

That morning the Huffmans' granddaughter, Ida Carrier, who was almost seven years old, walked over from her parents' farm to be with her grandparents. Years later she remembered that when the cavalrymen informed her grandmother, Christiana Huffman, that they had orders to burn the barns and mills of the Valley, she told them that they had "come too late to burn the barn. A hand more powerful than yours has taken care of that—it was struck by lightning and burned to the ground two weeks ago." The soldiers had to be content with the mill and the store, which were quickly destroyed by an intense conflagration.

Ida ran back to her own home, arriving just in time to witness the discovery by the Federals of "a lot of pies" that her mother had been baking. The interlopers breakfasted on the pies before moving on.[9]

Soon it was time for the regiments that had been left at Port Republic to catch up to the rest of the division. They dashed through miles of charred and smouldering rubble in their effort to reach their comrades and the safety of numbers. Following them was Col. George Imboden's Eighteenth Virginia Cavalry which, only a couple of days before, had been trading newspapers and tobacco with the men of Custer's Third Division. The Confederate horsemen carried vengeance in their hearts but lacked the strength to do anything more than observe the devastation wrought by the Northerners and pick up the rare straggler.

The ground changed suddenly as the burners exited Rockingham County and entered Page, which nestles between the Blue Ridge on the east and the Massanutten on the west. A large area of the southern part of the county comprises hollows, ridges, hills, and ravines, some of which seldom feel the touch of the sun. A sergeant in the Twenty-second Pennsylvania Cavalry wrote in his diary for Sunday, October 2: "Our regiment formed the advance column to-day.

8. (Hutton 1976, 18; Interview: Mary Elizabeth Kite)
9. (Harrisonburg *Daily News-Record*, December 8, 1948)

We passed through the rough country . . . and on through the town of Luray, which has been a fine place, and camped on an elevation one mile below the town." The "rough country" was prime territory for ambush, so the troopers did not tarry but pressed quickly on to the upper reaches of the Mill, Hawksbill, and Little Hawksbill creeks. From the headwaters of these streams, northward toward Luray, was the first-rate farming and grazing land of central Page County. Many mills lined the creekbanks, fed by the abundance of local wheat and corn.[10]

When they reached Columbia Ferry on the South Fork of the Shenandoah, the Northerners burned Noah Kite's mill, which was "full of grain and feed." As they moved along they came to the remnants of the bridge that Stonewall Jackson had ordered burned near the end of his 1862 Valley Campaign to keep Gen. John Frémont and Gen. James Shields from joining forces.[11] Now, two and a half years later, the Federals splashed across the swollen ford, then split into several columns. One followed the course of the South Fork itself, while another moved cross-country northward along Mill Creek to the spot where it flowed into the river downstream. Another force cut farther to the east until it came to the Little Hawksbill and then turned north; a detachment was sent on to the Hawksbill proper, where it also turned north. The high concentration of mills and fat barns kept each of the raiding parties busy for most of that Sabbath day.

By nightfall on the 2nd Powell had most of the division bivouacked around Luray; most of its damage had been done in a thirty-six-hour period. For the next five days the horsemen would use the county seat as a base of operations from which Powell would send out units on missions of one sort or another. Many of the assignments involved tracking down bushwhackers. Guerrillas had been attacking nearly every wagon train on the pike north of Harrisonburg even before Sheridan began his retrograde movement down the Valley.[12]

The weather during this period was mostly clear, with occasional rain squalls in isolated areas. The changeability of the weather played an important role in the life of one family whose farm was in the path of destruction. A couple of miles north of Columbia Ferry, near the village of Leakesville, Martin and Peggy Strickler had set up housekeeping on the eve of the war. By 1864 they had a three-year-old daughter, Clara, and Martin's sister, Mary Catherine, had come to live with them to help out around the farm. On the day of the general burning, Mrs. Strickler looked to the east and south and saw "many barns blazing." Not long after that hard men swarmed into the yard and began to apply their torches

10.   (Farrar 1911, 401)
11.   (PCPL, WPA Historical Inventory for Page County, Virginia, 559)
12.   (Walker 1869, 127)

to the Strickler's outbuildings and barn. Aunt Catherine, as she was called in the family, ran to the barn and called on the soldiers to stop what they were doing. They paid no attention to her and continued to build their fires around the structure. When she saw that her words had no effect, she did the only thing that she felt would give her power over the situation: she turned her eyes to Heaven and, raising her arms, invoked God's help in this moment of extreme distress. Almost immediately, according to the family legend, clouds rolled over the farm and a brief torrent of rain fell, completely quenching the fires at the barn.

When the rain passed the soldiers scrambled to the Stricklers' kitchen to reignite their brands, and soon they had new fires kindled against the walls of the barn. Aunt Catherine fell to her knees in the shallow mud slick in the barnyard and prayed for more rain. Sure enough, another band of rain passed over the farm and doused the flames a second time. When the same scene was repeated yet a third time, the frustrated soldiers mounted up and rode away, leaving the barn slightly scorched but still intact.[13]

A half mile farther north, along Mill Creek, was an area that was one of the first to be settled in the Shenandoah Valley, where ancestral beliefs and customs were still very much alive. A squad came to the farm of Martin Coffman, a well-to-do, peaceful farmer who was believed to have powers. Coffman was known locally as a fire witch—a person who through the use of incantations could take the pain from a severe burn and do other mysterious things as well. The farmer used his gift for the good of his neighbors, yet they said of him, "he could do more than eat cake." This old Pennsylvania-German saying meant that he had the ability to hurt as well as help.

When one of the Yankees entered the barn, the old man followed him in. The soldier scraped together a pile of tinder and was lighting it when Coffman laid a hand on his shoulder. The little blaze immediately went out. The bluecoat restarted the fire. Again Coffman laid his hand on the Northerner's shoulder, and again the flame died. This time the Federal unholstered his revolver and ordered the farmer to leave the barn.

"I can't stop you from doing this, but you are going to a bad end," the old man said. He walked out onto the barn bridge, turned to face the cavalryman, and said, "I *could* cause you to burst into flames." He then left the scene without demonstrating this power.

13.   (Strickler 1977, 302-3)

When the squad left, the barn was fully engulfed in flames. Somewhere a little to the east the Federals ran into some Confederate irregulars, who killed all of them. The Federals were buried, and corn shocks were built over the graves to mask them.[14]

Another mile and a half to the northwest, in a bend of the South Fork below the New Market and Sperryville Turnpike crossing, there was a thriving commercial complex called Old Fredericksburg after the busy port on the Rappahannock. One of the largest flour mills in the county—with a log upper structure over a dressed limestone foundation—was fast by the river. It had served the area for sixty years.

Joel Mauck owned the mill and most likely had an interest in the docks and warehouses that lined both sides of the river. Here flatboats were loaded with country produce, flour, iron, and other items for shipment downriver to Harper's Ferry. A Union burning party rode in and ended it all when its soldiers fired all of the buildings, including Mauck's barn. The glow of the burning logs that had been the mill could be seen for miles as night fell.[15]

On a hill overlooking Old Fredericksburg stood River View, the brick home of Rebecca Kauffman, a widow, and her two Confederate soldier sons. In the family cemetery below River View was the grave of a third son, Joseph, the eldest, who had been killed at the battle of second Manassas. Although the house dated from 1820, the family of Rebecca's late husband, Daniel, had owned land here since before the Revolution.

Enoch Kauffman, age twenty-four, was a sergeant in the Tenth Virginia Infantry. He had been caught up in the rout of Early's army at Fisher's Hill on September 22, and rather than risk being overtaken and captured by Sheridan's pursuing men, he had headed into the Massanutten range. On the morning of September 30, after a wearying week in the mountains, he had crossed the river and come home.

Seventeen-year-old Philip Kauffman, a private in the Thirty-fifth Battalion Virginia Cavalry known as the Comanches, was visiting his home while in the county on a scouting detail. The Comanches were considered by federal authorities to be a guerrilla outfit just a small degree above bushwhackers.

Someone informed the burning party that the Confederates were in hiding on the place, and both were taken into custody. As they were mounted on horses and led away, Mrs. Kauffman could do little more than weep; her pleas to the

14.   (Interviews: Jesse Thomas Modisett and John H. Modisett)
15.   (PCPL, WPA Historical Inventory for Page County)

cavalrymen to spare her sons fell on deaf ears. The men were taken to Luray, where Powell had set up his headquarters on a knoll on the western edge of town. There they were locked up and held under guard until the colonel could find the time to deal with them.[16]

In the meantime Powell sent out detachments on various missions paramount to the security of his division and Sheridan's flank. One unit was sent into the Blue Ridge Mountains when Powell was informed by a Northern sympathizer that a band of bushwhackers was camped at a certain location. The Union horsemen attacked and destroyed the camp, killing one man. Powell reported that his men had "surprised a party of bushwhackers, destroyed their rendezvous, capturing 2 prisoners, 10 wagons (loaded with plunder of every description), medical supplies to the value of $5,000, horses, mules, etc., and sent one bushwhacker to his long home."

As that detail was returning from the Blue Ridge with the two bushwhackers in tow, a Union soldier was found dead near Luray with his throat cut. Powell flew into a rage at the news and ordered the Kauffman brothers to be executed in retaliation. The prisoners were informed that death awaited them on the morrow; there was nothing they could do but resign themselves to their fate.[17]

Rebecca Kauffman and her daughter, who had come to town for information about Enoch and Philip, were told of the summary sentencing and imminent execution. In an audience with Colonel Powell Rebecca pleaded for the lives of her sons but was told nothing could be done; the decision would stand. The bereft women left in tears.

16.   (Murphy 1989, 159; Devine 1985, 96)
17.   (OR, Series I, Vol. XLIII, Pt. 1, 508)

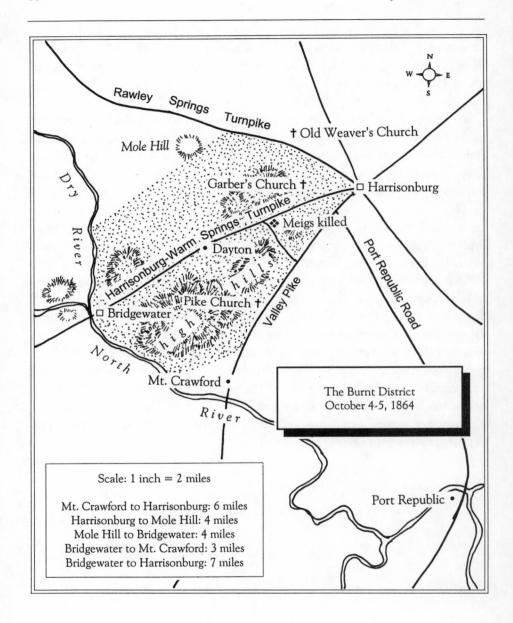

Rawley Springs Turnpike

Mole Hill

† Old Weaver's Church

Garber's Church †

□ Harrisonburg

Dry River

Harrisonburg–Warm Springs Turnpike

✜ Meigs killed

• Dayton

Port Republic Road

high hills

□ Bridgewater

Pike Church †

Valley Pike

North River

Mt. Crawford •

The Burnt District
October 4-5, 1864

Port Republic •

Scale: 1 inch = 2 miles

Mt. Crawford to Harrisonburg: 6 miles
Harrisonburg to Mole Hill: 4 miles
Mole Hill to Bridgewater: 4 miles
Bridgewater to Mt. Crawford: 3 miles
Bridgewater to Harrisonburg: 7 miles

Chapter Ten

THE BURNT DISTRICT

While following Early's retreating forces, Sheridan had moved farther and farther from immediate and strong support in his rear. He had been plagued by the raids of Southern partisan rangers even before leaving the Lower Valley; the raids seemed more acute now, with every hill, ravine, woodlot, and window being places of concealment from which to fire on small parties of Union soldiers. In addition to the active, recognized bands of partisans, other groups formed to harass Sheridan's supply and communication network. A Richmond newspaper reported that "our guerrillas and irregular bands in the Valley have completely cut Sheridan's communications with Winchester."[1]

A few squads of regular Confederate cavalry scouts were sent into the Union lines to gather information about the dispositions of the federal forces so Early could be on firmer ground should he decide to renew the contest with Sheridan at Harrisonburg. On the afternoon of Monday, October 3, a small band of scouts slipped across the North River in drizzling weather and wound its way among the federal camps. Sadly and unintentionally, that action unleashed a firestorm of devastating proportions.

Lt. John Meigs and two orderlies had been out since daybreak that Monday, making the rounds of the camps to verify the position of each brigade so they could be moved efficiently at Sheridan's command. They ended their circuit near dusk, about a mile north of Dayton. A light rain was falling as they headed

1. (Richmond *Examiner*, October 7, 1864)

Lt. John Rodgers Meigs in his U.S.
Military Academy uniform. (U.S.
Army Corps of Engineers)

back toward headquarters at Harrisonburg. They passed the pickets at the junction of the Warm Springs Turnpike and
entered the Swift Run Gap Road, which ran
over a set of low hills to the Valley Pike.

There was a belt of woods about a hundred yards from the junction, on the right.
Suddenly, about thirty yards ahead of Meigs's
party, there emerged three riders wearing
oilcloths for protection against the drizzle.
The trio turned away from Meigs and continued at a walk, riding three-abreast up
the hill. Meigs urged his horse into a trot,
and the orderlies followed him in single file.
As he neared the unknown men, he called
for them to halt. They slipped into single
file but kept moving at a relaxed pace.

The men Meigs had surprised were Confederate scouts from Wickham's brigade
sent to gather information about the disposition of Union troops between Dayton and
the Valley Pike. Benjamin Franklin ("Frank")
Shaver of the First Virginia Cavalry, whose
home was close by, was guiding troopers George Martin and F. M. Campbell of
the Fourth Virginia Cavalry on the mission. Campbell, who was General
Wickham's chief scout, was actually in command. Shaver had been included in
the detail because it was thought he knew "every cow path" in the area. He had
remarked when assigned to the task that he "would like to go home and see the
folks and get a good square meal."[2]

When the Southerners had crossed the North River earlier in the day, they
had been five in number. Near the river they captured two federal pickets; one
of the Confederates suggested they shoot the prisoners. Shaver strongly ob-
jected, saying, "If you want to kill them, give them their arms, and two of you
fight it out with them. I will kill the first man who attempts to kill them."
Campbell then ordered two of the scouts to take the prisoners back into
Confederate lines while he, Shaver, and Martin continued.[3]

2.   (Staunton Yost's Weekly; Wayland 1973, 187; Interview: Joseph H. Meyerhoeffer)

In an attempt to miss the Warm Springs Turnpike picket post, they had turned eastward, hoping the dreary weather and the approach of night would allow them to reach Shaver's father's home unde-tected. When the scouts realized that fed-eral horsemen were approaching from behind, Campbell asked Shaver, "Shall we run or fight?" To which Shaver re-plied, "Fight!" Campbell ordered them to widen the gaps between their mounts to enable them to wheel around at the mo-ment of confrontation. In preparation, each had drawn his revolver under his oilcloth cape. Perhaps these movements, in addition to the manner in which they had entered the road, had alerted Meigs to draw his own weapon.

As Meigs drew up beside Martin, the Confederate showed his revolver and de-manded the lieutenant's surrender. Meigs discharged his weapon from its place of concealment and shot the man through

Just to the left of the two trees is the spot along the Swift Run Gap Road where Lieutenant Meigs was killed. (Author's photo)

the groin; Martin pulled the trigger of his own weapon and slumped forward in the saddle, yet he held on. The shots that followed in quick succession were muffled to flat pops by the damp air. Shaver aimed his revolver at Meigs's head and pulled the trigger. Campbell fired his weapon into the officer's body. Meigs reeled, fell from the saddle, and lay dead in the roadway. In the confusion, one of his orderlies leaped from his horse, jumped a split rail fence, and disappeared into the enclosing gloom; the other orderly threw up his hands and surrendered.[4]

The wounded Martin pleaded with his companions to get him away from the federal lines. The prisoner was warned to keep his mouth shut and was given Meigs's horse to lead, while his horse was led by one of the scouts. The party

3.   (Staunton *Yost's Weekly*)
4.   (Ibid.) Frank Shaver died in 1895. His personal account of the Meigs affair was found among his papers. He always maintained that the confrontation could not have been avoided. Friends of his reported, "That Lieutenant Meigs had fallen by his hand was a grief to Shaver." It was found that the hammer of Martin's revolver had fallen on a defective percussion cap.

galloped back down the road toward the picket post, blew past it at full speed, crossed the turnpike, and rode up the wooded hillside to the west, where it vanished into the trees. The confused pickets did not fire until the scouts were well off into the woods; their shots had no effect but to urge the riders to greater speed.

The scouts and their prisoner rode on into the night for some distance, looping back south and west of Bridgewater to the vicinity of Spring Creek. Near there they left Martin at the home of Robert Wright, and Wright sent to Bridgewater for Dr. T. H. B. Brown, who came to look after the man's wounds.

Shaver and Campbell, with their prisoner, re-crossed North River and made their way back to the camp of the First Virginia Cavalry at the village of Milnesville, about four miles south of Bridgewater. From there Campbell rode on to his own regiment's camp on the Valley Pike near Burke's Mill; his Fourth Virginia was part of Thomas Rosser's Cavalry Division, which had arrived from eastern Virginia the day before.[5]

With Rosser was the Laurel Brigade, whose greatest strength was that most of its men were native to western Virginia. They had seen much hard service recently, yet their spirits were buoyed—they were going home. They felt they could not be beaten on their own turf, the difference in numbers notwithstanding.

At the news of Meigs's death Sheridan flew into a rage; he had been constantly irritated by guerrillas and bushwhackers since coming to the Valley in August, but now they had killed one of his favorite and most promising young officers. The orderly who escaped reported that the trio had been fired on by civilians and that the lieutenant had been shot down in cold blood while trying to surrender. It is likely that, because of the turmoil, and in his haste to save himself, he had heard Martin's demand for surrender and nothing else. He also reported that he had thought the men ahead of them had been their own because they were wearing "rubber overcoats."

Sheridan considered Meigs's death to be murder, not an act of war. Even after it became known that the men on the road were Confederate cavalrymen on a scouting mission, the story persisted that Meigs had been ambushed and killed in cold blood. The question that should have been raised, but was not, is this: why would three Confederates, surrounded by thousands of Federals, want to draw attention to themselves by ambushing Meigs?[6]

5.   (Driver 1991, 101)
6.   (*Rockingham Register*, August 16, 1895)

The following morning one of Sheridan's aides, Maj. George A. Forsyth, was sent to find the scene of the encounter. A sergeant of the provost guard on the road reported that he had just come upon the body of a lieutenant a few hundred yards ahead and pointed Forsyth to the spot. Meigs was fully stretched out, with one arm partially raised. His other arm was extended at his side, and just beyond the hand was his revolver. Upon examination it was found that one round had been fired. There was a wound just under his right eye and another in the left side of his chest. Forsyth speculated that Meigs had been "murdered by members of either Mosby's or White's gang" when he made his report that evening. In closing he lamented, "I have never been so pained in my life as I have at the death of little Meigs."[7]

Sheridan did not wait to see if more information would be forthcoming. His frame of mind toward bushwhackers in general and this incident in particular is reflected in one of his reports: "Lieutenant John R. Meigs, my engineer officer, was murdered beyond Harrisonburg, near Dayton. . . . Since I came into the Valley from Harper's Ferry, every train, every small party, and every straggler, has been bushwhacked by the people."

Chaplain Edwin M. Haynes of the Tenth Vermont Infantry was incensed over the Meigs killing and wrote:

> This, every living soldier who was in this campaign knows to be true. The people were meek-faced citizens by day, and in the presence of any considerable body of Union troops; but as soon as the troops were out of sight, when darkness came on, they became desperate and bloodthirsty guerrillas; and in this character they stole upon our men like savages, and shot them down or dragged them away to the woods where some of them were found hung up by their heels with their throats cut. . . . Concealed in their houses, or in the guise of friends, they made bloody capital of our conversation, counted our files for the Confederate Chief, and pounced upon the weary soldier who, lame and panting, had fallen a few rods behind the column, to drag him away a prisoner, or butcher him on the spot. Could anything justify their course? Could any punishment be too severe?[8]

7.   (NA, Forsyth Letter) For years Col. James Forsyth, Sheridan's chief of staff, has incorrectly been identified as the officer who found Meigs.
8.   (HRCHS, Civil War Files) There is a tradition that along the Back Road near Brock's Gap six or seven burners from Custer's division were captured and hanged.

In direct reprisal for this act of "murder," Sheridan ordered that the town of Dayton and surrounding houses be burned to the ground. Meigs had not been dead more than a few hours when Custer was summoned to headquarters and in person received orders to begin burning homes and barns in the condemned area. The legend is that as Custer and Sheridan took leave of one another in the yard of the Byrd house, the young brigadier sprang to his horse and called back over his shoulder, "Look out for smoke!"

Chaplain Louis Boudrye of the Fifth New York Cavalry of Custer's division wrote that Captain Lee, the provost marshal of the division, issued orders to the regiment to "burn every building within a circle of three miles from the scene of the murder."[9]

While the cavalrymen of Custer's Fifth New York made ready to go to work in the area around Dayton, the men of the 116th Ohio Infantry learned to their dismay that it would be their job to burn the town. They had come to know and like many of the inhabitants during their short stay. In the early hours of the morning of October 4 they went from house to house, waking the families and informing them that the town was to be destroyed that evening.

The older folks and small children were bundled up in blankets against the cool and damp fall air as the more able-bodied residents began to remove as many possessions as they could from their condemned homes. Some of the people later related unexpected acts of kindness—some of the Northerners helped them to move their belongings to safer ground.[10] Lizzie Coffman remembered that a Union guard was posted to discourage "foragers" from helping themselves to items from the pile in front of her home.[11]

Sarah Shrum, whose husband Samuel was away with the local reserves, had a parlor window open when a soldier rode right up to the house. His horse's head was inside the room as he informed her that she had to leave. She could feel the horse's breath on her arm. She and her seven-year-old son Joe began to move their belongings with the help of a Union soldier.[12]

One Ohio soldier later recalled "such mourning, such lamentations, such crying and pleading for mercy. I never saw nor never want to see again, some were wild, crazy, mad, some Cry[ing] for help while others would throw their arms around yankee soldiers necks and implore mercy."[13]

---

9.   (LCMD, Rodgers Family Papers, Series 1; Boudrye 1865, 176)
10.   (Sites and Hess 1962, 65; Interview: Joseph H. Meyerhoeffer)
11.   (Leigh Private Collection, Coffman Letter)
12.   (Sites and Hess 1962, 65)
13.   (Grimsley 1995, 184)

One Union cavalryman in Custer's division described the scene in a letter to his wife: "In the town of Dayton everything was carried out of the houses and left out till morning. . . . [T]he soldiers carried off whatever they had a mind to but I did not touch a single thing." He also noted that the "people here had made large supplys of apple butter but the Yankees used it up."[14] Lizzie Coffman reported that the bands of cavalrymen wandering around were the main culprits when it came to thievery.[15]

• • •

The targeted area reached south to Bridgewater, east to the Valley Pike, and north to Harrisonburg and the Rawley Springs Turnpike. The Dry River, which runs eastward from the mountains for a number of miles before turning south-ward near the village of Rushville, marked the rough boundary on the west side of the proscribed area.

The townsfolk saw homes beyond the town's environs engulfed in flame as the Fifth New York Cavalry began to carry out its assignment. One of the first places targeted was the farm of Noah and Sarah Wenger, just fifty yards from the spot where Meigs had been killed. Whether or not the Wengers accepted Sheridan's offer of transportation is not known, but Wenger loaded personal items on a wagon while his wife baked bread for their journey and tried to keep five-year-old Peter close to her. Their preparations were hindered, however, as the soldiers appropriated her baked goods as soon as they came out of the oven. The Wengers complained to an officer, who put a guard on the house. Without the harassment, it did not take them long to finish packing. They pulled out into the road where Meigs had been shot less than twenty-four hours before and drove over to the Valley Pike, where they joined a refugee train made up of some four hundred wagons.

Soon after their departure, a group of cavalrymen arrived to burn the place. Andy Thompson, the fourteen-year-old boy who worked part-time for the Wengers, watched as the soldiers piled hay against the barn, broke up some weatherboarding for kindling, and set it ablaze. After seeing it well-caught, they rode on to another farm. Before too long a second squad of federal horsemen arrived. They entered the house, emptied the chaff from bed ticks against a wooden partition and kindled it, then withdrew to the yard as smoke began to roll from the top of the doorway. Andy, under their gaze, grabbed a crock that

14.   (USAMHI, Martin Papers)
15.   (Leigh Private Collection, Coffman Letter)

Susan Swope, who answered a Union soldier's question with one of her own. (Swope Family)

was upended on a fence paling and filled it with water. He threw the water on the fire, then stamped out the lingering embers with his feet. For some reason the men did not restart the fire or punish Andy for his interference in their work. When the Wengers returned during the next year, their house still stood because of the courage and loyalty of their hired boy.[16]

Across the field and the Swift Run Gap Road from the Wenger farm Waverly, the old brick residence of the late Judge Daniel Smith, did not fare as well. Flames roared from its windows and ate away at its beautiful mahogany double-front doors.

Detachments of the Fifth New York Cavalry worked their way out from the storm center. A person standing on the roof of the house on the highest eminence in Dayton would have seen smoke rising from burning homes in every direction.

One group of tough, blue-clad horsemen descended on Reuben Swope's farm, which was on a side road about a half a mile north of town. Swope begged them to stop, but to no avail. His wife, Susanna, and their three grown daughters looked on in disbelief as the Northerners set all of the outbuildings on fire. The girls were, however, given permission to enter the house and retrieve family heirlooms they wished to save from the coming conflagration. One of the soldiers asked twenty-year-old Susan Swope, the youngest daughter, if she thought that the women of the Valley would ever forgive the Northern soldiers for burning their homes. A quick light flashed in her eyes as she replied, "Do you think if it were Southern soldiers burning the houses of your mothers and sisters they would be forgiven?"

Once the girls had gathered what they could from the house, the soldiers shooed them out and set fires in each of the downstairs rooms. The soldiers left, but before departing they warned the family that they would return later, and if

16.   (Sites and Hess 1962, 66-67)

they found that the fires in the house had been extinguished, they would shoot them all. Despite the warning, as soon as the burners were out of sight the Swopes immediately filled the hogs' slop buckets with water and, with much exertion, saved their home.

A little later, as he and his family surveyed the loss of all of their other buildings, Swope considered what they had done. Fear for the lives of his wife and children prompted him to set the fires anew, thus becoming an unwilling yet compliant accomplice in the destruction of his own home.[17]

The blue horde visited every farm in the three miles between Dayton and Bridgewater. At Joseph and Abigail Coffman's, all eleven of the slaves ran off, including the trusted Harence and Lee, who "told the devils where our stock was." Even with the treachery of the two slaves, the federal horsemen did not find the hidden horses

Abigail Lincoln Coffman, Abraham Lincoln's first cousin once removed. (Estate of John W. Wayland)

and cattle, but the soldiers did kill all of their hogs and burn the barn, new smokehouse, and granary besides destroying most of the fencing on the place. The house was spared, although the details of the event have been confused by time and telling.

The most often-told story is that sixty-four-year-old Abigail Coffman stood on her porch and called to the soldiers that they dared not burn her house because she was a first cousin of Abraham Lincoln's. In reality she was Lincoln's first cousin once removed; her father and Lincoln's grandfather were brothers.

Another story holds that Mrs. Coffman's devoted slave woman went to Union headquarters and told the officers that her mistress was a near relation of the U.S. president and that she personally had been treated kindly during her servitude with the family. This story is brought into question by another that maintains the house was spared because it was used as Custer's headquarters;

17. (Swope Family History Committee 1977, 32; Interview: James O. Swope)

instead of going to headquarters, the slave woman would have been there already.

Yet another story is that a Union officer found Joseph Coffman's Masonic apron when he entered the house to burn it, and that that brought about a reprieve. Whatever the truth, the house was left standing while most of those around it were reduced to ashes.[18]

Illness in a home in some cases brought mercy and in other cases did not. It all depended on the temperament of the man in charge of the particular detachment. Just to the east of Dayton a house was spared because the owner's old aunt was bedfast. Just to the north of town, at the Abraham Paul home, a similar situation spared the house, but the barn was torched.

A little farther down Cook's Creek from the Coffmans' was Retirement, the home of John Alexander Herring Sr., whose son was a sergeant in McClanahan's battery in Imboden's brigade. The Herring family was one of the oldest in the region; the farm was extensive and the house, built in 1776, was a fine one. The story goes that the elderly Herring was ill, and that the soldiers carried him from the house and dumped him in the yard. From his position on the ground, with his wife standing over him, he watched as household goods tossed from the windows smashed on the earth below. Following this needless destruction, the house was set on fire, along with the barn and other outbuildings.

Across the creek from Retirement, a tenant house on the Herring property was occupied by the Valentine Bolton family. Bolton, age forty-five, was either away with the county reserves or off hiding livestock for his landlord. When the burning detail arrived, Mary Bolton, her three young children, mother-in-law, and sister-in-law were told to vacate the premises as the house was about to be destroyed. Some of the soldiers slipped inside to plunder the family's belongings before applying the torch. Others, with more helpful dispositions, carried furniture from the house so that all of the Bolton's property would not be lost in the flames.

As Mrs. Bolton stood comforting her children, a soldier approached holding out a book he had found—a Masonic manual. He asked, "Is your husband a Mason?" She was not pleasantly disposed toward the men who had come to burn the roof from over her head, and snapped back, "Yes, he is!" She must have been somewhat surprised at the magical properties of this answer, for in an instant the other soldiers were told that the house was not to be burned. Property that had been removed was taken back inside, and a guard was left to protect the

18.   (Wayland 1973, 196; Interview: Joseph H. Meyerhoeffer)

premises from other details that were crisscrossing the area. Thus the tenant house survived, yet the manor house burned within sight of it.[19]

Another estate near those of the Boltons and Herrings belonged to Lewis Byrd, who had enlisted at the first call for troops in 1861 and had served faithfully as a sergeant in the Tenth Virginia Infantry. He had been wounded and captured at Chancellorsville in the spring of 1863, and his left leg was amputated below the knee. As he languished in the federal prison at Elmira, New York, a burning party from that very state destroyed every building on his property.[20] The Rockingham *Register and Advertiser* reported, "The enemy burnt Mr. Byrd's barn with all its contents, two dwelling houses, his shop, lumber house."[21]

David Landis, a young Mennonite clergyman, had taken advantage of Sheridan's offer and had been given a six-mule team and wagon to move his family away. The Landises quickly packed what they could, mostly bedding and clothes, and went to Harrisonburg in a falling rain the evening that Meigs died. They stayed out in the open for the next couple of days while waiting for the refugee train to get under way. During the wait Landis became uneasy about his farm. He recalled later, "I went back to see the state of things there, and found the destruction completed. The dwelling house and barn with all their contents and all the outbuildings were entirely consumed by the flames."[22]

Another Mennonite who thought it would be folly to stay in the Valley after Sheridan was done with it left this vivid account of his feelings at the time:

> The Union army came up the Valley sweeping everything before them like a hurricane; there was nothing left for man or beast from the horse down to the chicken; all was taken. So we felt as though we could not subsist; and besides, they were burning down barns and mills in every direction around us. Not feeling willing to stay and again have the rebel army over us, searching for something to eat, I went to Harrisonburg Head Quarters to see about getting away.[23]

Benjamin Wenger, a successful farmer and Mennonite deacon in the area, suffered heavily during this time. He had worked hard to build up his farm so he would have something to give his children when it came time for them to set

19.   (Wayland 1973, 194-95; Sites and Hess 1962, 66; Interview: Joseph H. Meyerhoeffer)
20.   (Murphy 1989, 143) In this work Murphy has incorrectly recorded Lewis Byrd's name as Levi.
21.   (Rockingham *Register and Advertiser*, February 10, 1865)
22.   (Horst 1967, 105-6)
23.   (Ibid., 105)

up housekeeping on their own. To that end he had just built a new home on his property; the old home was to go to his son Abram and his young family. But on that terrible Tuesday one of the Northern cavalry details cantered down his lane, and soon both houses and the barn were engulfed in flames. Three thick towers of smoke pushed against the leaden sky. Horses and cattle were driven off, and forage and produce were loaded onto wagons and taken away.[24]

Less than a mile east of Bridgewater a squad of Custer's cavalry swooped in on the Byerly farm and merchant mill complex.

In 1833 young Joseph Byerly had been closing up the mill late one night when he looked up into the dark sky and witnessed a long and spectacular meteor shower. Having never seen anything like it, he concluded that the world must be coming to an end. He woke the members of his family, gathered them together, and spent the night reading the Bible and praying in preparation for Judgment Day. With the coming of dawn the Byerlys realized that the Lord had "fooled 'em," and they returned to their normal existence.

Byerly had passed away before the war began, and his widow now ran the farm and managed the milling enterprise. On this day, with the wind rustling through the yellow leaves of the poplars along the river, it seemed to the family that the world really was coming to an end. The soldiers carried out their work quickly, and both of the Byerly barns and most of the outbuildings were already fully ablaze before the widow Byerly was fully aware of what was happening out on her property. When the burners turned their attention to the house and mill, Mrs. Byerly pleaded that these two structures at least should be spared. After questioning her, they learned that she was a widow, and the cavalrymen, per orders, remounted and rode on without inflicting further damage.[25]

Over on the west side of the Valley Pike, near the Pike Mennonite Church, the farmers had been warned the day before to pack up and clear out as their homes and farm buildings were to be destroyed. Michael Shank, whose farm was some two hundred yards north of the church, decided to leave with the other refugees who were gathering at Harrisonburg. He and his wife, Lydia, had packed their possessions in the wagons, and his five children stood crying in the rain as he hitched up the teams.

His wife rode with the youngest child in the wagon while Shank led the team on foot. The other four children, including nine-year-old Kate, also walked. Kate

24.   (VSL, WPA Inventories, Rockingham and Scott Counties) Even after all of this, the Wengers did not lose their faith. At the end of the hostilities they built anew, with Benjamin living to see his family prosper once again. Abram was ordained in the ministry of their church.

25.   (Ibid.)

weighed all of thirty-six pounds that day. At birth she had weighed only a pound and a half and was so small she could be placed in a quart cup and covered with a hand. Her own hand was so small that its palm could be hidden by a kernel of corn. As little as she was, she came from stock that had weathered adversity over the centuries; she walked all the way to Pennsylvania and later told the story of those difficult and confusing times to her fifteen children.[26]

The Shanks moved along the congested pike toward Harrisonburg and were hardly out of sight of their home when a burning detail arrived and set about reducing their once thriving and prosperous farm to a scorched mark on the earth.[27]

As the burning continued in the outlying area around Dayton, the townsfolk awaited their fate.

26.   (Interview: Emma Shank Delp; Delp 1990, 3-6)
27.   (Horst 1967, 102)

Chapter Eleven

THE BURNT DISTRICT WIDENS

Back in Dayton, the townspeople waited in fear within the eye of the storm. Some huddled with their possessions in the fields and on the hills around the town while others moved back and forth between their homes and the makeshift camps, ferrying whatever they could from their condemned property. They spent the night in the open "with great fires raging on every side and what little sleep that was had was taken on sleeping couches stretched on the sod." In the morning they saw "a dense blanket of smoke and fog that had settled over the country," hiding from view "the awful effect of the great holocaust of fire of the evening before."[1]

Although it must have seemed as if the end of the world were coming, even then forces in the guise of Lt. Col. Thomas F. Wildes were attempting to lessen the blow. Wildes commanded the First Brigade of the First Infantry Division of Gen. George Crook's Army of West Virginia, which included his old regiment, the 116th Ohio Infantry. He was sensitive to the situation in which his boys had been placed, admitting later that the people of Dayton "were very kind to our men." Because of this relationship and his own reservations about retaliation against civilians, he wrote a note to Sheridan in which he "urged and begged [him] to revoke the order in so far as Dayton was concerned."[2]

Wildes gave his messenger strict instructions to place the plea directly into

1.   (Horst 1967, 102)
2.   (Wildes 1884, 192)

*Lt. Col. Thomas F. Wildes
requested that Dayton be spared.
Years later the citizens of Dayton
erected a monument in his memory.
(USAMHI)*

Sheridan's hand and no other and to tell the general that he had been ordered to wait for an answer. The messenger reported back that Sheridan had "read the note and swore, read it again and swore, examined and cross-examined the messenger. He was in great grief over the death of his valued staff officer." Despite his outburst, Sheridan held Wildes in high regard and was perhaps persuaded by the plea. He reflected in silence for a moment, then yielded. The order to burn the town was rescinded, although the order to burn the outlying homes still stood.

While this was happening, word of the order to destroy Dayton and the reasons behind it filtered through the Confederate lines to the camp of the First Virginia Cavalry, where Frank Shaver and his Yankee prisoner were resting from their exertions of the previous night. Shaver, upon hearing the news, took the Federal to Wickham's headquarters, where he was offered his freedom if he would go to Sheridan and tell him there had been a fair fight between Meigs and regular Southern cavalrymen. The man readily agreed, and he was immediately taken to the North River and released.[3] Apparently Trooper Shaver's prisoner did not make his way to Sheridan's headquarters in time to add his testimony to Colonel Wildes's reasoning, or many other houses might have been saved.[4]

The firebrands were prepared and ready to be ignited when the 116th was called together and the announcement was made that the order had been revoked. One of the Ohio boys, who was seventeen at the time, later noted that "there was louder cheering than there ever was when we made a bayonet charge." Colonel Wildes observed a great deal of "clapping of hands and shouts

3.   (RPLGR, May 1976, 434)
4.   (Wayland 1912, 149-50; Wayland 1973, 193)

The Rawley Springs Turnpike, looking east toward Harrisonburg. The Burnt District is to the right (south) side of the pike. (Nancy Hess)

of gladness of the little children over the good news," and he saw this was "too much for even the grim and sturdy old soldiers. The sleeve of many a blouse was wet with their tears." Wildes took a measure of comfort also in the thought that in Dayton at least, if in no other place in the South, there were people who believed there were "some Yankees who had some humanity in them."[5] The thankful townsfolk moved back into their homes, and many of the men of the 116th Ohio cheerfully helped them.

Caution was still called for, however, as there were plenty of lurking scavengers bent on going through any unprotected belongings in their quest for plunder. At Lizzie Coffman's, an infantryman guarded the family's possessions as the owners set about the task of moving their things back into their home, Social Hall. She wrote to her cousin Julian that she had "carried as hard as I could until I gave out, then I said to the guard to give me his gun + I would guard the rest while it was carried in, for we had it some distance from the house. About fifty of their cavalry was standing in the road ready to plunder, when they saw the guard leave one of them came down where I was (not knowing I was

5.   (Wildes 1884, 192)

armed) finding I was raising the gun he exclaimed 'what are you doing?' I replied 'you have forced me to take up arms.' Perceiving I was in earnest he walked away and they all left, to my relief."[6]

All of the army had heard of the order to burn the town, and on the morning of October 5 many soldiers in Harrisonburg still thought the order had been carried out. George Bucklin of the Tenth Vermont Infantry of the VI Corps wrote to his father that morning:

> Sheridan is making thorough work here in the Valley, destroying every thing that would help feed the rebel army. The Town of Dayton, four miles from here, was burned yesterday afternoon in retalliation for the Murder of a Union officer there. I believe Gen. Sheridan to be the man for this place after all. It will not do to trifle with him. Though it may seem brutal to burn the homes of women and children, justice to our own brave men sometimes demands it.[7]

His misconception is not surprising since so many fires were still being set in that area. The retaliatory burning in the surrounding countryside continued into the next day.

Col. Charles Lowell, commanding the reserve brigade of the First Cavalry Division, was in camp with his brigade near Mount Crawford on the morning of the 5th. He awoke long before dawn, when the sky was surprisingly clear. He wrote to his wife:

> Did you see the new moon last night within a quarter inch of the evening star, and turning her back on him? They must have been close together an hour before I could see them; for an hour after, they were still less than an inch apart. They looked very strangely calm and peaceful and almost reproachful in the west last night,—with the whole North and East, far and near, lighted up by burning barns and houses.

He told her that his men were not ordered to participate in this assignment, although he felt "if it would help end bushwhacking . . . I would cheerfully assist in making this whole Valley a desert from Staunton northward."[8]

---

6.   (Leigh Private Collection, Coffman Letter)
7.   (Elliott Private Collection, Bucklin Letter)
8.   (Emerson 1971, 352-53)

The Mole Hill country of Rockingham County, looking west. (Author photo)

• • •

Although Dayton had been spared, nearly all of the mills along the North River from Bridgewater to Port Republic had been destroyed—and yet the burning continued. The burning parties moved over to Dry River, a couple of miles west of Dayton. From there they turned northward into the country surrounding a local landmark known as Mole Hill. At 250 feet higher than the rolling land surrounding it, the eminence is too big to be a hill, yet not quite large enough to be called a mountain. In reality it is the plug of an ancient volcano and large enough to sport a good forest of timber that began in the first rising of the hill and covered most of its surface in 1864. At the initial word of the approach of the armies, the local men and boys gathered up as much of their livestock as they could and drove them to the top of Mole Hill.

By the time the burning parties reached the area, some of the people and animals had been in the woods for ten days. What kept the soldiers of both armies from reconnoitering the hill was the fear of bushwhackers, yet had they known the area well they would have realized that there was not much real danger from that quarter—the locals were mostly pacifist Mennonites.

The patriarch of the region was the rugged, God-fearing, seventy-four-year-old Gabriel Heatwole, known far and wide as Old Doc Gabe because he practiced a type of herbal medicine. He was an active farmer, miller and cooper, and it was said that he also delivered many babies in the area. He and his wife, Margaret, had an even dozen children, all of whom lived to adulthood and had families of their own in the immediate vicinity. Some of them worked in the family cooper shops and mill on Dry River where it arcs to the south, toward Bridgewater. The family all adhered to the Mennonite faith and teachings with the exception of one grandson, Henry Heatwole. He had gone off to the war in the Tenth Virginia Infantry but now rode with Buck Woodson's partisan rangers somewhere in Sheridan's rear or on his flank.

On October 4 Doc Gabe and his sons and daughters no doubt saw the flames and smoke from the Reuben Swope farm as it was only a mile or so from their farms across mostly open ground. They had to know their time was coming, and soon.

Many of the cavalrymen who filtered into the area on the 5th seem to have had their fill of house burning the previous day. On the second day, for the most part, they targeted agricultural and commercial buildings, like Doc Gabe's shops and mill. A large contingent rode into his complex and immediately set about putting it to the torch—the mill, cooper shops, storage buildings and sheds, barrels and stockpiled lumber were swallowed up by the flames. The beams and stones eventually crashed into smoldering rubble.[9]

The closest house to the Heatwole complex was the home of Doc Gabe's granddaughter Maria and her husband, Daniel Good. Two detailed yet very different stories of the burning at this place have been passed down.

The first legend holds that a squad of cavalry arrived to set fire to her barn as Maria Good watched her grandfather's buildings burning below her house, but first the Northerners entered the house and carried off anything that caught their fancy. As the others left, one lagged behind, and with true regret he reported that he had been ordered to burn the house. Mrs. Good was shocked; this she had not expected. Days earlier other soldiers had taken away most of the livestock; the burning barn was now beyond saving. That the house was also to be taken from them was beyond her comprehension. Her obvious distress affected the Federal, and his face lightened as he told her that he would set only a small fire so that he could say that he had followed orders. He noticed a crock of milk on a table in the room, and he whispered to her that after he set the fire and left she should take up the crock. "Outen' it with milk," he told her, "that's

9.   (Hess 1979, 121)

better'n water." He then set the fire in the corner of the room and quickly took his leave. She did as he instructed and doused the little blaze; the only real damage to the house besides the looting was a scorch mark on the floor.

The second story says that soon after the Good's barn had been burned a couple of cavalrymen rode up to the house. Their horses' heads poked over the porch railing as they informed the couple that they had come to destroy the home. The couple immediately left the house with their three small children. Good sent his wife and the little ones on to the home of her uncle Simeon Heatwole, then slipped behind the garden fence, where he could observe the house without being seen. When the soldiers departed Good rushed into the house and found that the two horsemen had raked live coals from a stove onto the floor and placed a child's rocker on them. The blaze had not caught well enough to spread very far, and Daniel soon had it extinguished, leaving only scorch marks on the wide floorboards.[10]

It is probable that one story refers to an incident on another relative's farm and that through the years the location and name were lost or confused. In this way one story may have been mistakenly joined to another frequently told about the Good family.

To the north, on the east side of Mole Hill, a detachment rode up the lane of John G. Heatwole's farm; John was Doc Gabe's second eldest son and Maria Good's father. Heatwole was gone with the stock, and his second wife, Elizabeth, had to face the troopers with her stepdaughter Bettie, age eighteen. Bettie and Bishop Coffman's son John had fallen in love the previous autumn at an apple-snitsing party in the neighborhood, and she wondered if they would ever be together again. The refugee train that bore young John and his friends to safety had started north on the Valley Pike that very day.

Bettie's thoughts about John were likely cut short as the spoilers dismounted and separated to carry out their orders. The two Heatwole women kept close to the men, hoping to head off whatever mischief they could or at least minimize the damage. No doubt smaller farm buildings were lost to the incendiaries, but when they came to the barn, Mrs. Heatwole could tolerate the abuse no longer. When the soldiers gathered tinder in the center of the barn floor and set it on fire, she grabbed a rake from against a wall and vigorously pulled the pile apart before it could fairly catch. Then she leaned on the rake with a resolute look on her face, as if daring them to try her again. Twice more the soldiers formed a mound of tinder, lit it, and were shooed out of the way as the determined woman

10. (Rosenberry and Showalter 1989, 27-29; Heatwole 1970, 136-37.)

moved in and scattered the material. The blue-coated soldiers must have decided finally that they had no more time to waste at this sparring game. They mounted and rode off, leaving the barn standing.[11]

A short distance to the north and just across Rawley Springs Turnpike from the Heatwoles' was Bishop Samuel Coffman's place. It seemed as if every day for the past ten the farm had been visited by soldiers who carted off grain and hay. When Frances Coffman baked bread, she hid it from the Federals in the tall case clock in the hall.[12]

Finally, one day, the officer in charge smiled cruelly as he informed her that she had a half an hour to remove what she could from the house, after which it would be burned down. Mrs. Coffman took him at his word, and she and a thirteen-year-old daughter "worked like mad" and got most everything out, even down to "the last crock of apple butter." Following all of their frantic work, the officer coldly informed them that he had changed his mind about the house and that they could put everything back in. The soldiers did, however, set the barn ablaze before they left. Despite the scare, the family at least still had a roof over its head, which could not be said of quite a few of the families living on the south side of the pike.[13]

Some soldiers had a difficult time carrying out their orders in good conscience. A member of the Second Ohio Cavalry noted that the men of his company helped "an old lady to move her furniture, as they had rec'd orders to burn the barn + this stood near the house, but as it was nearing evening, when the officer left them, the boys all left, not one of them would fire the barn."[14]

Samuel Weaver was Frances Coffman's father. His home and farm were a little way up the pike from his daughter and on the other side of it, across from the Mennonite church named for his family. During the past week and a half the Federals had used the church as a commissary and supply depot for that sector and even as a makeshift barracks. The church members were shocked that the long pulpit desk had been used as a bunk by men who did not bother to remove their spurs as they slept. Weaver's farm, meanwhile, had been stripped bare even before the burning was ordered. Every animal on the farm had been killed or taken away, and it was bereft of produce fit for man or beast. All of the

11.   (Interview: Paul V. Heatwole; Heatwole 1970, 93)
12.   (Interview: David Coffman)
13.   (Coffman 1964, 55) The bishop and his son Jacob were probably on Mole Hill with the remnants of their livestock at this time, as their names are never mentioned in connection with this episode.
14.   (Starr 1981, 302)

fence rails had gone to the camps for cooking fires and warmth as the nights turned colder. All that was left to Weaver when the cavalrymen went to work that day were his home and farm buildings. By nightfall even these had vanished in coils of smoke.[15]

Many squads of cavalrymen who had been burning homes and farms in close proximity to Dayton the day before now hurried down the Warm Springs Turnpike toward the outskirts of Harrisonburg, trying to cover as much territory as possible before dark. About two miles south of Weaver's Church, on a road that connected the Rawley Springs Turnpike with the northern end of the Warm Springs Turnpike near Harrisonburg, was Garber's Church, the anchor for an enclave of Dunkard farms that were well within the area marked for complete destruction.

One file turned onto the Jonas Blosser farm, just south of where Garber's Church Road entered the Rawley Springs Turnpike from the west. The Blosser family's large limestone home overlooked well-cultivated fields and even better pastureland. The soldiers rode directly to the barn and set it on fire. Their officer went to the house and informed the Blossers that their home would be torched in ten minutes. Some of the cavalrymen helped to carry belongings and furniture away from the structure, yet when the brief grace period had passed, they set a fire in every room and broke out the glass in the windows so there would be a good draft. Their work completed, they remounted and cantered down the road to the next farm.

Just behind the Blosser farm, and nearer to the church, was the Burkholder family farm. The officer who led his band onto this property was tired of destroying homes and had already decided to burn only the barn. When he realized just how close the barn was to the house and considered that the strong breeze that had come up would carry the fire to the other building, he called the whole thing off. Both structures were spared.[16]

Passing the entrance of the road to Garber's Church, the same party turned down the next farm lane to the left, which led to Daniel Garber's home, a large frame house with a double front porch. As the Northerners neared the house and barnyards they noticed that somehow the farm's pigs had been overlooked thus far. The infantry had driven off the rest of the livestock; perhaps the pigs were left because they were difficult to herd. Several men honed their sabers to a keen edge on a large grindstone that stood in the barnyard, then waded into

15.   (NA, Southern Claims Commission Files)
16.   (Hess 1979, 132)

Barbara Geddes, née Garber, in old age. She is third from the left. (Olen Landes)

the pig enclosure and slaughtered the swine. The squeals of the terrified animals rang sharp in the heavy air. A wagon was called in from the pike, and the carcasses were loaded and carted off.

The Garbers' son, Sgt. Daniel Garber Jr., had enlisted at first chance under Confederate cavalry officer Turner Ashby. Daniel was not a shoot-over-their-heads kind of Dunkard. Already in this war he had twice been sent home to recuperate from wounds received in action. He was at this very moment somewhere south of North River with the Twelfth Virginia Cavalry, chomping at the bit to get at the men in blue who were burning so much of south central Rockingham County.

Daniel Garber Sr., age sixty, his wife, Mary, and their teenaged daughters Susan, Barbara, and Polly looked on in disbelief as the invaders lit their torches from a stove in the kitchenhouse and set afire the barn, smokehouse, granary, chickenhouse, swine shed, and every other structure. Mr. Garber followed them, pleading that the destruction be stopped, but he was ignored.

At the dwelling house, soldiers went from room to room, plundering. An officer told the women that the house would be burned soon and warned them that they had better remove quickly anything they wanted to save. Mrs. Garber,

Susan, and Polly, age fourteen, began carrying possessions out and piling them in the house yard, moving in and out of their doomed house with tears streaming down their cheeks.

Barbara, age seventeen, tried to shoo the plunderers out of the house, but to no avail. She walked onto the second-story porch and leaned on the railing as she tried to comprehend the chaos spreading across the farm. Just below she could see her mother and sisters piling whatever they could away from the house, and she could hear their sobs as they re-entered the downstairs for another load. Two soldiers, holding horses, were also watching the struggles of the Garber women. One of the bluecoats laughed out loud. "I believe every dang one of em's crying," he said. Upon hearing that, Barbara's anger reached its limit. She leaned over the railing and shouted at the man, "I'm not crying! I wouldn't cry for ya!" The startled soldiers looked up just in time to see the girl pulled into the house by a soldier who forced her down the stairs and out of the ill-fated structure. Other men had piled all of the wooden chairs they could find into one room. With such a large stack of tinder, the house was soon ablaze.

As the soldiers waited around to make sure that the fire was entirely caught, they burned the platforms and wooden pumps on the two wells in the yard. Finally, their mission completed, they secured their plunder, mounted their horses, and rode away, leaving a very disconsolate group standing there with their meager possessions as smoke swirled around them. Watching the Federals turn from the lane onto the pike Barbara said, as much to herself as to the others, "They were wicked people."[17]

Earlier in the occupation Daniel Garber had sent a horse into hiding with his second son, John, and he had also managed to conceal a barrel of flour, so the family could get by for a little while. But with soldiers still moving about, he decided to spend the night near the remnants of their belongings to keep them from being stolen. He had another house in Dayton, a few miles up the pike, and he told his wife and daughters to go there straight away. As the soldiers seemed to be heading north, and none were coming from the other direction, he thought he would be able to join them before too long. So there he stayed, while the women walked toward town.

It was nearing the end of the day; the weather had turned cold and misty, and the air was heavy with drifting smoke. As Garber sat there, with night falling, who can know what thoughts passed through his mind? For a while, at least, he

17. (Liskey and Sherwood 1990, 46; Frye 1988, 129; Interview: Olen Landes) After the war, brave Barbara Garber married Stuart W. Landes, who rode with Buck Woodson's rangers that terrible season.

must have been acutely uncomfortable, for as the house and other buildings burned and then smoldered, he was at times engulfed in smoke that choked him and made his eyes sting and tear up. The burning of the wellheads made it impossible for him to quench his thirst and relieve his parched throat.[18]

The last destruction close to Dayton was the burning of two mills on the banks of Cook's Creek by members of the Fifth New York Cavalry as they withdrew from the area. A Union soldier near Dayton wrote in his diary, "A squad of cavalry has just passed coming from the country where they have been carrying out the General's order. The whole country around is wrapped in flames, the heavens are aglow with the light thereof."[19] A young boy, looking out over the region from Mole Hill toward Harrisonburg and Dayton, filed away in his memory his impressions of the aftermath of Sheridan's retribution. In later years he wrote, "The morning after the terrible burning, gray smoke hung over Mole Hill. A stench filled the air."[20]

Lizzie Coffman, writing to her cousin Julian on October 10, summed up the opinion of many people, especially those in the outlying areas, when she wrote: "The *detested* Yankees have left."[21]

Later, in explaining to Grant the circumstances that caused him to order the homes around Dayton destroyed, Sheridan noted, "The people here are getting sick of the war. Heretofore they have had no reason to complain, because they have been living in great abundance." The statement seems a contradiction, though the first sentence certainly describes the effect of his actions against the truth of the latter one.[22]

Soon after the war the words "Burnt District" began to appear on local maps to mark the area where so many barns had been consumed by fire and where more than two dozen homes had been destroyed—a brutal act of reprisal for a death that was no more than the result of an accidental meeting in the fortunes of war.

18.   (Interview: Olen Landes; Brunk 1959, 169)
19.   (Grimsley 1995, 184)
20.   (EMU, Heatwole Scrapbook, Pt. 1, 48)
21.   (Leigh Private Collection, Coffman Letter)
22.   (Pond 1892, 199)

Chapter Twelve

On October 5 Colonel Powell issued an edict to the citizens of Page County:

> The undersigned, commanding the Second Cavalry division, Department of West Virginia, United States army, having learned that armed citizens, commonly known as bushwhackers, have been engaged in deliberately murdering Union soldiers belonging to this command while in the discharge of their duties while under orders from the Major General commanding the army, will in retaliation for such offenses committed, hang or shoot until dead two (2) Confederate soldiers, (now held by him as prisoners of war,) for every one of his command, murdered by such parties, and will also destroy all property belonging to these parties, now engaged as "bushwhackers" wherever found. (signed) W.H. Powell, Colonel commanding division[1]

Powell's report says that on October 4 he "had two bushwhackers shot to death in retaliation for the murder of a soldier belonging to my command by a bushwhacker."[2] The men who were executed were not the Kauffman brothers who had been picked up at their mother's home, but two others captured in the mountains. The colonel had reversed his order concerning the Kauffmans, who

1.   (Richmond *Examiner,* October 17, 1864)
2.   (OR, Series I, Vol. XLIII, Pt. 1, 508)

John R. Burner, a Page County farmer who resigned himself to the destruction of his barn. (Burner Family)

were sent off to the prison camp at Point Lookout, Maryland, to sit out the rest of the war. Both lived into old age knowing how close they had come to facing a firing squad under somber skies in October 1864.

On a great shelf of land above the broad plain known as Old Field to the American Indians, the substantial brick home of the Burner family overlooked the Page Valley. The New Market–Sperryville Turnpike ran just below the bluff before turning and rising up into New Market Gap.

John R. Burner, the owner of the farm, watched the columns of smoke advancing. He herded his cows out of the stockyard and drove them over the hill just north of the house, seeking safety for them in the ravine beyond. As he made his way back to the house he saw a party of men from the Second Pennsylvania Cavalry driving some of his neighbors' cattle up the pike toward the pass. Their charge was to drive them over the Massanutten on October 6 and deliver them to Sheridan's quartermaster somewhere near New Market. Having made the delivery, they were to recross the range and return to Luray.[3]

The sound of cows lowing and the clanking of their bells reached Burner's ears as the herd came under his hill. Unfortunately he was not the only creature to hear the sounds; as he looked back over his shoulder he saw his own cows coming over the hill, lured by the sounds of their sisters in the road. He tried to turn them, but to no avail—they were determined to be captured. He could do nothing but watch them trot down the lane and melt into the herd moving west.

The crestfallen farmer sat down on his porch, certain that the worst was yet to come. To fortify himself against the ordeal, he began to sing hymns aloud, which puzzled his three sons, Isaac, Danny, and Davy. It was not long before two federal horsemen turned up the lane. One of the men called out, "We've come to burn your barn!" Burner stopped singing, pointed to the building, and

3.   (USAMHI, Stevens Papers)

said, "There it is. Burn it."

The soldiers headed toward the barn with the three boys following close behind. As they searched for materials with which to start the fire, Davy cried out, "Let me get the eggs!" He dashed into the barn and returned shortly with a sack containing "four or five dozen." The soldier in charge, perhaps thinking of a son of his own back home, said to Davy, "Captain, I'll take your eggs and leave your barn." Davy immediately handed over the sack—he recognized a good deal when he heard one—and the cavalrymen departed.

Seeing the soldiers leave with the barn still intact, John Burner asked his boy what had happened. Davy said, "We traded— they took the eggs and left me the barn."

Later that night an old yellow cow who had deserted the cattle herd came wandering home, so Mrs. Burner at least had some milk for her boys for the rest of the war.[4]

A 1929 oil portrait of Davy Burner, who as a boy traded eggs to save the family barn. (Burner Family)

Near the headwaters of Hawksbill Creek, in an area known as Ida Valley, the burning had begun by mid-morning on October 2. Sometime before noon a small file of Northerners rode into the yard of Gideon Hoak's farm and reined up in front of the large, two-story log home with a split-shingle roof and stone chimneys. Gideon was away with the stock in the Blue Ridge, but his wife, Ann, was home with their six children. She stood on the small, square front porch watching the men dismount and was surprised when she recognized one of the soldiers as a cousin who had gone north before the war. The men had already been about their work for some time, and they asked for something to eat. Mrs. Hoak went to work in her lean-to kitchen and gave them a good meal, and as they cleaned their plates she asked them not to burn her house and barn. They were grateful for the food and agreed not to harm her property.

The cousin apparently carried a grudge against one of her neighbors, however,

4. (PCPL, WPA Historical Inventory for Page County; Interviews: Burner Family Members)

because he announced that they would instead "go down and burn old man Varner's mill." Emanuel Varner, a forty-four-year-old bachelor, and his brother Reuben farmed and also ran a grist mill about an eighth of a mile down the creek. Mrs. Hoak watched the bluecoats ride away, no doubt with a sigh of relief. Before too long smoke billowed from the Varners' place, and the party of horsemen arced north and west, following the course of the stream toward Luray.[5]

All along the Hawksbill and Little Hawksbill creeks during that first week in October, barns, flour mills, sawmills, granaries, stables, tanneries, and lumber yards were destroyed.

Near Luray the two creeks met and flowed on a short distance before entering the town, splitting it almost in half, east and west. From there the Greater Hawksbill flows into the broken ground north of Luray and winds its way several miles to its confluence with the South Fork of the Shenandoah.

About a mile above the point where the two Hawksbills meet, on the west side of the Greater Hawksbill, was the farm of Henry Pendleton Hershberger. Late one afternoon Elizabeth Hershberger and six of her children watched smoke rising in every direction. From their vantage point on the high porch of their five-bay brick home they could see a half a mile to the west, on the far side of the Little Hawksbill, where the large barn on Abraham Kendrick's farm blazed, the leaping flames cutting through the lurid smoke. Looking north, toward the spot where the streams joined, they could tell that great destruction was also occurring around the Willow Grove Mill.

Mrs. Hershberger and the children were anxious and fearful that their barn would be next. Pendleton Hershberger and his second-eldest son, sixteen-year-old David, were up in the Blue Ridge with the farm stock. The eldest son, John, a Confederate soldier, had been captured in the bloody fighting at Spotsylvania Court House back in May and was being held at Elmira Prison in New York State. As dusk approached, three Northern cavalrymen rode up the lane and stopped at the front gate. One of the soldiers dismounted and approached the porch on foot, accompanied by another who was still mounted. Looking up at the family, he announced in a "loud and boisterous" manner that they had come to burn the barn, but that it could be spared if the Hershbergers would give them "$30 or $40 in gold or silver." Mrs. Hershberger offered them nothing, suspecting that they or someone else would burn the barn anyway. She pulled her children close to her and pleaded with the men, who she thought were drunk, not to

5.   (PCPL, WPA Historical Inventory for Page County; 1860 Census Records for Orange, Page and Patrick Counties)

destroy the barn. The three soldiers boasted about the destruction they had already been involved in and demanded matches, as they had "run out of them."

From their elevated vantage point, some of the Hershberger children noticed a body of horsemen who had emerged from the edge of the woods on the far side of the orchard and were riding toward the house at a brisk pace. Mrs. Hershberger reported this to the Northerners below, who could not see them for the trees and outbuildings, saying that she could not tell which army they were from. One of the Yankees swore, but other than that no one seemed too concerned. They continued with their loud talk and threats as if unaware that a potentially dire situation might be developing.

The horsemen were ten mounted Confederates led by a local man, Sgt. Frank Long of the Seventh Virginia Cavalry, who was home on leave because of a head wound he had received at Ream's Station in August. When they reached the main road near an ancient oak tree, they stopped. To the Hershbergers it seemed as if their attention had been drawn to the burning buildings farther down the creek, but it was later thought that the Southerners had heard the loud voices and halted to listen. The men in gray would have been sensitive to the probability that they would likely encounter enemy units that day.

Sergeant Long and two other Confederates rode down the lane, and the Union horseman who had stopped at the gate immediately surrendered himself and his comrade's horse. One Confederate stayed with the prisoner and the other two rode into the yard and demanded the surrender of the remaining two Federals, confident that they would give up without a fight as their comrade had done. But that was not to be.

The Northerner on foot drew his revolver and leaped onto the porch yelling, "I will surrender you!" He fired a round at almost point-blank range at Sergeant Long. The bullet whistled just past his head. The frightened mother quickly drove her children into the house and slammed the door behind her. A few more shots were fired, then all was quiet. Although no one was in sight when the Hershbergers gained enough courage to peek out, they remained indoors, fearing the worst.

After dark more visitors arrived, a group of men from Luray who were known to be connected with the Confederate army. They asked if Mrs. Hershberger could spare them some supper. As she fed them, she related what had transpired earlier. She told them that she feared the Federals would come and exact terrible retribution if any of them had been killed on Hershberger property.

The men reported that they had put their horses in the barn upon their arrival, and as they walked toward the house they had stumbled over the body of one of the Federals. They had carried the corpse down by the Hawksbill and had buried it in a shallow grave, covering the site with "bundles of fodder" to make it look as if feeding livestock had disturbed the ground surface there. It was apparent that the Yankee trio had earlier extorted Samuel Stover's gold watch as a ransom for his barn; they found the watch on the body.[6] When the men took their leave, they reassured the family that they would keep watch in the neighborhood for the rest of the night.

The next afternoon a detachment of Union cavalry arrived. The commander, who appeared very agitated, told Mrs. Hershberger that it had been reported in Luray that the body of one of their soldiers was lying in a field north of the house. Mrs. Hershberger related a version of what had happened the evening before, saying that she thought the mounted man had escaped, but evidently he had been killed by the Confederates who had stayed out in the public road. The officer seemed to feel that her story was honestly told. They were "courteous" to her from that moment, but threatened dire straits for the "Gray-Jackets" when they were captured. Some of the men were detailed to bury the body in the field, and, with this job completed, the troop cantered back down the road toward Luray.[7]

Although the Hershberger property was spared, a price was paid for the deaths of the Federals. Two Marylanders of Sturgis Davis's command were probably the two Confederate soldiers mentioned in Powell's proclamation of October 5. They had been caught off guard by a squad of Union cavalry led by one of Powell's staff officers. It was said that Confederate trooper Churchell Crittenden fought them until he had emptied every load from his pistol and wounded "a Yankee lieutenant very severely." Despite his efforts, he and his companion, John Hartigan, were taken prisoner and carried into Luray. Crittenden had been "slightly wounded" but was still handled roughly. The two were brought before Powell, who ordered their execution. According to local observers they were not even allowed time to write a last letter to friends and loved ones before being shot. A Richmond newspaper called the incident an "atrocity" and declared, "The reason assigned for shooting them was that some of their men [Federals] were shot while burning barns."[8]

Some of the smoke that the Hershbergers had seen on the afternoon of the 2nd was from the Willow Grove farm and mill complex. Samuel Moore of Shenandoah County owned this milling operation and one near Mount Jackson,

6.   Samuel Stover's farm was next to the Kendrick place, to the west of the Hershbergers.
7.   (Kerkhoff 1962, 99-102; 1860 Census Records for Orange, Page, and Patrick Counties)
8.   (Richmond *Examiner*, October 17, 1864)

on the other side of the Massanutten. The mill at Mount Jackson had come to him through his marriage to Amanda Morgan, whose grandfather, John Penny-witt, had built the second mill on the site. The milling operation at Willow Grove had been purchased from Samuel Gibbons in 1860. Amanda's uncle, Ben Morgan, oversaw the day-to-day business at Willow Grove during the war.

The miller's house at Willow Grove was considered one of the finest brick dwellings in the county. It was situated on the north bank of the Little Hawksbill, and the tail of the millrace ran just in front of the yard. The mill was built of logs supported by a high rock foundation and was powered by an eighteen-foot overshot wheel. An up-and-down sawmill connected with the place used the same energy source. Orchards and a distillery were also a part of the operation. Of the destruction at Willow Grove, Amanda Moore remembered, "we had the Mill, Saw Mill, barn + all the stabling, grainery, corn crib, and everything burnt. . . . [T]he barns were full of wheat and there was also a great deal in the Mill."[9]

A little farther up the Greater Hawksbill, just on the southern edge of Luray, a New Yorker named Peter Borst had established an extensive tannery operation that covered a number of acres. Besides the tanning pits, there were storage buildings for finished hides, a leaching house, and large buildings where the tanning bark was stored. Borst had arrived in the area more than a decade before as a young, ambitious lawyer. He married a Virginia girl, rolled up his sleeves, and prepared to make his fortune. By 1864 his roots were sunk firmly in the soil of the Old Dominion, and he had fathered four children whose births were evenly spaced at two years apart. Peter Borst was an ordered man who had set his goals and met them. He had been accepted by his neighbors—indeed, he had been embraced by them. When the war clouds had begun to gather he was the commonwealth's attorney for Page County, and the people sent him to the Secession Convention to represent them. As one of the wealthiest men in the county, he was worth a regiment or more to the Confederacy. His tannery and harness shops supplied an immense amount of leatherwork to the war effort.[10]

It is almost certain that Colonel Powell himself visited Borst's tannery grounds before ordering the whole concern leveled by fire on October 6. In his report of his activities in Page County Powell remarked that Borst's tannery had been "used for the exclusive benefit of the rebel army. Unfinished leather to the value of about $800,000 was destroyed here."[11]

On October 7, with the stench of the burned tannery still in the air, the

9.   (PCPL, WPA Historical Inventory for Page County; Burruss 1993, 138-39)
10. (Strickler 1977, 377-86)
11. (OR, Series I, Vol. XLIII, Pt. 1, 508)

Second Cavalry Division pulled out of the Luray area and moved quickly northward through the rough territory of the narrowing Page Valley toward Warren County and the railroad line at Front Royal.

Many Page County slaves had departed with the Northern horde, leaving some families who had lived comfortable lives with servants as overseers of their own labor. A few homes had been destroyed, either by accident or by heartless or drunken individuals who disregarded the orders forbidding such practice. The affected people moved in with more fortunate family members or tried to fix up abandoned cabins against the coming winter. So disrupted was life in Page County that on October 24 the county court petitioned the Confederate government for relief from conscription, stating that there was "just and sufficient reason to fear starvation will be the fate of some of our citizens should the order call for all men be enforced."

When it was all over in the eastern section of the Valley, it was obvious to Sheridan and all who had taken part in the operation that there had been an able man at the helm. One member of the expedition later wrote that Sheridan "subsequently expressed his satisfaction with the choice he had made. Colonel Powell handled the division with good judgement, and for this efficiency was finally commissioned as brigadier general of volunteers."[12]

12.   (Sutton 1892, 162)

Chapter Thirteen

OF STIRRINGS GREAT AND SMALL

During Sheridan's tenure in Harrisonburg a considerable amount of restless activity occurred behind his lines. Some Confederates worked to augment Early's thin ranks by pressing local men into service, and it seemed as if every Confederate officer who had come home from the war, no matter what the reason, was prepared to annoy and disrupt the blue movement whenever the opportunity presented itself.

Confederates home on horse-gathering details in the area took the opportunity to let Uncle Sam supply the needed remounts. It was a "dangerous method of securing mounts," remembered one soldier, but it was "often the only way for them."[1] Some Valley men were afield to capture Union booty with little risk of attention from the many small units of soldiers in blue moving up and down the Valley. Other groups of pick-up irregulars comprised Confederate officers and men who were at home recuperating from or retired because of wounds or illnesses. Their actions were at most a deadly nuisance so far as the military impact on the federal forces was concerned. The greater number of these opportunists confined their activities to the periphery of the Army of the Shenandoah. The real danger for them was in having limited avenues of escape. They left the important, nerve-wracking, behind-the-lines intelligence gathering to the soldiers operating within regular commands.

In fact, the presence of the irregulars was far more important than their

1.   (Surber 1921, 24)

actions. When the general burning began, the perceived threat of being ambushed without warning and of being cut off from their unit kept the incendiaries moving quickly. The direct result was that a number of outlying farms were overlooked, thus sparing them from the harshest realities of almost total war.

Maj. George Chrisman of the Rockingham and Augusta County Reserves operated from his father's plantation north of the Mount Clinton Pike, a few miles northwest of Mole Hill. Unlike most of the farmers in his area, the major's father was a slave owner and, for Rockingham County, a large one, with twenty souls in keeping. In a hamlet called Mount Rock the Chrismans had a store and a mill which no doubt were run with the help of slave labor. Most of his own Third Battalion of Virginia Reserves were south of Richmond digging entrenchments and guarding artillery positions at Manchester.[2] Chrisman was told to gather in conscripts to augment Early's depleted forces, but he did not have much luck on his home turf. The few men who reported were kept busy riding out with the major as he tried to round up others who were not keen to serve.

Many of the Mennonite and Dunkard youths who lived in the country near the Chrisman place fled toward Shenandoah Mountain instead of making for Sheridan's camps at Harrisonburg. Chrisman and his squad tried to head some of these men off, and, since they had been neighbors, he hoped that his appeal for help in this time of crisis would be heeded at least by some. If those he brought to bay were not swayed by his arguments, they would be forced into line.

Henry VanPelt was a Mennonite who opposed the war on peace principles, yet he was not averse to violence if it were his only recourse in protecting himself or his immediate family. He was a noted hunter in western Rockingham County, and he and the major had known one another since they traipsed the local fields and hills together as children. One day, while the federal forces were still in Harrisonburg, Chrisman and his men pursued some conscientious objectors, including VanPelt, into a gap in the western mountains. Chrisman pressed the group hard. He was in front of his men and closing in on VanPelt, who was only a little over a hundred yards ahead and on foot. Suddenly the Mennonite turned, took aim with his rifle, fired, and ripped a bullet through the major's coat. This hot passage so close to his skin got Chrisman's attention and brought him and the men following him to an abrupt halt. The major had been in his share of desperate fights in this war and had been wounded in the battle at Piedmont in June; he was not about to give up his life to a neighbor. The pursuit was broken off before someone really got hurt.

2.   (Sommers 1981, 470)

Later, back at his home place, Major Chrisman gave his uniform coat to his old mammy to have the bullet hole mended. The black woman fingered the hole and snorted. "Humph! I know who put another button hole in the major's coat," she said. "Only one person can shoot like this—was Hank VanPelt!"[3]

In the north central part of Rockingham County, up along the North Fork of the Shenandoah River at the town of Broadway, a retired captain, John Q. Winfield of the Seventh Virginia Cavalry, set about collecting men who were not on active duty because of wounds or illnesses and those who had been cut off from their commands by Sheridan's advance up the Valley while in the area on horse-gathering details. He planned to put as many men as he could in the saddle to harass Sheridan's wagon trains and lines of communication.

Before the war Winfield had been a physician, having received his medical training at Jefferson College in Philadelphia in 1845. He also owned a mill and was developing interests in the natural resources of western Virginia. When the war loomed on the horizon, he organized a company of infantry named after Virginia's governor and the area of Rockingham County where the men were from, the Letcher-Brock's Gap Rifles. Their service as ground troops was brief, as they were asked to change over to a mounted company in the Seventh Virginia Cavalry. There they quickly gained a reputation for hard fighting. Captain Winfield's dependability and fearlessness as a combat leader were recognized almost from the start.

Soon after Turner Ashby's promotion to brigadier general, and almost immediately after Ashby's death in battle, Winfield's name was mentioned as a worthy successor, but the captain was ill. He had a cancer in his nose that plagued him and eventually caused him to resign his commission and return home to try to regain his health. He rested from his arduous service and treated his affliction with the prescribed methods of the period, all to no avail. In the end, the cancer could only be stopped by the removal of his nose. Now, after more than a year's recuperation, he was again strong and had grown as accustomed as he ever would to the triangular silver plate that covered the place where his nose had been. He, like Chrisman, was attempting to enlist men of the area into Confederate service.

Winfield wrote to Gen. James L. Kemper, commander of the Virginia Reserves, that before he could attend a rendezvous to enroll conscripts at the county seat in Harrisonburg, Sheridan had arrived and covered the area with his camps and patrols. Winfield instead called together a few comrades from

---

3.   (Interview: Joan Sparks)

Albert Curtis Lincoln, Confederate guerrilla leader. (Carmelita Kammann)

Ashby's old Laurel Brigade and a couple of rangers from McNeill's command, along with the odd fellow from this unit or that, and eventually he had a party of about twenty men. Although most were not fit for sustained active service, they were nonetheless veterans led by a highly competent and respected officer.[4]

Albert Curtis Lincoln, a native of north central Rockingham County, had, like John Winfield, commanded a company in the Seventh Virginia Cavalry—but there the similarity ends. The daring and reckless Lincoln had a talent for creating opportunities where none actually existed and was known for an utter disregard for danger that was seen by most people not as bravery but more like something approaching insanity.

It was the day-to-day tedium of camp life and company paperwork that finally turned Lincoln from his regular army duty. His every nerve ending tingled for adventure and release from the ordinary. Wild impulses pulled at him and distracted him from the protocol an officer was expected to follow if he wished to resign his commission. Regimental records show he went absent-without-leave in June 1864. The truth was that he had jumped and headed for home. Men who went AWOL in the Civil War because they had lost their nerve were referred to as having flanked a fight. Lincoln did not flank a fight—he retreated from boredom and discipline.[5]

Once back in his old stomping grounds, Lincoln put together a guerrilla band that attacked unwary Federals who traveled a certain section of the Valley Pike or wandered into the area between the pike and the southern reaches of the

---

4.   (Wayland 1973, 290; NA, CSR, Capt. John Q. Winfield) Winfield's service records indicate that he had to retire from the regular cavalry because he suffered from scrofula, which had begun to affect the area around his eyes. Local tradition is very strong that he had cancer in his nose. Correspondence and interviews with descendants have failed to produce even the memory of a likeness, though the tradition of the cancer is also known to family members.

5.   (Miller 1994, 194)

Massanutten Range. Most of the men who rode with him early on were deserters like himself; others were old cronies, mostly local roughnecks. In the area known as Mountain Valley and up in the Massanutten fastness, Lincoln quickly became known as a "notorious bushwhacker." Burners who ventured into his territory looked over their shoulders constantly, and with good reason.[6]

In the area near Lacey Spring, named for an early settler but sometimes referred to as Lincoln Spring, Union soldiers learned to stay particularly alert—the region was home to a number of Lincolns. An inn kept by the family had been a stage stop in the village for several years. One resident Lincoln might have caused the army to pause had he been sighted—Jacob Lincoln looked so much like his cousin, the president, that they could have been mistaken for one another.[7]

Jacob Lincoln of Lacey Spring, a cousin of President Lincoln. (Author's collection)

Everyone from Linville to Mountain Valley knew of Al Lincoln, and nearly everyone had an opinion as to the state of his sanity, but probably no one would have voiced it out loud. His wild, reckless war against small parties of Federals made him famous locally. Ten to twenty local fellows who craved unrestricted and unregulated adventure heard his claims to have killed numerous Yankees and put themselves under his banner. Legend has it that during several raids against Custer, Lincoln and his men made off with a number of federal horses, including Custer's white stallion, which the former captain rode for the rest of the war.[8]

On one occasion Lincoln made an off-hand reference to his relationship to the president of the United States. "As long as Cousin Abe keeps sending 'em

6. (Arrington 1982, 292; Interview: Marie Arrington) According to Mrs. Arrington, stories of the exploits of Al Lincoln still abound in Mountain Valley. To some he was a folk hero, yet others remember that his story was passed down in a negative light because of his ruthlessness.
7. (Wayland 1987, 197)
8. (Armstrong 1992, 184; Interview: Marie Arrington)

down the Valley," he said, "Cousin Al will keep killin' 'em."

In the week before Sheridan ordered the retrograde movement of his army, Lincoln had attacked small parties of Federals moving in both directions on the pike. The rowdy band would charge a group on the road, its members firing their revolvers and yelling at the top of their lungs, then wheel around and melt into the timber. If their ploy were successful, a few Union soldiers would peel away in pursuit, never to be seen alive again.

The story is told that after one such raid, during which he had killed two Federals, Lincoln rode to the farm of his cousin, Harriet Koontz, a mile and a half east of the pike. She was a young widow with five children of her own and one stepson in the Seventh Virginia Cavalry. Another stepson, 16-year-old John, had deserted from the Seventh with Lincoln and now rode with him. Having Lincoln nearby made the widow Koontz very nervous. Once he had scared her near to death by riding onto a hilltop near her house, standing up in his stirrups so as not to be missed, and waving his hat to some Federals on the pike. Harriet pleaded with him not to lead the Yankees to her place; she was afraid she and her children would be killed in retaliation for his acts. He laughed at her plea, tipped his hat, said, "Cousin Harriet, I wouldn't let one of them touch a single hair on your lovely head," and then rode off into the pine thickets.[9]

The Federals took him seriously enough to mention his activity in official correspondence. On October 1 the acting provost marshal general of the Army of the Shenandoah had written to Sheridan's chief of staff, Col. James Forsyth, that stragglers from Early's defeat at Fisher's Hill had fled into the Massanutten and that some of these were "acting under the leadership of one Captain Lincoln, who commands a band of guerrillas. They are every day becoming more troublesome, as they are getting better organized and armed."[10]

Now that the Valley was thick with Federals, Lincoln had to modify his mode of attack. His rash bravado was reined in for awhile, though not completely. Local people noted during this time that "Al Lincoln took a wounded Yankee and threw him into [a] burning barn."[11] The Northerner had been with the party that set the fire.

9.   (Armstrong 1992, 179; Arrington 1982, 294)
10.   (OR, Series I, Vol. XIII, Pt. 2, 250) How the life of Albert C. Lincoln finally ended is shrouded in legend. At the close of the war he married a cousin, Mary Elizabeth Koontz, with whom he had a son and four daughters. By 1878 he had gone west and was either murdered by a business partner or killed while stealing horses.
11.   (BCA, Wayland Diaries)

Infantrymen detailed to gather in fodder and food for the troops had to be especially vigilant; they made it a point to go about their tasks in large parties. The lack of supplies was a serious one and may have been caused in part by the lack of transport; Sheridan had tied up a great number of wagons in his generosity to the refugees of Rockingham County. A Vermont soldier remembered, "There was not enough transportation in the Department to feed us at that distance from our base, and moreover the guerrillas were attacking every train."[12]

Other impromptu guerrilla warriors also ranged about looking for opportunities to kill and plunder the men from the North. At this point in the war the sanctioned Confederate partisan bands were disorganized for various reasons. Hanse McNeill had been mortally wounded while attacking a camp of Ohio infantrymen south of Mount Jackson, in Sheridan's rear, on the day Meigs was killed; for the time being his men were riding with whatever group seemed to have a healthy commander. Harry Gilmor's leaderless Maryland partisans were operating all over the Valley in pairs or in small groups while he recuperated from wounds received in the Lower Valley in September.[13] Buck Woodson's small company had received recognition from the Confederate government only that summer and did not have much experience operating independently, but Woodson was a well-thought-of leader in his own right, and some of McNeill's men had attached themselves to his command.[14]

Although the partisans had suffered some losses in leadership, their activities and those of the pick-up guerrillas were terribly aggravating to the Federals. Their sporadic hit-and-run tactics were irritating, like the whine of a gnat in the ear—but sometimes the irritations were deadly.

• • •

Sheridan had decided that his cavalry divisions and part of his infantry would withdraw down the Valley to Strasburg and Front Royal along four major routes,

12. (Walker 1869, 127)
13. (Wayland 1987, 337)
14. (*Memorials of Edward Herndon Scott, M.D.* 1873, 18) This may be the only monograph printed that touches on Woodson's men after they became a ranger unit. After being captured at Vicksburg, Woodson's company was sent to Virginia to be exchanged in the late summer of 1863. Assigned to the Sixty-second Mounted Infantry, the rangers took an heroic part in the battle of New Market on May 15, 1864, suffering many casualties. The survivors requested that they be allowed to remain in Virginia to form a ranger company. Most of their recruiting seems to have been done in Rockingham County and in the eastern counties of West Virginia.

burning from mountain to mountain as they went. His object was to get to Strasburg with his army intact and to leave the country behind him, an area about fifty miles long and twenty-five miles wide, as near to a wasteland as possible. Orders were that any farm animals too difficult to drive were to be shot and burned or left to rot. The property of widows was still to be left alone, and from now on the burning of private residences would be either aberrations or accidents.

The infantry started off first, on October 5, with the artillery, corps wagon trains, refugee train, and cattle and sheep herds gathered in the Upper Valley; the caravan would keep to the area immediate to the main pike. While en route the soldiers would continue to gather in supplies, fodder, and all the livestock within reach. The four hundred wagons of the refugee train carried civilians and their possessions. Peter Hartman and John Coffman rode alongside with the other conscript-age boys. Hartman estimated that there were about sixteen hundred wagons altogether, covering close to sixteen miles of road. For most of the journey they traveled in a dismal, cold rain.[15]

Although they were promised relative safety, traveling with the refugee train was not necessarily less dangerous for the civilians. Coffman noted that their progress was slowed by bushwhackers operating near the pike. These raiding parties ran the gamut from duly recognized Confederate ranger units to vagrant riff-raff out for what they could get in the way of booty at little risk to themselves. Some cloaked their acts in patriotic rhetoric when in fact their only intention was to enrich themselves and brutalize anyone who challenged their wishes.[16]

Far ahead of this train was a wagon carrying the body of John Rodgers Meigs, now a posthumous major. Escorted by a cavalry detail, his corpse was to be shifted to the first railroad train leaving the Lower Valley for his birthplace, Washington, D.C.

The wagon train stopped about 10 P.M., and refugees camped for the night between New Market and Mount Jackson. Margaret Suter, a refugee from Rockingham County, later recalled that the horses pulling her family's wagon had thrown some shoes and were in pretty bad shape by the time they approached New Market; a farrier in the town put new shoes on, and afterward the horses moved at a trot to the camps.[17] Some of the travelers were very thirsty from the trek even though a light rain was falling. Peter Hartman and some friends went down the road about a quarter of a mile and found a pond from

15.   (Hartman 1964, 25-26)
16.   (Steiner 1903, 18)
17.   (Suter 1959, 492)

which they carried water back to their campsite. The next morning, in daylight, they saw two dead mules in the muddy pool.[18]

A correspondent traveling with the main column wrote, "Hundreds of nearly starving people are going North. Our trains are crowded with them. They line the wayside. Hundreds more are coming—not half the inhabitants of the valley can subsist on it in its present condition."[19]

A refugee later recalled that during their perilous journey, whenever they camped for the night, the civilians would gather together and sing, and the soldiers would crowd around to listen.[20]

Early in the predawn hours of October 7 the columns began to move northward once again, their numbers swollen by the livestock sent over from Page Valley by Colonel Powell.

The camps in the Harrisonburg area were vacated before noon on the 6th. Only litter remained, covering hundreds of acres and leaving the grounds looking like the site of a vanished carnival. By midday there was not a Union soldier to be seen in southern Rockingham County. A pall of smoke hung in the low places, and the normal sounds of farm life, once taken for granted, were now eerily absent. It was as if the land were in the grip of a hushed predawn.

Sheridan directed his cavalry to follow up the retrograde movement of the infantry by taking to the series of parallel roads that angled toward the northeast. As the cavalry units withdrew they were to spread across the Valley from mountain to mountain, burning as they went. Custer and the Third Division were assigned to move down the rough Back Road that hugged the western side of the Valley. Two brigades of Wesley Merritt's First Division were ordered to move on the Middle Road and a parallel drovers' road that ran through prime farm and grazing land to the town of Broadway. The remaining brigade of the First Division, Colonel Kidd's Michigan Brigade, was to act as the infantry wing's rear guard on the Valley Pike. Powell, with the Second Division, was already moving down the east side of the Valley, guarding the army's flank, destroying barns and mills, and gathering information about movements of the enemy.

If Sheridan had not begun his withdrawal when he did, in all probability there would have been a battle somewhere south of Harrisonburg on October 6. Jubal Early had left Brown's Gap and was on the Valley Pike in Augusta County. The few days that his infantry had spent encamped around Mount Sidney had been used to prepare to move against the federal army to the north. There was all too

18.   (Hartman 1964, 26)
19.   (Tomes undated, 42)
20.   (Hartman 1964, 26)

little left in the vicinity to support even Early's small force—often a day's rations had to be spread over two or three—yet the soldiers were able to grind some grain in a mill that Custer had missed. Even with the realization that their strength and ability to gather in supplies was at best marginal, the soldiers were anxious to close with the enemy and bring them to battle.

"Our hearts ached at the horrible sight," one Confederate remembered later, "our beautiful Valley almost a barren waste and we with an army so inferior in numbers as to render success almost hopeless. Yet the sight carried with it unseen power and determination to avenge this dastardly warfare, making us doubly equal to such an enemy."[21]

Sheridan hoped that even if Early or some other Southern commander thought to follow, the Confederates would be in no condition to fight after a pursuit with empty haversacks and minimal forage for their animals.[22] Nevertheless, as the Federals began to move northward, shadowy horsemen from the South began to appear through the acrid mist.

21.   (Buck 1925, 121-22)
22.   (OR, Series I, Vol. XLIII, Pt. 1, 442, 508, 520)

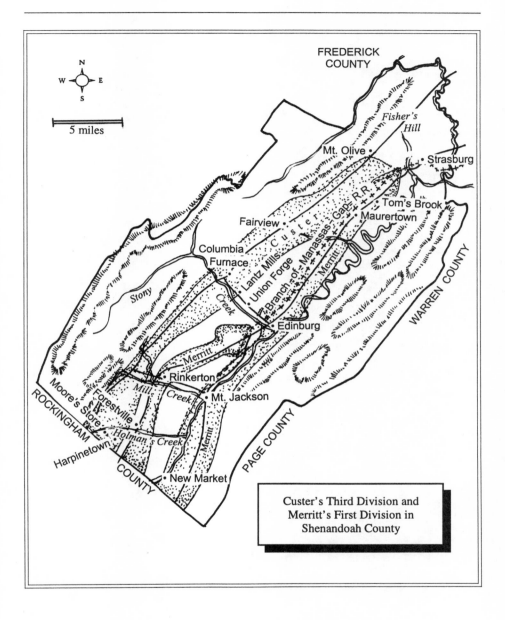

Custer's Third Division and
Merritt's First Division in
Shenandoah County

Chapter Fourteen

CUSTER TAKES THE BACK ROAD

Sheridan had given permanent command of the Third Division of Cavalry to Custer because he considered him to be an officer who led by example and one in whom the men would have confidence, and he wanted the fiery general with him when this campaign ended. Sheridan knew that eventually he would once again command the cavalry of the Army of the Potomac. He expected that the Second Division would be kept with George Crook's Army of West Virginia, so he had readily handed it back to Powell.

Custer's meteoric rise to the rank of general officer has been portrayed popularly as a fluke or an outright mistake, but the truth of the matter is that Sheridan's predecessor, Alfred Pleasonton, had recognized Custer's energy and ability to act quickly and decisively in combat situations. Some of the men who served under Custer might have debated his leadership qualities—they were led into the hottest encounters and their ranks suffered an inordinate number of casualties whenever Custer was in command—yet others revelled in their association with Custer and the fame that was growing around him.

It is doubtful that more than a few, if any, of the farmers, millers, and shop owners who lived and worked along the western side of the Valley had heard of Custer prior to this campaign. Contemporary local stories told about him are mostly derogatory and can probably be attributed to his flamboyant lifestyle and spectacular death in the west after the war. Surprisingly, though, there were people in the Valley who experienced his mercy in this merciless time.

The scant surviving records of Custer's first foray along the Back Road are revealing in that they seem to point to a young man who weighed circumstances and did not destroy just for the sake of destruction. His outburst at Sheridan's headquarters in Harrisonburg, when he supposedly exclaimed, "Look out for smoke," may have been more a hasty vow of retaliation for the death of John Meigs than an overpowering urge to lay waste to the farms.

The Third Division pulled out of the camps around Dayton at dawn on October 6 to embark on its final mission of general destruction in the Valley. The Federals rode westward, crossed Dry River a little north of Bridgewater, then followed the north bank of the North River for three miles to the quiet little village of Spring Creek, where they entered the Back Road.

A large portion of the southwest quadrant of Rockingham County was made up of farms inhabited by peaceful Mennonites and Dunkards. The well-tended, fruitful, and prosperous farms in the area attested to the industriousness and agronomic skills of the God-fearing families who ran them. Custer seemed moved by the nonviolent stance of the people; while he destroyed the mills at Spring Creek, Ottobine, and Clover Hill, there is no record of a single barn being burned along the Back Road from Spring Creek to its crossing of the meandering Dry River about six miles farther on.[1]

Once the division crossed Dry River, the burning under Custer began in earnest. One of the first farms to be hit belonged to a thirty-six-year-old Mennonite potter, John Heatwole. Potter John had suspected early on that the war would not be a brief struggle, and he had a plan that he thought would protect him from prolonged involvement in it. In 1861 he enlisted in the Confederate army for a year. He told his wife, Elizabeth, that he would not shoot at anyone, and at the end of his year's enlistment he would come home, having served his time. In that way they could live without fear of being molested by the authorities.

He was shocked when in April 1862 he was informed that his earlier enlistment had been nullified—the Confederacy had drafted him for an additional three years. He felt he had served his time in good faith and petitioned his officers to be allowed to return home, but the request was denied. He was one of hundreds of men serving under Stonewall Jackson who were in the same fix.

Heatwole continued to serve in his regiment, the Thirty-third Virginia Infantry of the Stonewall Brigade, for another four months, but after the battle at Cedar Mountain on August 9 he returned home and went into hiding, coming out of a nest in a haystack to visit his wife and children only at night. The provost

1.   (Rockingham *Register and Advertiser*, April 11, 1867)

marshal's office in Harrisonburg feared that the well-known potter would become a heroic symbol to younger Mennonite and Dunkard men, who would follow suit and also hide out to avoid reporting for duty. Consequently, a reward was offered for his capture, and squads were sent to look for him near his home. Even rangers from McNeill's band questioned local people as to his whereabouts. The pressure finally drove him into the mountains, where he built a lean-to in a remote hollow.

Potter John's defiance of Confederate authority did not buy his farm a reprieve from Custer's burners, however. The Heatwoles, like everyone else, had watched the smoke columns rising to the east and south, and word had spread across the countryside that anything that could be herded would be taken by the Union cavalrymen. The eldest Heatwole son, Bud, took the family's two horses into a nearby woods.

In the late morning a squad of horsemen thundered over the hill from the Back Road, passing the pottery shed and pug mill on their way down to the house and barn lot. Mrs. Heatwole stood outside in a cold, light drizzle while her children looked on from the porch and windows. She was told they had come to burn the barn and outbuildings. She asked what she was to do to keep her children fed, but the officer in charge only shrugged his shoulders and waved his men to their work. In no time the farm buildings were ablaze and the unit had disappeared back over the hill.[2]

A few more barns were fired between the Heatwole place and the crossing of the Rawley Springs Turnpike. On the other side of the pike the Back Road entered a region of ridges with small fertile vales that fell off to the east and west.

A unit burning in the vicinity of the village of Mount Clinton, east of the Back Road, experienced difficulty on the farm of Henry and Elizabeth Heatwole. Henry Heatwole was away riding with Buck Woodson's guerrilla outfit. The Federals moved through the fields surrounding the house and barn, setting the standing crops ablaze with no interference, but when they tried to burn the barn, Mrs. Heatwole flew at them, knocking apart the mounds of tinder and beating out the small flames. Her efforts failed, however, as finally some of the soldiers held her while others reset the fires and allowed them to catch. To make matters worse, the combination of the burning barn and the blowing sparks from the crackling fields caught the house on fire. Ironically, although they had destroyed everything else on the place, the cavalrymen went to work to save the home. When the structure was out of danger, the Federals mounted and rode away.[3]

2.   (Interview: Paul V. Heatwole)

*Brigadier General Thomas L.
Rosser commanded the division of
Confederate cavalry that harassed
Custer's rear October 6-8. (Library of
Congress)*

The troops took the Back Road along its upper course until it approached Hopkin's Mill and the mills belonging to Major Chrisman's father along Muddy Creek at Mount Rock; these they disposed of in short order.

The detachments swept forward, burning and gathering all of the livestock that had not been taken to safety. Trooper Isaac Gause of the Second Ohio Cavalry remembered that "it was our orders . . . to take all the stock, and to destroy all the supplies on the back road." None of the groups tarried long. They knew that Confederate horsemen would be following as soon as they realized Sheridan had pulled out and was moving down the Valley.[4]

Indeed, Thomas L. Rosser, commanding a force that included his own Laurel Brigade and Wickham's brigade, was already on Custer's trail. Pvt. Beverly Whittle of the Second Virginia Cavalry noted in his diary that on the morning of October 6 he was riding picket when "about 9 o'clock our cavalry began to advance + we were ordered to join our regiment, which we did near a place called Dayton. . . . All along our route were burning barns houses etc. The beautiful + fertile Valley of Virginia is in one vast cloud of smoke, + the very air is impregnated with the smell of burning property. I found a plank left by the Yankees, on which was written 'Remember Chambersburg.' " [5]

Pleasant Kiser, a native of Rockingham County who was riding with the Eleventh Virginia Cavalry, was on familiar ground. He had grown up a little downriver from Bridgewater, where the regiment crossed that day. As his unit reached Dayton and turned to the left, Kiser had the impression, and later stated in his diary, that "almost every Barn & a good many Houses Burned."[6]

3.   (Kauffman 1940, 322; 1860 Census for Rockingham County, Virginia)
4.   (Gause 1908, 326)
5.   (UVAL, Whittle Papers)
6.   (Evans Private Collection, Kiser Diary; Armstrong 1989, 157)

W. H. Arehart, a Confederate home on sick leave, had been hiding in the mountains about five miles west of the Warm Springs Turnpike to avoid capture. On the 6th he made the following entry in his diary: "Reported the Yankees are falling back this morning and burning all the barns as they go. Gen. Rosser's brigade marched through Dayton today."[7]

In Rosser's division—in fact, in his old brigade—rode Pvt. Levi Getz of Woodstock, a member of the Seventh Virginia Cavalry. On October 6, in the morning, he passed by the grave of his older brother, Davy, without realizing it.[8]

A few years earlier, as cadets at West Point, Custer and Rosser had been very close, and in some ways they still acted like two boys trying to best each other in a field sport. They were known to send each other playful messages through the lines that usually included wagers on who would be

Cpl. Pleasant Kiser, Eleventh Virginia Cavalry. (Beverley and Jeffrey Evans)

victorious in their next encounter. On this day Rosser's men were not in a playful mood, however, since many troopers in the Laurel Brigade regiments were Valley natives. Understrength, underfed and in many cases mounted on horses past their prime, the Southern cavalrymen nevertheless had their hackles up and were anxious to close in and grapple with their enemies.

The Union horsemen kept their eyes on their backs, being very aware of the danger in that quarter. Charles Farr of the First Vermont Cavalry noted that "the . . . Rebs followed us all day"[9] as they burned the western part of the Valley.

Two of the young men in Rosser's force were the Pennybacker brothers, lieutenants Joseph and Derrick of the Seventh Virginia Cavalry. They had served under the silver-nosed Captain Winfield before his illness caused his resignation from active service. Their father, Derrick Sr., was one of the wealthiest men along the North Fork of the Shenandoah River. As they rode

7.   (Alexander Private Collection, Arehart Diary)
8.   (Interviews: John A. Getz and Bennie Getz)
9.   (USAMHI, Farr Papers)

toward the river at the head of their company they watched the ominous smoke pillars ahead and noted a tight group of columns rising just down from Cootes's Store, the site of their home place. Perhaps Custer or one of his officers had been informed that the Pennybackers were slaveholders and staunch supporters of the rebellion, because someone decided to make an example of the place. Two houses were burned, plus three barns and three mills.[10]

Rosser, Lunsford Lomax, and John Imboden followed the main bodies of the burners as they moved northward, but Winfield's guerrillas, who had been swooping down on wagon trains and small parties of the enemy in Sheridan's rear for more than a week, suddenly found themselves in front of the advancing might of the Army of the Shenandoah. They were unsure what was happening and did not know what to do. Winfield disbanded them temporarily and made his way to his second home near Brock's Gap, just beyond Cootes's Store.

Newton Burkholder, who had grown up in this region, was the Confederate military telegrapher assigned to Harrisonburg on the line that ran from New Market to Staunton. With the approach of Sheridan's army, he had closed the office and ridden off to join Winfield's pick-up force. Suddenly left to his own devices, he embarked on his own course of action.[11]

He and a few others found themselves on high ground east of Custer and west of the Broadway-Harrisonburg Road, where Col. Thomas Devin's brigade of the First Division of Cavalry was working. The Confederates noted that the forces moving toward and around them were accompanied by quite a few wagons—too many for a foraging party. Burkholder tried to work it out in his mind:

> What was Sheridan doing? A retreating force never left the Valley pike—the great highway and a magnificent road—so no one thought of retreat. We could not grasp it, it was too bad to think. Falling back along all roads and burning as he comes did not suggest itself to one of our little party, till at last, as we sat on our horses there on that lone peak, motionless and horror struck for our country, we saw the awful work come toward us.[12]

10. (Rockingham *Register and Advertiser,* February 10, 1865; Wayland 1973, 293-94; Armstrong 1992, 208; 1860 Rockingham County Slave Schedules) The Pennybackers never rebuilt at the site.

11. (Garber Private Collection, C. S. A. Military Telegraph Records) When Burkholder returned to the office on October 10, he made a note on his monthly account that he had had to close the office between September 24 and October 9 because of the enemy.

12. (Richmond *Dispatch,* July 22, 1900) "The Barn Burners" is the finest account written by a

The Confederates' first inclination when they realized what was happening was to fall on the first burners within their reach and throw them in the burning barn, but they were wise enough not to act on it. They recognized that they were greatly outnumbered and would be swept up by the tide of Union horsemen if they did not take immediate action to get away.

They wished to reach home, near the western mountains, and turned their horses in that direction, but they did not have a clear path as cavalrymen in blue seemed to be on all sides. In their flight they came upon a Northern trooper who, it was found out later, was riding a stolen horse while leading his own. The rider was separated from his comrades, both fore and aft, by just a hundred yards or so—close enough that Burkholder could hear their voices, although they were hidden by trees and the contours of the land. The Southerners took him prisoner and continued along warily but as swiftly as possible. A little farther on, near Trissel's Mennonite Church, they met a neighbor who recognized the prisoner as the man who had come to burn his barn but who, at the last moment, had given in to his wife's plea to spare it.

They rode within sight of a Union patrol that fired on them at long range and were driven into the timber by this encounter, where they hid in a deep ravine. There they came close to being discovered by yet another party of Custer's men who were driving cattle through the cedars on the steep hillside above them.

When the cattle drivers disappeared, Burkholder and his friends turned toward the south and were delighted to come upon Rosser's men moving forward, closing the distance between themselves and the burners. The little band, upon recognizing the Southern horsemen, cried out, "Huzza for the Laurel Brigade! Huzza! Huzza!" The prisoner, who had told them that he was from Vermont and had a wife and two children, was turned over to Rosser's provost marshal. Afterward Burkholder learned that the man had been killed trying to escape.[13]

By the late afternoon of October 6 most of the men of Custer's division had crossed the North Fork and were preparing to go into camp on the high ground beyond the river bottom. Two regiments left on the south bank, the Fifth New York Cavalry and the Eighteenth Pennsylvania Cavalry, prepared to bivouac on ground between the river and an imposing hill on John Fulk's farm. The camp was less than a mile down from the hill and part of it was on the Jacob Neff farm,

Confederate soldier who witnessed the Burning in his home county. While others made brief comments that were later included in memoirs, family histories, and genealogies, Newton Burkholder left an almost hour-by-hour account of what he experienced on October 6-7, 1864.
13.   (Ibid.)

not a quarter of a mile from Cootes's Store.

Susanna Neff had prepared for the day when Northern invaders might drop by. The Neffs were not well-to-do people, but what Susanna lacked in wealth she more than made up in common sense. She had reasoned that they would be safe from thieves if she hid their few pieces of silverware in a pitcher of sour milk. She was right—the first Federals who entered her house took what food they could find, but eleven-year-old Molly Neff observed that they wrinkled their noses at the noxious liquid and turned away from it.[14]

No sooner had the soldiers left the Neff house than gunfire was heard up the road. A Union picket line was seen racing back toward the camp, and the two regiments hastily prepared to mount, as men on foot fired up the road at the charging Laurel Brigade. The Federals formed a mounted line and were able to slow the advance of the Confederates for a time, but Rosser had the advantage of position and numbers. Trooper Whittle of the Second Virginia Cavalry reported in his diary, "My regiment dismounted + were rapidly driving them when they attemped a flank movement and the 4th came to our assistance, + the Yankees broke + ran in confusion."[15]

The Federals saw their resistance as dogged, although they realized they had not retired in very good order. The Union horsemen streamed through Cootes's Store and crossed the river, where their retreat was now covered by artillery; the Confederates had no field pieces with which to answer.

One cavalryman in the Twelfth Virginia, Americus Vespucius Bull, who apparently had imbibed a considerable amount of strong whiskey, rode headlong into the retreating Yankees. He was mortally wounded and died the next day at Cootes's Store, not far from his home, which was just a little way downriver.

Without artillery, Rosser was stuck on the south bank. When Custer moved out, he would pursue and try to bring his old friend to battle on ground where artillery would not be a factor. While he waited, General Rosser rode off to have supper with Captain Winfield.[16]

Earlier in the day Susanna Neff's twelve-year-old son, George, had been sent to Little North Mountain to guard the family cattle and some belonging to neighbors. From his vantage point above the Third Division encampment, it looked like a band of fires stretched across the Valley from mountain to mountain. He worried that details would be sent up into the mountain to look for hidden stock. When dawn approached on October 7, he decided to try to

14.   (Interview: Alice Crider)
15.   (UVAL, Whittle Papers)
16.   (Harrisonburg *Daily News-Record*, December 1, 1948)

throw them off the scent. He said a prayer and walked down to the nearest camp, where he told the soldiers, "Boys, you better move back, the mountains are full of 'em [rebels] back there." It was more than enough to discourage the curious, who were already skittish.[17]

As it was, the day before about seventy-five men from the Fifth New York Cavalry—who had been sent through Brock's Gap to burn haystacks and ricks near Fulk's Run and along the North Fork west of the gap—had been the targets of shots fired from concealment. That put them off their work, and they went into a cold camp that night, not wishing to blunder into enemy soldiers in the dark. The next morning they narrowly avoided being cut off by Rosser's videttes as they galloped out of the gap.[18]

Local tradition holds that Custer spent the night of the 6th in the farmhouse owned by seventy-year-old Jacob Shoemaker. About a dozen of his men killed in the action with Rosser were buried on the farm. While some of the troopers picketed the river and others herded the livestock farther on, the rest of the division slept, having ridden twenty-five miles since breaking camp that morning.[19]

17. (Interview: Alice Crider)
18. (OR, Series I, Vol. XLIII, Pt. 1, 102)
19. (Interview: John Elliott; 1860 Census of Rockingham County, Virginia)

Chapter Fifteen

CUSTER ON THE BACK ROAD

On October 6, after forcing the two Union regiments across the river and before taking supper with Captain Winfield, Rosser met with Newton Burk- holder and Sgt. Erasmus Neff. Both were local boys, so Rosser sent them on a night scout in an attempt to determine whether Custer would stay on the Back Road course or cut cross-country to link up with the main army. It was not quite dark as they rode over to Cootes's Store and turned their mounts eastward along the south bank of the North Fork. As they rode along they saw many barns burning across the river. It became obvious to them as they made their way that Custer had no intention of trying to recross the stream farther down to get at Rosser's flank or rear by stealth.

Passing between the sawmill and tannery at Alger's, they rode up a little hill where George Brunk kept a fenced garden. From this point they spotted two horsemen on a hill across a hollow from them; they were silhouetted in the quickly falling dusk by fires burning behind them over on the Broadway Road. The two Confederates were not sure if the men were friend or foe, so Neff dismounted and, using the garden fence as a rest, took aim at the strangers with his carbine. He had not loaded the weapon but had only capped it. When he pulled the trigger there was a sharp crack, but the strangers did not move. Burkholder, however, saw movement in the hollow below—about a dozen riders appeared from behind some farm buildings. He urged Neff to remount, and they galloped away under a hail of bullets. Soon they splashed across Alger's Ford in the thickening gloom and were north of the river.[1]

Once camp was broken on the morning of the 7th, the Third Division rode on down the Back Road into an area where the ground just to the left of the road rose to the heights of North Mountain. The division had not proceeded very far when the detachment of the Fifth New York that had sojourned in Brock's Gap overnight caught up with the regiment, much to everyone's relief.[2]

To the right, the Northerners could see almost to the Massanutten, where columns of smoke and fires by the score could readily be observed as Merritt's cavalrymen operated along the Middle and Broadway roads and the infantry pushed along the Valley Pike. Behind Custer, the barn at Jacob Shoemaker's, where the general supposedly spent the night, burned like a torch in the crisp air.[3]

One of Rosser's officers recalled, "The sight of burning barns and stack-yards, banished everything from minds but the thought of vengeance. The fires of destruction were partly visible. Clouds of smoke hung across the Valley, extending from the Blue Ridge to North Mountain, hiding the movements of the incendiaries but clearly showing the fiendish character of their work."[4]

Rosser's division pressed Custer closely, and while the work being done and the pursuit was hot, the weather had turned decidedly cool.

With the mountains crowding his western flank, Custer had his men spread farther to the east; that flank was in close proximity to Merritt's men operating at mid-Valley. Trooper Gause of the Second Ohio said the ground they passed over "was rough and interspersed with woods and fields."[5] The Third Division left Rockingham before noon on the 7th and crossed into Shenandoah County.

The hamlet of Moore's Store on Holman's Creek was a charming little settlement that had slept quietly during the war until Custer's men descended on it. Nothing on Joseph Moore's farm was left untouched, perhaps because he was a slaveholder and well-to-do Southerner. Every building, including the house, was put to the torch. The Moores lost everything they owned, save for the land, having been given no time to rescue any possessions. The old Moore Mill, which had stood in the hamlet for three score years and longer, was also burned to ashes. That night Moore, his wife, Virginia, and their five children had to seek shelter elsewhere.

A little farther down Holman's Creek, which flows to the east, was a grist mill,

1.   (Richmond *Dispatch,* July 22, 1900)
2.   (Boudrye 1865, 177)
3.   (Interview: John Elliott)
4.   (McDonald 1907, 300)
5.   (Gause 1908, 326)

General Custer watching the work of the men of his division. (Battles and Leaders of the Civil War)

sawmill, and several homes of people by the name of Harpine. On this morning Harpinetown lost both of its mills and all of its barns to the fires set by the Northerners. Another half mile farther downstream was Peter Myers's mill, which at fourteen years of age was relatively new compared to most Valley mills. It did not reach age fifteen. The Myers barn, also doomed, was so close to the house that the window sills became hot to the touch.[6]

A quarter of a mile beyond, Samuel Hockman ran the old Andrew Zerkel mill in the village of Forestville. Looking upstream, Hockman saw the smoke rising from Harpinetown and then the fire at Myers's mill. Thinking quickly, he ran to the top floor of the mill, leaned out of a small window under the eaves of the structure, and nailed a United States flag to the peak of the roof. He hurried back downstairs to meet the Union officer and his squad, who were approaching briskly from the west. Standing before the group he told them how happy he was to see them and professed his loyalty to the old flag. When they saw the Stars and Stripes so visibly displayed on the mill, they were convinced of his sincerity. The officer waved his men away from Hockman's mill, making it the only one spared along the creek that day.[7]

6.   (Wine 1985, 163-65; Interview: Blair and Maxine Zirkle)

Between Forestville and Moore's Store was the farm of Elder Jacob Wine, a minister of the Dunkard church. A group of Federals bent solely on acquiring plunder swooped down on the Wines. Jacob was absent, but his wife, Catherine, daughters Catherine and Anna, and son Daniel bore witness to the raid. The men had a wagon and team with them and may have been members of an advance stock-raiding party. While some of the men entered the house with bags in which to stuff their loot, others fed their horses oats out in the yard. Everything that was stolen was brought to the yard and loaded in the wagon. All of this took place in great haste, yet the Wines followed the soldiers and noted all that was taken: "1 dozen coverlids; 4 quilts; 4 blankets; shirts; pillow slips; bedding; 2 stands of bees and honey; 125 pounds of homemade maple sugar; 2 barrels of flour in bags; 20 bushels of oats in bags; 2 buckets; 1 large jug; saddle pockets; 6 pounds of bacon; 12 to 15 bushels of sweet potatoes; 8 or 9 gallons of molassas; 1 felling ax; [and] 4 or 5 men's hats."

It is interesting to note that as all of this was taking place Elder Wine was about thirty miles away, at Mossy Creek in Augusta County, selling produce to Confederate purchasing agent James Hooff. How he got through country that was literally crawling with Union cavalry without being stopped is a mystery.[8]

The looting that took place during this campaign was not condoned by the majority of the Northern soldiers in the Valley. A Union staff officer, Capt. Hazard Stevens, had already noticed the propensity of some of the soldiers to loot when he wrote to his mother in August, "They pillage and plunder and the Generals take no measures to prevent them." Many of the Federals who were of a like mind felt the destruction of mills and barns might be justified as necessary to bring the war to an end, but the looting would cast an ugly shadow that would mark them as nothing more than thieves.

As the burners moved a couple of miles into Shenandoah County, Col. William Wells, commanding the Union Second Brigade, shifted part of his rearguard line—including the cattle herd that had been gathered before the crossing of the North Fork the previous evening—over to the Middle Road. He also moved some of the division forge wagons, which were necessary to every large mounted unit for the quick repair of cast-off horseshoes. As these elements moved cross-country Rosser made a strong attack.

The cavalrymen drove one another back and forth in sharp, close contact for what seemed like hours, especially to the men of Wells's harried Union brigade.

7.   (Ibid.)
8.   (NA, Southern Claims Commission Files)
9.   (LCMD, Stevens Papers)

It was remarked upon at the time how aggressively the Confederate cavalrymen dogged at the heels of the foe, when many thought that they should have been played out from hard marching and lack of supplies. George E. Pond wrote in the early 1880s that Rosser's "zeal was probably due in part to the excitement of his men at seeing their farms and homes in flames; for many of Early's cavalrymen were from the region. Their eagerness to exact retribution brought upon them double mortification and suffering."[10]

A dispatch to the Confederate War Department reported: "General Sheridan is still moving down the Valley. A large force of his cavalry was attacked by us on the 7th and we drove them handsomely, capturing a number of horses, several ambulances, some wagons, nine forges with teams, and about fifty prisoners."[11]

From early that morning most of the Second Brigade, under the command of Colonel Wells, acted as a rear guard for the burning details. Wells was in a thankless position. His men were being hit somewhere along their line almost constantly by small, fierce attacks. The First Vermont Cavalry was part of the rearguard force, and trooper Farr said that the "Rebs pitched into our rear . . . and captured a part of our cattle and Sheep and 8 Forges we had a sharp fight and lost about 25 men." While Wells and his men were stubbornly attempting to hold off the highly motivated Confederates, the burning parties with their torches were moving along at a brisk pace; they knew very well what they could expect at the hands of the Valley soldiers, whose property they were destroying.[12]

Wells suffered the humiliation of losing most of the herd, seven forge wagons, a few ambulances, and several men.[13] Maj. John Phillips of the Eighteenth Pennsylvania Cavalry wrote in his diary, "The enemy follow close all day and give the 2nd Brigade fits. They get many of the sheep we have picked up and some of our Forges."[14] The capture of the forges infuriated Custer; they were impossible to come by this far from a secure supply line.

Corporal Kiser of the Eleventh Virginia Cavalry noted with satisfaction that they had come into "contact with the Yanks giving them a pretty good threshing Capturing a good many Stolen sheep . . . and nearly all their wagon train."[15] What Kiser and most of the Confederates did not realize was that, once expended, the energy of man and beast could not be replenished on almost

10.   (Pond 1892, 204)
11.   (Richmond *Dispatch*, October 12, 1864)
12.   (USAMHI, Farr Papers)
13.   (Boudrye 1865, 77) Although various numbers were reported, seven forges were captured.
14.   (Phillips 1954, 116)
15.   (Long Estate Private Collection, Kiser Diary)

nonexistent rations. The Federals were consuming all the forage that time would allow, and the rest was being carried off or destroyed. When strength would count for everything, the Southerners would be in a sorry state.

The Third Division remained on task as its men crossed the old Howard Lick Turnpike, also known as the Orkney Grade. They were now working the upper reaches of the aptly named Mill Creek, which flows east toward the town of Mount Jackson in countryside that was mostly rolling pastureland and wheat fields cut by small feeder streams. A squad of Custer's men followed Crooked Run down from the Back Road. They set their barn fires and moved on, their officer following a few minutes later to make sure the owner had not extinguished the flames. In this manner he could obtain an accurate tally of property destroyed by his command, which he would turn in at the end of the day.

This detail reached the farm of forty-four-year-old Moses Fry as it neared the mouth of Crooked Run. A lane ran between the house and the barn. Fry and his wife had seven children, five of whom were still at home; their eldest son, Erasmus, was an enlisted man serving in the Twelfth Virginia Cavalry under Rosser. Farmer Fry had a reputation as a good neighbor, but he was not someone to be played around with when riled. "Big, mean and a brawler" was how he was styled by some in the community.

Fry watched with blood in his eye as the Northerners set about kindling the fire in his barn. Despite his reputation, he realized that there were too many of the raiders to handle, so he fumed quietly, hoping they would soon depart.

Keeping to their operating procedures, the cavalrymen remounted and cantered downstream to the next farm once the fires were set. Fry lost no time leading his family into action stamping, smothering, and dousing the flames. In less time than the Frys thought possible, they had saved the barn. As Fry checked to make sure that they had missed no ember that might start a fresh fire, his wife called his attention to the arrival of a lone Yankee officer.

The mounted man surveyed the tired, smoke-smudged family standing by the barn and knew what had happened. He dismounted, saw something in Fry's demeanor that he did not like, drew his revolver, and motioned for the big man and his family to stand together in the road where he could see them. The Frys were held at gunpoint with the barn in front of them and the house behind.

The officer, keeping an eye on the family and especially Fry, gathered straw and other dry tinder in a pile beside a wall of the barn and ignited it. He relaxed a little as he watched the flames bite into the wall and stretch toward the roof. It was obvious he would not leave until he was sure the blaze was beyond control.

Fry could not rush the man and risk having one of his family hurt. He turned away and walked slowly toward the house. The officer in his youth and inexperience must have assumed that the farmer had given up, because he made no effort to stop him. Fry closed the front door behind him, grabbed the rifle that stood beside it, and went upstairs. One of the front windows was slightly raised, and there he knelt, taking deadly aim at the young officer. The rifle cracked, and his target crumpled to the ground. Coming out into the yard again, Fry lifted the lifeless body and carried it to the inferno that had been his barn and, braving the heat and roaring flames, inched close enough to throw the corpse in.[16]

Other farmers who tried to stand up to the spoilers were less successful than Moses Fry. "One man stood on a haystack and fired into a marching column and he fell riddled with bullets. Another man stood in his barn door and shot the soldier that was ordered to set the barn on fire. He was tried by court martial." The trial was most likely a quick, informal, and unrecorded affair, like the one Custer held for Davy Getz.[17]

Later that afternoon part of the Laurel Brigade under Lt. Col. Richard Dulany forced a crossing of Mill Creek, and a sharp rearguard action ensued. Capt. William McDonald of the brigade wrote, "The Confederates, eager to get within sword range of the detested barn-burners rode at them furiously." The Federals under Wells did what was called for, again falling back doggedly, allowing the burning units time to move along behind them to a safe distance. During all of the pursuit the Southerners had to pass through country that had felt "the blasting and savage hand of war."[18]

By midday the burners were well into Shenandoah County with the Confederate horsemen nipping at their heels. In Rockingham County, south of the North Fork, the country was virtually clear of soldiers of both armies. Near Trissel's Church, less than a mile from the scene of the fight between Custer and Rosser the day before, was the home of Americus Bull, the Confederate cavalryman who was killed in that action. It is not known if his wife yet knew of his death when she saw a Yankee horseman ford Cedar Run and ride toward her barnyard leading another horse. She could not help but be aware of the wholesale destruction of the barns and mills in the area the day before and was afraid with this man's unexpected appearance that her barn would not escape the flames as she had hoped.

David Showalter, a young local miller, was concealed at the edge of a thicket and heard and observed what happened. Another neighbor watched from a

16. (Interview: Daniel Warrick Burruss II; Frye 1988, 128)
17. (Gause 1908, 327)
18. (McDonald 1907, 302)

different vantage point, but he was not close enough to hear the exchange of words. Mrs. Bull followed the Federal to the barn and summoned up her courage to ask, "Now, you are not going to burn a poor woman's barn down, are you?" He replied, "No, indeed, Madam. I just stopped to change saddles and then I am going on my way."

It is possible that this man was one of the soldiers in Sheridan's army who were thoroughly disgusted with orders that called for the destruction of civilian property. Perhaps he had had enough and decided to take himself out of the war altogether. Whatever his motive, after changing the saddle he was true to his word and rode off without molesting Mrs. Bull or her property in any way.

The neighbor who had been out of earshot hurried away and reported to some friends, who have been described locally as "a gang of idlers," that Mrs. Bull had pleaded desperately with the man to spare her barn and then somehow had driven the Yankee marauder away. The "idlers" got on his trail and before too long overtook and captured him. They led him across the Back Road and up into the mountain near Brock's Gap, where they relieved him of his valuables and horses and told him to "run now." Before he had gone very far he was gunned down and his body left where it fell.[1]

The Third Division rolled inexorably through Shenandoah County, bringing the war to the farms of rich and poor alike. The fires of hearth and blacksmith shops commandeered by the begrimed strangers brought ruin to farms and businesses en route. As evening closed, the Valley had been scarred deeply.

Custer, with the bulk of the division, camped for the night near the Columbia Furnace. It seemed as if the works at the furnace were set afire every time a federal force came through; when the wreckers left it was rebuilt and again struggled to resume operations. The most recent destruction had taken place the previous May. Apparently there had been enough new construction completed to provide quite a bit of fuel, because when Confederates passed through the next day one soldier noted that "the furnace and some other buildings were burning." Resources and will were finally stretched too thin, and this time reconstruction would wait until the end of hostilities.[20]

Valley historian T. K. Cartmell wrote of the events of that day: "By eleven the atmosphere was stifling with smoke; the livid flames, that shone in the early morning from river to mountain, were obscured by the increasing pall of darkness that rested on the once beautiful landscape." A pursuing Confederate cavalry-

19.   (HRCHS, Nair, 30-31, 59)
20.   (UVAL, Whittle Papers)

man wrote, "The Yankees have destroyed everything in their course."[21]

Before daylight on the 8th Custer's troopers were up and fed and presently moving. The Third Division continued moving to the northeast, approaching Strasburg. The end to its participation in the Burning was in sight, yet more miles had to be covered before sundown, and many farms lay in the path of this portion of Custer's force.

The Confederates were slow to move on this day, probably because many of their horses were breaking down. The Federals were destroying all of the forage within their grasp—they burned what they could not feed to their own mounts. Horses that had escaped confiscation by the Yankees were hidden in the mountains, also out of reach of the Confederates, who sorely needed remounts.

Just north of the village of Fairview on the Back Road was the home of Levi and Mary Gochenour, whose son Philip was a private in White's Comanches. The Gochenour's barn was built very close to the dwelling house. When the soldiers set the barn on fire, flames and flying embers scorched the dwelling's shake roof. Gochenour climbed up on the roof, and his wife and children handed up buckets of water that he used to douse the hot spots. It was so hot on the roof that his eyebrows were singed off, but he stayed at his work and kept ahead of the threatening flames. The house was saved, but the barn was a total loss.[22]

By the time Rosser's men came pounding northward again, much new destruction had occurred. A Confederate captain reported that "every home was visited, the proud mansion and the humble cottage feeling alike the blasting and savage hand of war."[23]

One of the "proud mansions" about to be overrun and trampled was the Miley family home, Clover Hill, which had grown and prospered through the hard work of four generations. The house is sited east of the Back Road, built into the gentle slope of a hill. Its brick foundation, rising almost a story high on three sides, is surmounted by a large frame structure with two internal brick chimneys, one on each end. Under the roof is a handsome dentil molding. The plantation had two fine, large barns, a granary, "commodious sheep shed," school for the benefit of local children, spring house, and many lesser farm structures.

Martin Miley and his wife Catherine had five children, two boys and three girls. George and James were in Confederate service; George had been captured during the battle of Spotsylvania Court House in May and was sitting out the war in the Elmira, New York, prison camp. The two eldest daughters had

21. (Neese 1988, 319; Kellogg 1903, 213; UVAL, Whittle Papers)
22. (Evans 1977, 46-47; Spratt 1992, 240-41)
23. (Phillips 1954, 116)

Martin Miley, the blind master of
Clover Hill. (Mary Jo Miley Keller)

Bettie Miley, who wrote down her
impressions soon after the Burning.
(Mary Jo Miley Keller)

returned to Clover Hill with their children. Mary Ellen's husband, Joseph
Holtzman, had been mortally wounded at Chancellorsville in the spring of 1863.
The youngest daughter, Bettie, and her cousin, Mary Hisey, both nineteen years
old, were also at home.

When Miley was a young man he had begun to lose his eyesight. By 1864 he
was totally blind, yet even in his blindness he was a superb farmer and stock
raiser, well known for the quality of his cattle and horses.

For two days the family members had their attention riveted to the south,
where they had watched the smoke moving in their direction. When the
columns were seen rising around Fairfield, only a few miles up the road, they
knew they were in for trouble, too. Miley had set his mind to the probability of
massive destruction in the Valley. His home had been threatened several times
in the past couple of years, yet so far the losses had never amounted to much
more than stolen food or trampled fields and gardens. This time his sixth sense
told him something was different; it may have been the malevolent odors carried
on the wind. When the women of his household related what they saw, he
decided it was time to go to work.

Clover Hill, the Miley estate in Shenandoah County. (Mary Jo Miley Keller)

One of the two barns that had been built by his grandfather contained "smooth and nicely finished" troughs that had been crafted with care by his ancestor. Miley considered saving them, but the grain had to take priority. For almost two days, with the help of his wife and daughters, Miley carried boxes and barrels of wheat to an orchard, where they were stacked at the base of a large oak tree in the hope that they would remain undiscovered.

On the afternoon of the 8th a burning party arrived, fresh from having torched Benjamin Layman's barn just across the fields from Clover Hill. Young Bettie Miley remembered, "With no mercy to the helpless, or to the blind and aged . . . the barns were burnt to the ground." All of the outbuildings were destroyed, and the few animals left on the place were herded off or scattered. The next day Bettie noted that the "smoldering fires of burned barns were seen in all directions." To make matters worse, the Union cavalrymen returned the next day and found the wheat, fed some to their horses, carried some away, and scattered the rest. Considering the futility of their efforts to save the grain, for the rest of his life Martin Miley carried a deep regret that he had not responded to his initial impulse and saved the troughs made by his grandfather.[24]

Levi Pitman was a fifty-seven-year-old clockmaker, jack-of-all-trades, and staunch Union man who lived north of Clover Hill, at the lower end of the village of Mount Olive. On October 8 he wrote in his diary: "The Federal Army commenced burning barns and dwelling houses early this morning. We could see dark and large volumes of smoke and still approaching nearer and nearer until they set I. N. Maphis's barn and also William Baker's and J. Rosenberger's barn on fire. They did not disturb our property."[25]

Another Union man near Mount Olive was stonemason and farmer Joshua Stump. During the war he had helped refugees and Confederate deserters get clear of the territory and into Union lines. Once, when he shouted "Hurrah for Abe Lincoln," he was threatened with arrest.

The evening of the 8th a large contingent of Custer's forces arrived at the Stump farm; as they neared their reunion with Sheridan and the main army, the small parties were coming together as regiments once again. Some of them went into camp on the road, while others pitched camp around the house. The summer had been a dry one, and the corn crop was not very good. Stump's ten-acre field had already been raided by Confederate soldiers, and now the rest of the crop was used as fodder. The Northerners cut it up and fed it out right on the place, along with a stack of hay and clover "10 feet broad and 15 feet high." During the night they burned about a thousand rails in their campfires and ate about ten bushels of apples from the trees in the orchard, but "they did not take them all." The worst thing that Stump's eighteen-year-old daughter Sarah witnessed was the shooting of a sow down by the road. Later Stump and his daughter walked down to the Back Road and found that the soldiers had cut the hams from the sow's carcass and left the rest to rot.[26]

Just before sundown most of the Third Division left the Back Road and rumbled east toward Strasburg. There they turned south on the Valley Pike and went into camp. Custer later reported that between September 25 and October 9, 1864, Sheridan's Third Division of Cavalry had destroyed: "10 mills; 150 barns; 1,500 tons of hay; Staunton railroad and railroad property; 10,000 bushels of wheat; 2,000 bushels of oats and rye; 400 head of sheep; 100 head of cattle."[27]

Bettie Miley later wrote of this period, "There is desolation and sorrow where the fire and sword of war have been. War is abominable in that men born brothers, bound mutually, are destructive of one another."[28]

24.   (Ashley 1988, 5-6; Interview: Mary Jo Miley Keller)
25.   (SCPLHC, Pitman Diary)
26.   (NA, Southern Claims Commission Files)
27.   (OR, Series I, Vol. XLIII, Pt. 1, 529)
28.   (Keller and Dudas Private Collection, Boyer Memoir)

Chapter Sixteen

MERRITT DOWN THE MIDDLE—BROADWAY ROAD

Brig. Gen. Wesley Merritt, whose First Division of Cavalry was charged with the burning in the middle of the Valley, planned his actions along two roads. The Middle Road ran north from Harrisonburg into Shenandoah County, where it turned back to the main pike just south of Edinburg. The early settlers of German origin referred to the road simply as the *Stross*, and it was commonly known for years to local farmers as the Ox Road.[1] The Broadway Road split from the Middle Road just north of Harrisonburg; the two roads ran parallel toward the town of Broadway. The Broadway Road, to the west, roughly followed Linville Creek through the village of Edom and then crossed the creek at its confluence with Joe's Creek. Just as the creek meandered in a series of twists and turns, so did the road, each heading toward its terminus at Broadway and the North Fork of the Shenandoah. The two roads were never more than a mile apart.

Merritt's name and likeness did not appear in the illustrated papers as often as Custer's, but he was capable, reliable, and constant, and he did not court disaster as his mercurial fellow brigadier was known to do. Sheridan had a place in his heart for each man; of all of his cavalry officers, these two were like a chieftain's favorite wolfhounds. While Custer strained at the leash for action, Merritt stood quiet and alert, ready to spring upon command; he was still moving through the dawn of what would be an illustrious military career. Between the two, Sheridan would have almost any situation covered.

1.   (VSL, WPA Historical Inventory for Shenandoah County, Virginia)

Brig. Gen. Wesley Merritt, commander of Sheridan's First Division of Cavalry. (USAMHI)

Merritt's assignment on October 6 was to spread the First Division from the Valley Pike into the country to the west of it and to within a mile or so of Custer's force on the Back Road, a front almost five miles wide. He was up well before dawn, knowing that Custer with the Third Division would pull out of the Dayton-Bridgewater area at an early hour. He did not want Custer to get the jump on him.

The Second Brigade under Colonel Devin would work out from the Broadway Road and be closest to Custer's flank. The reserve brigade under Colonel Lowell was to move directly down the Middle Road, with Lowell's men stretching from close to the Broadway Road on their western flank to within a mile or so of the Valley Pike on the east. Units of the First Brigade under the command of Colonel Kidd were to cover the withdrawal of the infantry, artillery, and wagons on the Valley Pike.

The infantry moved out of the Harrisonburg area before first light on the 6th, giving it a two-hour head start on the cavalry. As Merritt's cavalry brigades filed out of Harrisonburg, Devin's men took the lead. They angled to the left down the Broadway Road while Lowell and his troopers moved along the Middle Road toward the villages of Linville and Timberville. Near Timberville the two brigades would link up again; Lowell had the more direct route of fifteen miles, but Devin's was still less than twenty.

Around the village of Edom and the nearby hamlet of Greenmount there was a large community of Mennonites who had settled the fertile lands along Linville Creek and its feeder streams before the Revolution. When they first plowed the already cleared fields on both sides of the creek they turned up pipes, stone gorgets, and other relics of American Indians who had also enjoyed this particular region. As had their predecessors, the Mennonites waded in the creek searching for the large mud turtles that hid under its banks, from which they made stews from the various flavors of meats found in the reptile. Mills flourished all along Linville Creek, and other farming-related businesses enjoyed a healthy

custom in the villages and at the crossroads. In the fields some of the corn was
already in shocks, although many acres
stood uncut. The wheat harvest was over,
and the grain was in the barns waiting to
be threshed or in the granary waiting to be
delivered to the mills. It was an area blessed
with natural prosperity.

As Devin's troopers approached Edom,
some of the units turned to the country
immediately to the west of the road and
began burning the farms around the hamlet of Greenmount; others proceeded on to
Edom itself, where they found full barns
and livestock as yet undisturbed.

The patriarch of the many Wenger families in the vicinity was sixty-eight-year-old
Joseph Wenger, a self-made man who had
educated himself through hard work and
determination. He spoke English and German and knew some French, Greek, and
Latin.

*Brig. Gen. Thomas Devin. As a
colonel, "Uncle Tommy" led
Merritt's Second Brigade down the
Broadway Road in Rockingham
County. (Library of Congress)*

His energy, intellect, and example were
reflected in the successes of his children.
Around him his sons and daughters lived on well-established farms of their own,
and his son Isaac was the owner of several farms and a fine mill below Edom. In
the weeks prior to the burning Wenger had come down with a fever, and though
his wife, Barbara, had nursed him back to reasonable health, his constitution
still was not what it had been.

Once the troopers entered Edom, their attention would have been drawn
immediately to the Wenger home. The beautiful brick house with the magnificent stepped chimney ends and an interior chimney that was also stepped
occupied a rise on the east side of the settlement. Some of the Union troopers
rode boldly onto the property, and despite Wenger's protests began to set his
farm buildings on fire. They performed their tasks as quickly as possible, then,
at the shrill blast of their officer's whistle, they mounted their horses and left to
execute the same drill at the next farm—a procedure that would be repeated
many times that day.

The stubborn Wenger, drawing on the determination that had been so much a part of him through the years and against the entreaties of his wife, rushed into the barn and attempted to fight the fires that were blazing in every corner. Finally, overcome by heat, smoke, and fatigue, he had to give up. He backed out of the doomed structure choking, his chest heaving for breath. Perhaps it was the strain of the day, or maybe it was because he had failed to accomplish something he had set his mind to, but in any event the chord of vitality in Joseph Wenger broke that day, and by midwinter he was in his grave.[2]

Berry's Mill, just below the Wenger house, was also torched by the raiders. John and Salley Berry, who lived some distance from their mill, had seen the destruction coming toward their home and did what they could, but time to prepare was limited. A friend came by and told Berry that his mill was afire. He wanted to see for himself what was happening but was concerned for the safety of his wife and their newborn baby boy. Since the family could not know what besides fire might be visited upon them, John hid his wife and child in a nearby thicket. After making sure they could not be detected, he set off over the hill to the village to check on the mill.

When he was about halfway there he looked back toward home and saw smoke rising from the barn. He returned as fast as his feet would carry him and found that the burning party included some pyromaniacs who, not content with destroying the farm structures, had set some fires in the house. His wife had ventured from the hiding place with her baby, and together they pleaded with the officer in charge to spare their house. He looked at them briefly, then blew his whistle and quickly rode away with his men, allowing the Berrys just enough time to put out the fires in the dwelling.[3]

Over near Greenmount one of Devin's burning parties came to the farm of Joseph Wenger's son Jacob and his wife, Hannah. Jacob had been one of only three men in the precinct to vote against secession in the spring of 1861. He felt it to be a matter of conscience, and despite threats against him he held to his conviction and cast his negative vote. As the cavalrymen approached he had in his hand an affidavit stating that he had, in point of fact, voted to continue the Union. Before they could dismount Wenger handed the paper to the officer, who read it and nodded his approval, then returned the paper and led his men away. This routine was repeated several times as other units came to investigate the farm structures. Eight-year-old Solomon saw one federal soldier pat his

2.   (Interview: George L. Wenger)
3.   (Hess 1976, 207)

father on the back after reading the paper.

During one of these visits a cavalryman noticed nine-year-old Barbara holding her baby brother, Timothy. The trooper dismounted and took the infant from her arms, which alarmed Barbara greatly as "she did not know what the Yankees would do." The soldier passed Timothy up to one of his mounted comrades, who held the baby for a moment before passing him to another rider. Hannah Wenger, the baby's mother, was also alarmed, but when each of the soldiers had in turn held the child, he was returned safely to Barbara by the first man, who explained that they were homesick for the children of their own families. The group left almost immediately and did not molest the property.[4]

When it was felt that the neighborhood was free of menace, Wenger, his son Solomon, and a hired man climbed a hill on the northern edge of the farm. From there they saw the barns and mills aflame in every

The old Brenneman Mill near Edom in Rockingham County was saved by Hannah Shaver, Jacob Wenger, and Wenger's hired man. (Elma Collins)

direction. They suddenly heard an alarm sound from the old Brenneman Mill—someone was blowing the mill horn. Wenger sent Solomon home, and he and the hired man hurried to offer help.[5]

The mill, large and well kept, had been lovingly built in 1800 by Abraham Brenneman and was at this time owned by George Shaver and his wife, Hannah. It was a two-story brick structure on a tall limestone foundation with an overshot wheel powered by water from the west fork of Linville Creek. The heavy, hand-hewn beams and timbers inside were built some distance from the walls to cut down on structural damage due to vibration.

George Shaver, in his seventies, was very ill, and laid up in his bed in the miller's house. His wife, age seventy-seven, had to face the burning parties alone.

4.   (Interview: Norman Wenger; Wenger and Kratz 1961, 6; 1860 Census Records for Rockingham County)
5.   (Morgan 1962, 6; HRCHS Newsletter 1994)

When the troopers set the mill on fire, she attacked the blazes with a broom and beat them out. Several times she repeated this act as new parties arrived and attempted to destroy the structure. The last group to show up targeted a large barn that stood close by the mill. When the bluecoats departed she tried valiantly to extinguish the fires there, too, but was unsuccessful. Flaming material blew toward the mill and reignited it. It was at this point that she seized the old tin alarm horn and blew it for all she was worth.

Wenger and the hired man joined in her efforts and were able to keep the flames from gaining a foothold in the mill, but there was no hope of saving the barn. The men stayed as long as the hot, airborne ashes remained a danger. Once the mill was secure they made their weary way home, taking the old woman's gratitude with them.

A mile down Linville Creek from Edom stood one of the largest mills on the stream, the pride of Isaac Wenger (another of Joseph's sons) and his wife, Lydia. The younger Wenger owned sixteen hundred acres along Linville Creek and a distillery on the Back Road. In one of his mill account books he noted that a certain number of bushels would be held out for making whiskey from every load of corn brought in for grinding. He was much admired for his ability to manage his workforce, and was known as a fair employer who had an "easy, good-natured way" of superintending his business.

Wenger's home was on a bluff across from the mill, and from his porch he saw smoke rising in the vicinity of one of his four large barns. He and his eight-year-old son, Jacob, started up the road to investigate and were soon approached by a squad of federal cavalrymen. Reining in, the officer leading asked, "Old man, where are you headed?" Wenger pointed up the road and said, "I see you have one of my barns on fire." The officer nodded. "If that's your mill down there, it's next," he said, and he led his men on. Father and son turned back toward the mill, and Jacob later recalled that he "really had to trot to keep up with Papa."

By the time they arrived at the mill, the soldiers had already set it ablaze. Wenger asked if he might try to get some of the barrels of flour out of the burning building. The officer agreed, and Wenger sprang into action. He hurried up the mill ramp and began to roll barrels out into the yard. He saved about a dozen barrels in a very few minutes, but when the officer, who had been talking to one of his men, realized what the miller had accomplished, he declared that it was too much. He ordered his men to take all but three of the barrels back inside.

6.   (Wenger 1979, 120-21; Interview: John Wenger)
7.   (Hess 1976, 206; Interview: George L. Wenger)

By nightfall a blanket of orange embers marked the spot where the mill had stood.

Three of Wenger's four barns burned. The one that escaped was east of the home farm, nearer to the Middle Road, and was looked after by a hired man and his family who lived nearby in a tenant house. The hired man was absent when the burning party arrived, but his wife watched from the house with her children as the Yankees set fire to a shed that leaned against the barn and then carried their torches into the barn itself. The quick-witted woman went no farther than her water pitcher and bowl for a solution. She rubbed a bar of soap over her teeth, then took a mouthful of water and vigorously swished it around until suds foamed from her mouth. She then ran into the barnyard screaming, pulling at her hair, and rolling her eyes. The squad leader, taken completely aback, blew on his whistle repeatedly until his men came running to their horses. In almost no time they were

Isaac Wenger was the miller and a community leader in the Edom area. (Wenger Family)

mounted and fleeing from the farm and the madwoman. The enterprising lady and her children then battled the fires—the lean-to was lost, but they were able to save the barn.

About a mile farther downstream from Wenger's Mill were the home and mill of Levi and Catherine Baxter. Their family of ten children included twenty-year-old Jacob, who had been discharged from the Confederate cavalry because of his wounds. The family had already been visited by two burning squads when yet another showed up. The Baxters' old two-story log cabin home had not been

8.   (Interview: George L. Wenger) The flour was shared generously among their neighbors that winter. When his wife saw how much he had given away, she said to him, "You didn't keep enough for us!" To which he replied, "We'll all be hungry at the same time then."

9.   (Wenger, Wenger, and Wenger 1903, 53; Interviews: George L. Wenger and John Wenger) After the war several homes were constructed with a glassed-in cupola at the apex of the roof lines on the theory that in the event of another war, the residents would be able to see danger coming in time to prepare for it.

bothered, but the mill, which was built into the high creek bank behind the house, was a prime target. Each time the mill had been fired the Baxter fire brigade had rushed to its rescue, but this last group of Northerners was the clean-up detail and intended to see the job through. They set fires in every corner of the mill and then held the family at gunpoint until all that remained was the burning, crumbling framework, which eventually crashed, hissing, into the waters of Linville Creek.[10]

As the squads moved down the creek from Baxter's Mill, they entered an area in which the president of the United States had a number of relatives. In fact, the next farm in their path was once Capt. Jacob Lincoln's home place. The president's father, Thomas, had been born near there, in a log structure that no longer existed. Near the house was a cemetery where the presidential great-grandparents were buried.

The fine old house was now owned by Mary Homan Lincoln, widow of Col. Abraham Lincoln, Thomas Lincoln's first cousin. The colonel had been a well-known stockman and had made the home farm one of the best grazing establishments in the Valley. He left his widow comfortably situated, with domestic slaves to help her inside and field hands to tend the cattle, though probably not many of them were left by this time.

Colonel Devin's men, besides ignoring her late husband's blood tie to the chief executive, also ignored Sheridan's order concerning widows, which should have afforded her protection. It must have been apparent to the Northerners that the place was run with slave labor, and they may have let that fact influence their actions. On the farm where the president's father had been born eighty-six years earlier, Union troopers burned the barn, corncrib, and carriagehouse. They also consigned to the flames a reported 350 bushels of wheat and seventeen tons of hay and straw; if the barn actually held that much fodder, it must have been a tremendous fire.

Along with the burning, stock was rounded up and driven off or killed in the pens and fields. Here again, as at Mary Kyle's farm on the Warm Springs Turnpike, there were reports of soldiers driving iron spikes into the foreheads of the dead hogs in an attempt to render them unfit for later consumption.[11]

Just before reaching Broadway a squad came to the home and farm of Samuel

10.   (Harrisonburg *Daily News-Record*, September 19, 1992; Armstrong 1992, 110; 1860 Census Records for Rockingham County)

11.   (Wayland 1987, 55; Rockingham *Register and Advertiser*, February 3, 1865; NA, Southern Claims Commission Files) Several other Lincoln families living in north central Rockingham County lost barns, other outbuildings, and livestock during this phase of the Burning.)

Shank, a thirty-four-year-old, newly called minister in the Mennonite Church who had always considered himself to be a loyal citizen of the United States. The family consisted of Shank, his wife, Sarah, and three children age ten and younger, who were sent to an apple tree beyond the springhouse to keep them out of the chaos.

The soldiers set fire to the farm's out-buildings, then ransacked the house as the Shanks pleaded with them to stop. When their fairly new home was built, the young minister had endeavored to insulate it by filling the walls with sawdust. This proved to be a tragic mistake. As the barn burned and the cinders and hot ashes became air-borne, a spark found its way into a knothole in the house and ignited the sawdust. The structure was quickly and irreversibly en-gulfed in flames. Shank dashed into the house and carried out some bedding. He

Samuel Shank. (Shank Family)

returned and brought out a small walnut table, already scorched, and the family Bible that always rested upon it. His distraught wife ran back and forth between the house and the apple tree, trying to keep an eye on the children and make sure her husband did not stay in the burning house too long. Very soon the fire became so ferocious that it was dangerous even to approach it. The minister was still of a mind to try, but the soldiers stepped in and held him back.

The children, watching the goings-on in wide-eyed disbelief, saw one of the cavalrymen ride past with a firkin of butter, looted from the springhouse, held in the saddle before him. Once the house was beyond saving and the booty was loaded onto their horses and wagons, the cavalrymen mounted up and moved away, taking three head of cattle and leaving total devastation in their wake. That night the family stayed with various relatives, but the next day they returned to begin again.[12]

12. (Rockingham *Register and Advertiser,* February 3, 1865; Brunk 1959, 174-75; Burruss 1993, 135-36; Interviews: Randall and Samuel Shank, Emma Shank Delp) For a while the family lived in a small hired man's house while Shank fixed up the larger springhouse, where they made their home during the coming winter. When Rev. Shank rebuilt his house after the war

Shank was a very small farm operator, and for him the loss of the house and barn plus the other outbuildings, including the wash and butchering houses, was enormous. A threshing machine, cider press, other farm implements, fourteen hundred cap shingles, and six tons of hay had been sacrificed to the flames. Looted from this modest farm were 260 bushels of wheat, 8 barrels of flour, 125 bushels of corn, 18 hogs, 100 pounds of honey, a set of harness, 2 saddles, a pair of saddle bags, 50 pounds of bacon, 2 sacks of salt, 1 rifle, and 7 pounds of butter.[13]

Down from the Shanks, on the west side of Linville Creek, John Bowman owned a large commercial complex that included a large merchant mill, two barns, stable, carriage house, double shed, and corn crib. It was run by his large family and tenants who lived in a house nearby. The burning squad set it all ablaze, including the houses, before moving on. A squad on the east side of Linville Creek created a spectacular blaze closer to Broadway when it torched John Zigler's large tannery and bark-grinding mill. With Bowman's and Zigler's holdings both lighting up the sky, dusk would have been held at bay for a while.[14]

With miles of destruction behind them, the elements of Devin's brigade raced through the village of Broadway en route to the mills along the banks of the North Fork of the Shenandoah. Here the river turned northeast, toward Timberville, New Market, and Mount Jackson.

Captain Winfield's home and mill were nestled in the peninsula of land formed by the river and Linville Creek. By the time Devin's men arrived Winfield was gone, having returned from his raids on the Union supply lines to whisk his family out of Sheridan's path. He was probably at supper with Rosser at the general's retreat near the Back Road when the Federals entered his house and searched it from top to bottom in hopes of capturing the guerrilla leader. They found no evidence that the captain was anywhere nearby, so they set fire to the mill. When they finally moved on, billows of smoke were rolling down the river channel from the inferno.[15]

Having finished their task along the Broadway Road, Devin's men turned eastward toward a reunion with Lowell's brigade, with which they had left Harrisonburg earlier that day.

he used especially thick bricks so that "it could never be burnt again." Even the interior walls were eighteen inches thick.

13.   (NA, Southern Claims Commission Files; Shank Private Collection, Shank Enumeration Document, and Meyers Memoir)

14.   (Rockingham *Register and Advertiser*, February 3, 1865)

15.   (Ibid., January 27, 1865; Heatwole Private Collection, Massie Letter) Turner Ashby Winfield, the son of Captain John Winfield, became the first mayor of Miami, Florida.

Chapter Seventeen

MERRITT DOWN THE MIDDLE—MIDDLE ROAD

After Devin's brigade had peeled off toward Edom that morning, Colonel Lowell led the reserves down the Middle Road. Almost immediately they began to spread out over lands farmed by the descendants of "the barons," a group of well-to-do and highly educated Germans who had come into Rockingham County when it was still a part of Augusta County and George II was king of England and the Colonies.

General Torbert, Sheridan's chief of cavalry, traveled with Lowell's brigade. Torbert's was an oddly flat personality that did not inspire confidence in his immediate subordinates nor in the men they commanded. When told what was expected of him he was usually able to perform adequately, but when initiative was called for, something in Torbert was nearly always lacking. Generally speaking, staff officers were most often the first to defend their general's reputation, but one of Torbert's wrote that his "abilities were hardly equal to such large commands." The same man did, however, also note that the general was "brave as a lion."[1]

As the reserve brigade—two volunteer regiments and three regiments of regulars—started off, the soldiers turned their attention to the hay and grain stacks that filled the fields on either side of the Middle Road. Lt. Charles Veil, who led one of the squads, later recalled that "the entire Valley was ablaze, and the smoke settled over like a cloud. It was pretty severe medicine, but the Valley,

---

1.   (Wert 1987, 21)

one of the finest in the land, was a suitable granary; for the confederates in the army were allowed to come home for the winter and found plenty to subsist on, but not that winter."

Not far north of Harrisonburg the lieutenant and his men were met at the gate of an estate by an old gentleman who recognized that Veil was an officer and beckoned to him. The Northerner rode forward, and the planter spoke to him in a forthright manner. "I see what you are doing. My barn is full of grain. I have a lot of women, children and slaves here who will starve if you destroy my barn; not only that, but you will burn my house." He related that all of his young men were in the army, perhaps intimating that had they been at home a fight might have ensued for the old home place. In lieu of their presence, the old fellow offered Veil eighteen hundred dollars in gold that he had hidden in his cellar, saying, "Take my gold and spare my barn." Veil declined the bribe. He felt sympathy for the old man but left his squad to carry out the mission. He rode away as the barn was engulfed in flames, and he thought that perhaps the house was on fire, too, but he "did not wait to see." He seemed strangely detached from concern for its fate.[2]

The first community that Lowell's brigade reached was the town of Linville, which in 1864 was the center of a thriving grazing and stock breeding area. The land north of the town comprised vast acres of grazing land and wheat fields with only a few homes and farm complexes for three or four miles. Lowell's men moved through the area quickly, spending more time rounding up cattle than burning barns.

George Kratzer's four-thousand-acre plantation on the northern edge of town was one of the most extensive in that part of the county. The property was watered by springs on both the east and west sides of the Middle Road, and the Kratzers had devised a series of wooden water pipes that ran to the farthest corners of the estate. The portion of the Middle Road between Harrisonburg and Linville was known locally as the Kratzer Road. The family's late-eighteenth-century stone house had ten large, well-appointed rooms and nine corner fireplaces above an arched cellar; it was impressive by any standard. Near the house was an assortment of outbuildings that included two barns and a granary. Almost half a mile east of the house was a huge stone barn that had been constructed in the early nineteenth century.

The Kratzers, George and Matilda and their six children, were stock breeders, as were many of their neighbors. They had gotten used to men from one army

2.   (USAMHI, Veil Memoirs)

or the other coming onto their properties from time to time to requisition horses, cattle, hogs, sheep, or chickens. They were usually given vouchers for animals that were taken, but these were of questionable value.

No prior experience, though, could prepare them for the severity of the burning. Everyone in the district had heard tales or had read stories in the newspapers about the acts of destruction perpetrated upon private property by the forces under Franz Sigel and David ("Black Dave") Hunter in the spring and early summer of that year. Yet, just as a visit from the Angel of Death is unfathomable, none in the area thought that he would be touched by the hand of fate. Christly Kratzer, George and Matilda's eldest son, a private in the Stonewall Brigade, was at that time marching through the burned part of Augusta County. He was well aware of what was pointed at his home.

Col. Charles Russell Lowell commanded the Reserve Brigade of the First Cavalry Division. (USAMHI)

Had the Kratzers stood on high ground, they could have seen the dark columns of smoke stretching across the Valley like so many thick ropes dropped from the low blanket of cloud cover. Before noon they clearly understood that the fire demon was marching down the Middle Road toward them. Nevertheless, when the burning parties arrived, the family was amazed at the speed with which they worked. Within minutes, both wooden barns and all of the outbuildings on the Kratzer home farm were in flames. For some unknown reason, the massive stone barn that stood right in the path of the burners was not touched.[3]

The only settlement between Linville and Timberville was the hamlet of Cowan's, a small yet very busy place comprising mills, barns, warehouses, and a few homes. Daphna Creek, a tributary of Linville Creek, supplied the water-power for the mills. Fifty-two-year-old Jacob Cowan was the driving force here, and as he had had only daughters until he was forty-two years old, he relied on

3.   (1860 Census for Rockingham County; Agnes Kline 1971, 53; Reidenbaugh 1987, 128)

hired hands and slaves to keep his businesses up and running. Cowan was away when the burners arrived, probably with some of the livestock and his slaves.

The burning squads found barns and mills full of grain and corn shocks standing in the fields. They fired the mills and one of the barns and raced through the cornfields with torches, making bonfires out of the stacked cornstalks. When they came to burn the barn nearest to the house, Delia Cowan, Jacob's wife, ran in ahead of them, rolled a large keg of tobacco out into the yard, and sat down firmly upon it. Her behavior made the Federals suspicious, so they ordered her away from the keg, but she refused to move. They threatened her, but still she refused to budge. Someone suggested that they shoot her, and several men were raising their weapons when a high-ranking officer, realizing their intentions, rode in among them and ordered, "Disarm!"

Mrs. Cowan was left unmolested after the officer's intervention, and soon thereafter the cavalrymen departed. It is not known if the spunky woman was overly fond of tobacco or if something of even greater value to the family was hidden in that particular cask.[4]

• • •

Lowell's reserve brigade soon came into contact with the troopers of Devin's brigade, and the two units spread out over a large area in their push toward Timberville, where they would encamp for the night. In quick succession they burned barns at Harod Homan's, George Moyer's, David Holsinger's, Sam Wampler's, and Alexander Holsinger's farms. Trooper James Bowen of Devin's First New York Dragoons remembered that day as the time "[we] began moving down the valley, driving all stock before us, and leaving desolation in our wake."[5]

Leaving the area around the town of Linville, the reserve brigade approached rich farms watered by the North Fork. Squads flowed across fields, making pyres of grain-filled barns and mills. Their wagons and an artillery battery moved down the Middle Road toward the river, passing buildings already ablaze.

One of the artillerymen, seeing the river ahead and a town on the northern bank, became curious. He saw a country woman standing beside the road and called out a request for the name of the community. The woman was not favorably disposed to these agents of destruction and answered sharply and in no uncertain terms that her interlocutor should "go to hell—the Yankees has left me nothing but a bean to bite!"[6]

4.   (Kuhn Private Collection, Fox Letter)
5.   (Boudrye 1865, 242)

The two federal brigades crossed the North Fork at Timberville and clattered up the town's main street to high ground beyond, where they made camp for the night. Timberville was the site of a couple of significant horse fairs every year where traders, stockmen, farmers, and gypsies came together to buy, sell, and trade, but the town had never seen so many horses pass through in so brief a period of time as it did on October 6, 1864.

Newton Burkholder and Sergeant Neff continued their night scouting mission for General Rosser, having crossed the North Fork earlier in the evening. A brigade of Custer's riders moved down the northern bank of the North Fork, moving to the east to give the rest of the Third Division room to maneuver. To the west of the Back Road the ground was crowded by the mountains, and in this area the desirable targets of Custer's mission lay between the Back Road and the Middle Road. The Confederates followed the bluecoats almost to Timberville.

Burkholder and Neff had been in the saddle for most of the night, having removed their spurs so they could move as quietly as possible. The scouts mistakenly inferred that Custer had abandoned the Back Road and moved his whole force over to the Middle Road at Timberville. They rode into a wood north of the town, where Neff dismounted, handed his horse's reins to Burkholder, and left on foot to reconnoiter the land ahead. Burkholder, sitting on his horse, fell asleep almost immediately because, as he explained, he was "but a youth."

Neff returned and stumbled around in the darkness "for an age" looking for his companion and the horses and finally succeeded in rousing the sleeper with urgent whispers. They rode into another stand of timber, where they both left their horses and walked across the fields to the home of a "well known citizen." Coming near the farm buildings, they spotted straw or hay piled against the big barn doors and surmised this to be a sign that a Yankee was near and had prepared the tinder in order to burn the barn at first light. In the stall below the barn overhang, they found the enemy trooper's horse.

The scouts managed to awaken the young lady of the house without disturbing the rest of the family or their unwelcome visitor. In hushed voices they questioned her about the Federals who had come into Timberville that evening. She told them all she knew, including the rumor that General Torbert and his staff had taken over a little house just down the road for the night. Before Burkholder and Neff left, she asked them not to take the sleeping trooper's horse, because

6.   (USAMHI, Hanly Diary)

he might burn her father's barn in retaliation. They were brutally honest when they told her, "know that your barn is as good as burned right now—the preparation was all made by your noble guard before he went upstairs to pleasant sleep last night." Later they learned that they had been right—the barn was put to the torch the next morning.

As the scouts walked back to the place where they had hidden their mounts, they heard what they thought were sounds from Custer's camp. "One field lay between us," Burkholder said, and he and Neff made out "coarse voices, camp songs, laughter, blazing camp-fires and now and then the ringing sounds of the axe cutting rails." Regaining the woods, the scouts found their horses and rode down to the house where Torbert was billeted. They could not see a sentinel near the house, and all of the staff officers' horses "were picketed in the yard." Burkholder remembered that the sight of the fine horses tempted them, but already streaks of light were in the east, and they thought it prudent to get themselves away and back into friendly lines. Their mission now, as they saw it, was to avoid calling undue attention to themselves, which would be difficult at best.

Burkholder's description of what they observed from one especially good vantage point is remarkable for its lack of bitterness; he was, after all, viewing the area in which he had spent his youth:

> [F]or miles glowing spots of burning visible—tongues of flame still licking about heavy beams and sills—flames sometimes of many colors from burning grain and forage. These, with the numerous campfires lying nearer, bright spotting the black face of night. It seemed to us the firmament had descended—the stars had fallen. It looked just that way. Think of it we said: Looking downward to see the stars! The sight was unique, wonderful, awe-inspiring. Until this day no such desolation had been witnessed since the war began. What were we coming to? What would all this end in?[7]

General Torbert slept undisturbed as the damp and chilly dawn of October 7 roused the Union cavalrymen in their camps. They breakfasted heartily on the bounty of the land. While some felt they were engaged in a solemn business, the heartless and immature soldiers who also make up an army were having a field day.

7.   (Richmond *Dispatch*, July 22, 1900; *Rockingham Register*, July 13, 1900)

• • •

The Middle Road angled to the northeast, toward the Shenandoah County line, as it came out of Timberville. The North Fork turned slightly more to the east, toward the Valley Pike and New Market. The land between the road and the river formed a tilted **V**. The area was not extensive, and the First Division men moved across it in so tight a line that little escaped their attention.

At the point of the **V** was the old John Zigler homestead. Zigler, who had been an ensign in the militia during the War of 1812, came to Rockingham County in 1814 from Pennsylvania. On land that would eventually become part of Timberville, he established a tannery, extensive orchards, and a pottery kiln. He affiliated himself with the Dunkards, who were numerous in the area. When the war erupted, Zigler's sons and grandsons took a strong stand against it, and some family members paid the five hundred dollar exemption fee to avoid carrying arms. They were adamant that they were people of peace, not war, and were recognized locally for the sincerity of their convictions.

The soldiers who came to the Zigler home, when appraised of the family's opposition to the war and adherence to peace principles, were moved to make an exception to their orders. But they did not want to be brought up on charges of disobedience, so they devised a plan. Working quickly, they assembled a large pile of brush in the garden. They told the family that they would light it and that the billowing smoke would make their comrades think that they had fired the barn. The tangle was set ablaze and the soldiers waited a few minutes to make sure that it could be controlled by the family; then they mounted and rode away with the thanks and blessings of the Ziglers ringing in their ears.[8]

As the Union cavalrymen had made their smoky approach to Timberville the evening before, Martin and Elizabeth Garber and their young children had watched from their farm, which was on high ground north of the river and slightly west of town, in the neighborhood of Rader's Church. They clearly understood what was coming in the way of the destruction of buildings and other material things; their concern was for the fate of the people. Already there were stories on the wind that spoke of killings and outright murder and even worse. The Garbers decided to protect their children by moving out of the way of the soldiers.

When Merritt's troopers arrived at the Garber farm that night they found a stream from which they could get water for themselves and their horses, two

8.   (HRCHS, Garber 1993, 2)

fields of standing corn (about twenty-five acres in all), and a barn full of hay. Enclosing all of that was an amazing sight: an undisturbed rail fence. After three-and-a-half years of war fence rails had all but disappeared from the Valley; soldiers from both armies used them to fuel campfires. And that was exactly the fate of these rails as the First Division set up camp. The hay was brought out of the barn and scattered around, and the horses were turned loose to graze until they were satisfied. Garber watched all of this from a hill a short distance away, and he saw that the hay not fed out was loaded onto wagons, along with some of the corn from the fields. A train of wagons a mile long was observed moving northward.

In the morning, as the Federals made ready to depart from the Garber farm, they set fire to the remaining corn standing in the fields. They spared the house and barn, though, perhaps as payment to their absent hosts.[9]

East of the Garber's place and the Middle Road were several large holdings. One of them belonged to Capt. John P. Brock, the Confederate commissary officer for the county, and his wife, Caroline, a Lincoln family member. Brock, who owned a few slaves, had served in the Mexican War and as a Confederate officer in the Tenth Virginia Cavalry in the first year of the war. He was gone when the raiding party arrived, having managed to get away with some of the livestock.

When the burners showed up, his wife and their two young sons were helpless to do anything but look on. The men split into two working parties. One file lit their torches from the kitchen fire and made for the barn, stable, and grain house, which were soon engulfed in flames. The other group headed for the fields and pens and gathered in three horses, forty-seven cattle, and eighty sheep, and finished up by shooting two hogs. When the Northerners departed, it was as if a whirlwind had passed through, leaving only the ashes of empty stalls and bowers in its wake.[10]

Not far downstream from the Brock farm a burning squad came across an even more prosperous operation. Joseph Shoup owned the land, with each of his three sons having an interest or share in the farm's productivity. Henry, age thirty-four, was the eldest and had seen Confederate service. John, age thirty-one, had originally served in Captain Winfield's company of the Seventh Virginia Cavalry as an enlisted man but now rode at the head of a company in that regiment as captain. He had already been wounded three times, and a note

9.   (NA, Southern Claims Commission Files)
10.   (Wayland 1912, 150-51; Rockingham *Register and Advertiser*, February 3, 1865)

in his records relates that in April 1862 he "shot a Yankee officer." Now Captain Shoup and his company were sparring with Custer's rear guard a little to the west of Shoup's home place. The youngest brother, George, had likely paid for a substitute to take his place in the army in order to help his elderly parents with the farm in the absence of his brothers. Another shareholder in the farm was Joseph's widowed sister, seventy-three-year-old Elizabeth Gochenour. In fact, hers was the largest share after Joseph's own, which indicates that the farm had originally belonged to their parents.

The Northern soldiers found a well-appointed, combination stock-and-grain farm where cattle grazed on the hillsides bordering the river. Fields of corn as yet uncut were framed by well-tended fences, while other fields, where wheat and hay had grown, now lay in stubble. The burners found five barns on the Shoup land, one of which belonged to Elizabeth, all full of wheat and fodder. The torches were applied to all five. The farm sheds were broken open and equipment that included a Pitt threshing machine, a grain drill, fodder cutter, and a large amount of harness was broken up and set on fire. The Federals also destroyed a wheat fan and took a horse and cow that belonged to Elizabeth, plus three more horses, seven head of cattle, and ten sheep. The wheat loss alone was estimated at two thousand bushels.[11]

As they curved away from the river and back toward the Middle Road, still in the **V**-shaped area, the burning units came upon a string of farms belonging to the Lohr family. The first belonged to Isaac and Malinda Lohr. They had six children, the eldest being William, age twenty-one, who was serving in the Twenty-third Virginia Cavalry in Imboden's brigade. William owned a modest acreage that adjoined his brother George Jr.'s farm, which adjoined their father's home farm.

The raiding parties rode through each place in turn, burning barns and outbuildings as they came to them and driving before them what little livestock they could find. Even though George Sr. was ninety-three years old, he was shown no mercy, and when the cavalrymen had finished their work the Lohrs had lost all three barns, a thousand bushels of grain, and an estimated ten tons of hay and farming implements, as well as seven horses and ten head of cattle.

Fourteen barns, one merchant mill, many outbuildings, and some farm equipment were burned in this small wedge-shaped area, which held only about one sixtieth of the total "productive" land mass of Rockingham County.[12]

11.   (1860 Census for Rockingham County; Rockingham *Register and Advertiser*, February 10, 1865; Armstrong 1992, 225) Captain Shoup never saw the destruction; he was killed in action two days later in the cavalry battle at Tom's Brook.

• • •

As noon approached on October 7, the two brigades of the First Division began to cross over into southern Shenandoah County. The Middle Road north of Timberville descended from a long, narrow ridge into gently rolling country watered by Holman's Creek. From the ridge Merritt's men could see Custer's men burning the mills on the upper reaches of the creek near Moore's Store.

The First Division boys entered an area just south of Forestville that had been settled before the Revolution by Dunkards with names like Garber, Wine, Good and Bowman. Their farms radiated out from their home church, which was built on an immense slab of limestone and hence was called Flat Rock Church.

Just to the south and west of the church stood another home of the extensive Garber family. Lydia Garber, age twenty-seven and known as Aunt Liddie to her nieces and nephews, lived with her elder brother and widowed mother in a house built against the western rise of a little vale. She had been watching the evidence of the approaching destruction since the previous afternoon. The scores of narrow smudges being pulled toward a leaden sky had gradually thickened as the Union horde drew nearer. In the night a band of coral—light from the glowing embers—illuminated the horizon in that direction.

Troops moving up and down the Middle Road during the past week and a half had stayed near the road as they gathered livestock or moved supplies for fear of the surprise raids of the Confederate guerillas. The Garber farm, nestled between the sheltering hills less than a mile from the thoroughfare, had escaped attention for that very reason. Now the Yankees were in force and spreading out across the land.

Aunt Liddie correctly deduced that the Garbers' period of grace was about to end. On the morning of the 7th she led their three horses up to the house, where she penned them in the living room. She then heated a large kettle of water on the cookstove. When the Union cavalrymen came to her door, she stood on the threshold with the kettle of scalding water and warned the unwanted visitors that if they tried to enter the house they would get the contents of the kettle in their faces. Her threat was greeted with nervous laughter. They had not enlisted to do battle with determined women, so they turned away. They set the Garber barn ablaze before riding on to the next farm, but Aunt Liddie had saved the horses and kept the house from being ransacked.[13]

12.   (Wayland 1912, 151) The lay of the land in this area has not changed much since the Civil War. From a high hill in the vicinity, and by using a little imagination, one can see the ground that Union soldiers saw in the fall of 1864 as they carried out their orders of destruction.

The Garber home, where three horses were hidden in the living room. (Author)

Only three hundred yards to the south, within sight of the burning Garber barn, was the Wine family homestead. The Wines had hoped to save their grain by moving it into their house, but unfortunately they were in the midst of the operation when the Northern cavalrymen arrived. Since both house and barn contained materials deemed valuable to the Confederacy, both were torched.[14]

Although the weather was cold and dank, the burning parties blew through the area like a hot summer wind. When they got to Forestville they found that Custer's men had destroyed the mills in the immediate area earlier—with the exception of Samuel Hockman's, where the U.S. flag was still on display.

Farther down the Middle Road, Mill Creek cut across the face of the land from the Little North Mountain to the west and eventually entered the North Fork at Mount Jackson. This eight-mile run of water was a major target, its banks lined with creaking, rumbling, groaning, and rasping grist mills, sawmills, woolen fulling mills, and cider mills.[15]

13.   (Interview: Allen Litten)
14.   (Interviews: Allen Litten, Arthur Martin, Edith Martin, Florence Gordon, and Frances Price; 1850, 1860, and 1870 Census Records for Shenandoah County)

Margaret Rinker, the quick-thinking
mistress of Rinkerton. (Daniel
Warrick Burruss II)

Levi Rinker of Shenandoah County.
(Daniel Warrick Burruss II)

Had there been a monarch of Mill Creek, it would surely have been fifty-five-year-old Levi Rinker of Rinkerton. A shrewd businessman who was generous in putting much of his wealth back into community projects, Rinker was one of the few people who, through the use of common sense, hard work, and perseverance, lived to see an area named for him. By the age of twelve he had already gained proficiency as a surveyor. At age seventeen he had come to live at this crossroads with his aunt, Elizabeth Rinker Hickle, and her husband, who were childless. The boy was devoted to them, and they came to look upon him as a son. When they passed away he inherited their holdings and continued to add to them. Eventually Rinker had a beautiful brick mansion built on a rise of ground where the Middle Road crossed Mill Creek and then immediately crossed the Orkney Grade Road (which paralleled the north bank of the creek).

In early manhood Rinker was recognized for his abilities and leadership qualities, and at age twenty-three he was commissioned a captain in the Virginia

15.   (Hardeman 1981, 134-35)

militia; by 1850, at age forty-one, he was a militia colonel. He married Margaret Jane Reed, his uncle's niece, in 1836. They met when she came to visit the Hickles from her home in Hampshire County. The ambitious but gentle Rinker was drawn to the quiet girl from beyond the mountains. She became his partner in all things and encouraged him with her unfailing support.

At the time of the war Rinkerton had a store that held the post office, a blacksmith shop, and a shoemaker's shop. There were several homes nearby, and others clustered down the creek near the other Rinker holdings. Between Rinkerton and Mount Jackson, no more than a mile and a quarter apart, Rinker had his store, home, grist, and sawmills, as well as the fulling and carding mill, where cotton, wool, and flax were cleaned and prepared for weaving into cloth. Below the fulling operation, on the edge of Mount Jackson, was the old Pennywitt Mill, owned by Levi and Margaret's son Lemuel; there had been a mill on that spot since 1734. If Levi looked up and down the stream from the portico of his home, he could survey much of his domain. In addition to the mansion at Rinkerton he kept a house in Mount Jackson; both were built of bricks from a kiln on the home property.

Rinker was worried that his house would be looted and burned, and so he rode over to Mount Jackson before the destruction reached him to request of General Merritt an order safeguarding his house. Family legend has it that Rinker and Merritt had had some kind of business dealings before the war and that Rinker drew upon this prior relationship to save his house. In any event, the request was granted.

As he returned home, he beheld the destruction that had taken place in his absence. The mills at Rinkerton—the fulling mill and his son's mill—and the barns were afire, and his store had been ransacked. The officer in charge was about to turn his men loose on the mansion when the owner rode up and produced the paper signed by General Merritt.

Margaret Rinker may have been sitting on the porch during all of this. She had devised a series of hidden pockets in her petticoats in which she hid "jewelry, silverware, money, and other valuables." Because she would "rattle" and "clank" if she walked, she sat extremely still and told the intruders that she was very ill and could not be moved. All of the small, very portable treasures that looters most covet were thus saved for the rebuilding that would start, in a very limited way, after the armies were gone for good.[16]

16.   (Burruss 1993, 68, 70, 121, 122, 133; Interview: Daniel Warrick Burruss II; 1860 Census Records for Shenandoah County) The huge losses Levi Rinker suffered on that rainy Friday afternoon might have soured a lesser person. Although he was never able to regain the level of

Upstream, only a couple of miles from Rinkerton, a portion of Rosser's old Laurel Brigade was again engaging the rear guard of Custer's division. Merritt's men must have been uneasy as they went about their work, because over the roar and crackling of flames they would have heard from time to time the sounds of carbines and revolvers being fired to the west.[17]

By late afternoon the cavalrymen of the Second and reserve brigades approached Stony Creek, which flowed toward the North Fork at Edinburg. Behind them the countryside was filled with smoke, and the wind carried the strong smell of wet ashes. At the bustling and lovely hamlet of Lantz's Mill, two miles west of Edinburg, they continued their acts of arson. The principle businessman at this location was Jacob Lantz, who had inherited the farm, storehouses, shops, sawmill, and flour mill from his father, George. Over the years he had built the business up even further, expanded the operations and prospered. He, like his neighbor to the south, Levi Rinker, was a strong supporter of the Confederacy, and whenever Union troops came into the area he was forced to go into hiding. On this particular evening he was secreted in a nearby thicket and could not avert his eyes from the destruction of every building on his property, including his house. About the only thing he had left to be thankful for was the fact that his wife, Rebecca, had not lived to experience this day's devastation and ruin.

Jacob Lantz's half brother, Samuel, a forge master, had married Levi Rinker's younger sister Becky in 1848. They lived a mile down Stony Creek from Lantz's Mill, in the great house at Union Forge. Samuel Lantz's forge took in the iron pigs from local furnaces and hammered them into manageable bar iron for the local blacksmith trade. He also ran a couple of farms in the neighborhood.

Samuel Lantz was forty-one years old when the war came. He probably would have been exempted from military service because of his age and the importance of his forge to the cause, but he felt it his duty to serve; the tall, gray-haired ironmaster enlisted in the Seventh Virginia Cavalry. In June 1862, having served more than a year, he received a saber wound in the head in combat and was captured during Jackson's Valley Campaign. Lantz was held as a prisoner-of-war for nearly nine months before he was exchanged. When he returned from captivity he found that he had been discharged from the Seventh Virginia, and, after a few months working his farms and forge, he reenlisted in the Twelfth

wealth he had known before the war, he displayed during the rebuilding a strength of character that few men could have mustered. He did not ignore the sufferings of his neighbors while looking to his own recovery; he truly had the best interests of the community at heart.
17.   (Pond 1892, 204)

Virginia Cavalry, where he remained until the end of the war.[18]

Thirty-eight-year-old Becky Lantz was home with six children (the oldest was age fifteen; the youngest a seven-month-old baby) when the burning squads reached them. One squad took special care to wreck the forge and the tools, then burned the structure and its support buildings to the ground. The soldiers made such a thorough job of it that the forge would never operate again. Other burning parties targeted the Lantz barns, and these were also sacrificed to the flames.[19]

The remaining mile of creek bank to Edinburg was crowded with small farms and a mill or two. Along this stretch the coils of smoke rose close together, like teeth on a giant comb.

On the night of the 7th the burnings along the Middle Road came to an end. Devin's and Lowell's men, exhausted from their exertions of the past two days, went into camp when they reached the Valley Pike just above Edinburg. They looked to their outposts and picket lines before taking care of their horses' needs and finally their own suppers. In the morning the First Cavalry Division would be together once more for the final push along the pike to Strasburg, which the horsemen had left fifteen days earlier. In their wake, bewildered farm families prayed and tried to think of what they should do first to ensure their survival in the approaching winter.

18.   (Spratt 1992, 355; Armstrong 1992, 18)
19.   (Lantz 1931, 226; 1850 and 1860 Census Records for Shenandoah County) Buildings made of wood, brick, and stone could be destroyed, but the land could not. When Samuel Lantz returned at the conclusion of hostilities, he concentrated all of his efforts on farming and was successful. As for Union Forge, only the name on a map remains to mark that endeavor.

Chapter Eighteen

The Valley Pike, the main thoroughfare in the Shenandoah Valley, was one of the first macadamized roads in the United States. Prior to the war it carried produce, butter, hides, iron, hemp, feathers, and beeswax in Conestoga freight wagons, also known as Baltimore or Knoxville teams, bound for the large Baltimore merchant houses. The wagons returned loaded with merchandise that stocked the shelves of Valley stores. Now the cheerful sound of harness bells was a faded memory; the only wagons that passed by were in one way or another tied to the exigencies of war.

By 1864 the pike was not in very good condition, as repairs had been put off for a number of years. Yet even in its worn condition, it was still the best highway in this part of the commonwealth. With Custer burning along the Back Road and Merritt on the Middle Road, Sheridan himself took the Valley Pike. There are many stories of Sheridan popping up at farms in all corners of the Valley, but the fact is that he accompanied the infantry down the pike so he could be easily located to receive reports and be available to direct his troops should the Confederates force a major confrontation. Most accounts of his attitude as he traveled amid the destruction indicate that he viewed it as a necessary military expediency, and that, aside from the refugees, he was not overly concerned about the welfare of the people whose homes and farms were put to the torch.

Crook's Army of West Virginia was moving down both sides of the pike by 5:30 A.M. on the morning of October 6, followed closely by the VI and the XIX Corps, which also took to the fields as the Union army left its camps around

Maj. Gen. Lunsford L. Lomax.
(Library of Congress)

Harrisonburg. The artillery and supply wagons rumbled down the bed of the pike.

A member of the VI Corps later recalled that "hundreds of refugees accompanied us from Staunton, Mount Crawford and Harrisonburg. Unionists who had endured persecution until it was no longer endurable, and who now left houses and farms to find relief in the north from their sufferings for loyalty; and negroes who sought freedom from their ancient bondage."[1]

The last federal infantry unit to abandon its camp was the Third Brigade, Second Division of the XIX Corps, commanded by Col. Daniel Macauley. Its men were predominantly New Yorkers, with one regiment from Massachusetts. Among various duties, they were to act as support for some artillery pieces that would be kept with the rear guard in case of trouble.

Sheridan felt that he was initiating the movement from a position of strength and as an integral part of his campaign strategy, and he felt that his front was where his troops were closest to the enemy. He wanted his infantry and artillery to have a good start before his cavalrymen formed their line from the Massanutten to Shenandoah Mountain. What would have been considered a withdrawal in any other context was an 'advance in reverse' to Sheridan's way of thinking. This explains the statement of one of the Third Brigade soldiers, who said that the cavalry was "acting as our skirmishers."[2] Colonel Kidd, commanding Merritt's First Brigade, was charged with keeping the pursuing Confederates at bay. He had the tedious job of directing the "skirmish line" to deal with feints from General Lomax's division of Confederate cavalry.[3]

The infantrymen who formed in shivering ranks along the cold road were expecting to start the long march to Strasburg and anxious to be on their way. Instead they were surprised to learn that they had been assigned to burning

1.   (Stevens 1866, 411)
2.   (Hanaburgh 1894, 159; DeForest 1946, 197)
3.   (Kidd 1969, 399-400)

parties and stock gathering and driving units. Until this point, the actual burning had been conducted by the cavalry.

One of the first farms visited by the infantry belonged to Jacob and Margaret Byerly, whose extensive holdings bordered the pike to the east. For two days they had watched homes burning across the wide fields and the pike, and they fully expected to be included in the destruction. Michael Shank's house, near the Pike Mennonite Church, had gone up in flames the evening before. On this morning, the 6th, the Byerlys saw the barns and outbuildings of neighbors toward Mount Crawford sending black plumes of smoke heavenward as rain-dampened siding caught fire. As the drier framing timbers ignited, the color of the smoke changed to a dirty gray.

Martha Jane Byerly in old age. (John F. Byerly Jr.)

The Byerly's eldest daughter, seventeen-year-old Martha Jane, took joy in her music but had played her concertina very little over the past couple of months. She, like so many who had believed Southern independence to be a real possibility, had come to realize that the end of the war was in sight and that it was not going to be what had been hoped for or imagined. And it was no longer a war of principle fought in far fields—this very morning it stalked up the lane in the guise of blue-clad infantrymen. Martha Jane clutched the concertina to her breast; it was her most prized possession, and she was not about to let it go without a fight. Other valuables had already been hidden away; a slave, Nanny, had even contrived to secure a five-pound sack of sugar under her skirts.

The officer in charge sent men to round up the livestock while the burning squads made their preparations. Besides the smaller outbuildings on the flats along the creek, two fine, large barns faced each other across the yard. The officer himself entered the Byerly home with a few of his men to announce his intent to destroy it. The family was told to get out. Byerly begged for relief, but it seemed as if his entreaties fell on deaf ears. Finally, having resigned himself to the loss, he told the unrelenting officer that he would stay and bear witness from the yard. Whether it was the father's fervent pleas, the sight of the distraught children, or something else that finally touched the officer will never be known, but he unexpectedly rescinded the order—the house was saved.

Martha Jane stood behind the house and watched in horror as the granary, pens, corncribs, smokehouse, and barns were engulfed in flames. The roar of the fire mixed with the cries of frightened animals as some of the soldiers chased stray pigs and sheep while others tried to hold the rest together in a little herd. Despite the chaos, the stunned girl focused on a single animal, a special pet belonging to her younger sisters, Fannie and Lucy—a little duck now waddling back and forth in great agitation. The sight of the frantic duck stirred Martha Jane into action. With tears streaming down her cheeks, she moved toward the men, crying out that the duck was a pet and should not be harmed.

Several of the soldiers, who probably were not much older than Martha Jane herself, laughed and elbowed one another in the ribs. One of them picked up the bird and told her teasingly that if she were to play them a tune, and if they liked it, she just might get the duck back. She wiped the tears from her eyes and slipped her hands through the straps of the concertina. With great deliberation she pulled air into the squeezebox, placed her fingers on the buttons, paused a double beat to summon up her courage, and then began to play with great passion. When the first few notes of the popular Southern anthem "Dixie" rose above the din, the soldiers were astonished. For a few long moments they seemed to be as stunned as Martha Jane had been. Finally the soldier holding the duck laughed good-naturedly and offered it to the plucky musician. She stopped playing immediately, pulled the quacking duck into the crook of her arm, and ran with it to the house.

When the Northerners departed, all was quiet but for the crackling of the fires and the muffled roar of a racing wind born of the flames.[4]

As Macauley's soldiers moved north of Harrisonburg, they came upon a small subsistence farm owned by Jacob Baugh, a fifty-two-year-old tailor. He and his wife, Catherine, and eldest daughter, Dorothy, had emigrated to America and the Shenandoah Valley from Germany twenty-one years earlier. Six more children were born in the Valley—four daughters and, finally, two sons. Two of the eldest girls hired out as house servants to local farmers to help their parents with their finances. By the time the soldiers arrived, the Baughs could see smoke and flames in every direction. They knew that if they were to stay they would face starvation, so they heeded the soldiers' suggestion that they leave and

4.   (Byerly 1994, 75-76; Interview: John F. Byerly Jr.)

accepted their offer of a wagon. The wagon was quickly loaded, mainly with clothing and bedding. When this was done the four oldest girls—Dorothy, Martha, Nancy, and Hannah—announced that they would not go with the others but instead would stay and look after the place. After some tears and the realization that the girls were in earnest, their father drove the wagon with the rest of the family on down the road.

With part of the family gone, the soldiers told the girls that they had better leave also, as the house was to be burned. As the men moved from room to room kindling the little blazes, the girls rushed to gather up what remaining possessions they could and carry them out into the yard. Some of the soldiers were moved by the sight and helped to save what they could, which turned out to be a considerable amount. When the soldiers had departed, one of the sisters walked to a neighbor's farm and borrowed a wheelbarrow. The girls made many trips back and forth to Reuben Armentrout's place, where they stored their household items. They then went to live with relatives and friends until the war ended and the family could be reunited.[5]

Beyond the Baugh place the troops passed Harrison's Cave, where John C. Frémont had camped his army during the Valley Campaign in 1862. In the road and on either side of it, squads of soldiers drove herds of confiscated livestock. One of the herds was too large to manage, and a couple of miles beyond the cave the decision was made to reduce the burden. A large number of animals were driven to the top of a broad hill, where the soldiers shot them down with their rifles. The corpses were dragged into a pile, and squads of infantrymen stacked dry tinder from a nearby woods on top of them. The brush was soaked with lamp oil and turpentine from neighboring farms, and when the pyre was lighted, the flames shot up with a loud whoosh. The heat was so intense that at one point small streams of grease flowed down the hillside.[6]

Farther down the road and east of Lacey Spring was the farm of Harriet Koontz, whose cousin was the notorious guerrilla Al Lincoln. Despite his promises of protection, her concerns heightened as she watched the columns of smoke approaching. She sent her children over to the lower slopes of the Massanutten with some of the livestock and instructions to stay there until she

5.   (Robertson 1971, 241-42; 1850 and 1860 Census for Rockingham County) Pvt. John O.
      Casler penned one of the liveliest memoirs to emerge from the American Civil War. Following
      the war he married Martha Baugh.
6.   (Interview: Thomas M. Harrison) Mr. Harrison owned Melrose Cavern, first known as
      Harrison Cave. The cave is very close to the Valley Pike, and its walls are filled with soldiers'
      inscriptions, most created by John C. Frémont's army in 1862.

sent for them. Soon after, the Federals swept over the hill from the pike and entered her yard. They wanted to know if there were any guerrillas nearby, where her valuables were hidden, and where the livestock had been taken.

She was so frightened that she could not find her voice, and some of the men told her that she had better start coming up with some answers. They seemed to her to be very "mean," but they did not harm her and eventually just ignored her as they set the farm buildings on fire. Had she found her voice and told them she was a widow, events might have transpired differently.

As it was, all of the structures were torched but for the house and the granary, which was empty except for a large kettle. One of the soldiers had looked in, announced, "Nothing in here," and passed it by. Had he known that the kettle was used for cooking down nitre from collected urine and 'night dirt,' he most likely would not have ignored it—nitre was an important ingredient in the manufacture of gunpowder.

The real horror of the situation struck the widow only after the soldiers had departed, when she heard the screams of the family dog, trapped in the barn and burning to death.[7]

After Devin's brigade had peeled off toward Edom that morning, Colonel Lowell led the reserves down the Middle Road. Almost immediately they began to spread out over lands farmed by the descendants of the well-to-do, highly educated Germans known as 'the barons' who had come into Rockingham County when it was still a part of Augusta County and George II was king of England and the Colonies.

Morgan Sellers, his wife, Julia, and their children had lived in the Staunton area before the war but had moved down the Valley Pike near Lacey Spring soon after Virginia seceded from the Union. Sellers joined the Seventh Virginia Cavalry, where he served in the same company with Al Lincoln. He was wounded in April 1864 and sent home to recuperate, but he did not return to his unit. He joined Lincoln's irregulars when the captain deserted in June.

When Colonel Macauley's troops approached Lacey Spring shortly after noon, Sellers was in the Massanutten with Lincoln's gang. His wife, at home nursing two children ill with typhoid fever, was worried for their safety. She had heard of the burning of houses around Dayton and did not know if that mode of warfare was continuing. She wanted the children out of the house. She roused them and dragged their beds out into the yard, helped them to get back in, and made them as comfortable as possible under the trees.

7.   (Interview: Marie Arrington; Arrington 1982, 294)

When the soldiers arrived they went right to the barn and outbuildings and set them ablaze, ignoring the children. According to local legend, Mrs. Sellers saw General Sheridan out in the road and pleaded with him to spare the house for the sake of her two very sick children, who needed a roof over their heads. He assured her that the house would not be touched, "however, he took all the chickens and everything that was loose."[8]

Near the Sellers's place was Jesse Carrier's farm. Carrier was very outspoken in his condemnation of the war, but his bitter feelings were directed more toward the Confederates than toward the forces of the United States. He felt that killing was wrong and that the Confederates were responsible for the bloodshed and sorrow that touched so many families. In 1862, when Gen. Nathaniel Banks's army had come up the pike chasing Jackson, seventeen-year-old Amanda Carrier had asked a federal band to play some of the "national airs"; she was "surfeited with Dixie." Carrier was a tanner by trade, and his wife, Leonah, noted that when Confederates bought leather from him he used the money to purchase tobacco, which he then presented to Union soldiers when he saw them. The Carriers left with the refugee train on October 5; on the 6th their home was ransacked and looted by soldiers who had no knowledge of Jesse Carrier's sentiments or generosity to their compatriots.[9]

Only a few miles farther on was the hamlet known as Sparta; its longer, more optimistic name, Spartopolis, never caught on. Many years earlier the settlement had been known simply as Hoy's Tavern in honor of a local purveyor of hospitality. In 1864 the community consisted of a few shops and the old stagecoach inn owned by Joseph Mauzy and his family. Mauzy had for years been lauded for the welcome he offered to travelers and customers. He was a man of affairs in the county and accorded the respect due a leading citizen. Unfortunately his reputation was of no consequence to the soldiers who swarmed down the pike toward the hopeful little wayside. Two of Mauzy's barns were already afire and the third and largest was at torch-point when the old man ran toward them waving a safeguard that had been given to him by General Banks in 1862. The paper was honored and one barn spared, but the other two were lost.

That evening Mauzy lost additional property that he thought had been safely secured. Some of the last of Sheridan's men to pass by heard the quacking of a flock of prized ducks in a makeshift pen beneath the inn's porch. They took the birds to their camp, where they and their comrades enjoyed a hearty duck soup.[10]

8. (Arrington 1982, 295)
9. (NA, Southern Claims Commission Files)
10. (Hess 1976, 158) The old stagecoach inn remains a landmark at Sparta [present-day Mauzy].)

As the infantrymen marched on toward the Shenandoah County line, they also trampled kitchen gardens, cut telegraph wires, and chopped down telegraph poles.[11] At first glance the destruction of a small garden plot might seem to be a minor insult when added to the horrors the farm families had already been subjected to, but it was part of a calculated plan to induce Valley soldiers to desert the Confederate cause in order to look after their kinfolk. Melchior Brenneman, a Rockingham County soldier in the Twelfth Virginia Cavalry, is an example of the success of this ploy, a case in point among many. During the Burning he deserted the Laurel Brigade. He and a few friends outfitted a wagon and, under cover of night, escaped with their family members over the mountains into West Virginia.[12]

· · ·

Over toward Keezletown, near the pike, General Lomax's Confederate cavalry was not having any real impact on Colonel Kidd's Michigan brigade, but the Southerners did capture about twenty of the burners. They must have been captured between farms and not in the act of destruction, as they were sent off as prisoners instead of being shot on the spot. In the ten regiments and four battalions of Lomax's division, which were spread from the Middle Road to the Blue Ridge Mountains, there were only six or seven companies that had any appreciable number of Valley men as part of their musters; most of the local men were with Imboden, stalking Colonel Powell's contingent in Page County.[13]

The Confederate infantrymen following the "smoky trail of desolation" were frustrated and anxious to come to grips with their Union counterparts. As they moved through the wasted countryside they were shocked at what they beheld. Henry Kyd Douglas of Early's staff reported "columns of smoke which almost shut out the sun by day . . . I saw mothers and maidens tearing their hair and shrieking to Heaven in their fright and dispair; and little children, voiceless and tearless in their pitiable terror." He also took notice of the daughter of a clergyman who was seen laughing wildly, having gone mad at the sight of her family's outbuildings in flames.[14]

It saw Stonewall Jackson's men pass by in 1862 and cadets from V. M. I. march through on their way to immortality at New Market in May 1864, and it witnessed the stern hand of total war in the autumn of 1864.

11.   (Alexander Private Collection, Arehart Diary)
12.   (Gerberich 1938, 501; Frye 1988, 112)
13.   (Lewis 1988, 62)
14.   (Douglas 1968, 315-16; Kleese 1996, 12; Delauter 1985, 2)

• • •

Before passing out of Rockingham County the burners wreaked their havoc in an area of broad wheat fields and superb grazing land surrounding the hamlet of Tenth Legion. Less than a mile north of the hamlet, between the pike and Smith's Creek to the east, was the farm of seventy-year-old Michael Roller, his equally aged wife, and an unmarried daughter. Like so many others, Roller was powerless to stop the fiery business. There was nothing he could do, he later recalled, "but to stand and look on." As he watched his barn being reduced to charred rubble, a soldier taunted him with a cruel question: "Old man, isn't that a pretty fire?" "Yes," Roller replied, "but when you die and go to Hell, you will see a prettier one than that."

Another mile down the pike the troops came to the farm of Roller's son Samuel. Here they were treated to a humorous sight. Bet Roller, age eighteen, had taken to heart the terrible stories she had heard about uncontrolled looting by the Yankees. "When I heard of the coming of the Union Soldiers and beheld the others taking steps trying to protect their property, I thought of my own little belongings and especially my wardrobe; and thinking certainly they would not take my clothes off me, I went and gathered them up and put them all on; underclothes, petticoats and dresses, and such a fat looking girl as I was the soldiers observed and had much sport because of the odd looking spectacle." Some family members said that besides fearing that articles of her clothing would be stolen she also, and more importantly, had a fear of being molested by the Northerners; whatever her motivation, "the soldiers laughed at her standing in all her clothes."

Samuel Roller's sons had taken almost all of the stock to safety in a hidden hollow up on Massanutten Mountain. The barn was empty of fodder and grain and, in keeping with orders, it was left alone. An old corncrib nearby was in such bad shape that it leaned over at a thirty degree angle, and it, too, was spared. After the soldiers had gone, a sow with a litter of new piglets crawled out from under the corncrib.[15]

Just to the east of Samuel Roller's, nestled against the slope of the Massanutten, was Rosendale, the home of George Washington Rosenberger and his wife, Barbara Ann. Rosenberger had opposed secession from the beginning, and he abhorred slavery. He had inherited a five-hundred-acre plantation and two

---

15. (Roller Private Collection, Roller Memoirs; Interviews: Robert Roller, Richard Roller, Minnie Wagenschein, Rachel White, and Paul Roller)

slaves from his father in 1858, but he had freed the black men and told them they were at liberty to go where they pleased or to stay and work for wages; they both elected to remain. Rosenberger was not interested in the war, yet he realized he would have to make some kind of arrangements if he expected to be left alone. To this end he was more than willing to pay the one thousand dollars in gold required to have a substitute take his place in the Confederate army.

Despite the fact that Rosendale's owner had never borne arms against the United States, had opposed secession, and had freed his slaves, the Union soldiers piled all of his farm equipment in the barn and set it ablaze.[16]

Back on the pike, not a mile from the county line, Jacob Williamson fared better than George Rosenberger. The Williamson farm was east of the pike, where the rocky fields gave it its name: Hardscrabble. Williamson had sold the farm to his nephew and adopted son, Jacob Williamson Jr., before the war, but he continued to reside on the place. The younger Williamson was absent serving the Confederacy as a major in the Quartermaster Department at this time.

Earlier in the war Union general James Shields had occupied the house for a time, and he and the senior Williamson had had many discussions about the causes of the rift in the states. It was said that each man pressed his case with great fervor yet also with "courtesy and restraint." A mutual respect grew between them, and before Shields moved on he gave the family a signed order of protection. When Sheridan's men came to Hardscrabble, the order saved it.[17]

When all of the Union troops had departed from Rockingham County, the officers of the county court appointed a committee to assess the destruction inflicted on the farms and businesses lying within the jurisdiction. The committee's final list, which was published in the Rockingham *Register and Advertiser* on November 11, 1864, did not include outbuildings other than barns or personal items looted from homes:

Dwelling houses burned: 30

Barns burned: 450

Mills burned: 31

Fencing destroyed in miles: 100

Bushels of wheat destroyed: 100,000

Bushels of corn destroyed: 50,000

Tons of hay destroyed: 6,232

Cattle carried off: 1,750

Horses carried off: 1,750

Sheep carried off: 4,200

Hogs carried off: 3,350

Factories burned: 3

Furnace burned: 1

16. (VSL, WPA Historical Inventory for Rockingham County)
17. (Ibid.)

Also not included in the list were diverse types of farm equipment, from hoes to McCormick reapers and threshing machines. Money, silverware, and plate were also not reported, perhaps because the people were ashamed to admit that they had been hoarding against defeat at a time when the Confederacy desperately needed hard currency.[18]

A newspaper correspondent traveling with Sheridan reported what he saw on October 6 as the infantry moved along the Valley Pike:

> The poor, alike with the rich, have suffered. Some have lost their all. The wailing of women and children, mingling with the crackling of flames, has sounded from scores of dwellings. I have seen mothers weeping over the loss of that which was necessary to their children's lives, setting aside their own; their last cow, their last bit of flour pilfered by stragglers, the last morsel that they had in the world to eat or drink. Young girls with flushed cheeks, or pale with tearful or tearless eyes, have pleaded with or cursed the men whom the necessities of war have forced to burn the buildings reared by their fathers, and turn them into paupers in a day. The completeness of the desolation is awful.[19]

Another correspondent observed, "The horses and all the able-bodied Negroes and field hands are being collected and sent to the rear."[20]

Yet another Northern correspondent noted:

> The amount of wheat we find in the Valley is astonishingly large. The mills are full of it. The barns are stored with it. Stacks as high as houses are found in the fields. . . . Almost every barn we come to is loaded with wheat, hay and oats. The destruction of these barns is being accomplished as fast as possible.[21]

Even the lives on the farms that were not in the direct line of one of the Northern units were affected as fear disrupted the daily routines by which people made a living. Men going into the mountains with their livestock could not work their fields. One farmer who lived near the base of Massanutten Peak wrote in

18. (Surber 1921, 33)
19. (Tomes undated, 492)
20. (Richmond *Examiner*, October 14, 1864)
21. (Ibid., October 13, 1864)

his daybook that he had lost thirteen days of work since September 26 because of "the Yankees."[22]

Some of the Union soldiers were only interested in getting back to a base at which they would be well supplied with certain necessities. One soldier reported, "The push up the valley and constant fighting had made our men look quite shabby, some being almost barefoot." Later this man's company was issued six pairs of shoes, "not half enough to supply the demand."[23] The Confederates, however, were faring much worse. At the battle of Cedar Creek, still almost two weeks away, it would be noted that many of the Union dead were "stripped of their clothing by the enemy."[24]

With the coming of darkness on October 6, Sheridan's forces along the pike went into camps; they were stretched out for six miles, from near the Shenandoah County line almost to Mount Jackson. Although they had not covered as much ground as the cavalry on the Back and Middle roads, considering the multiple burdens of livestock, supply wagons, and refugees they had had to contend with, they had done pretty well.

General Sheridan rode on to below New Market, where he stopped for the night.

22.   (Garber Private Collection, Sheets Farm Book)
23.   (Hanaburgh 1894, 160)
24.   (Ibid., 160,169)

Chapter Nineteen

SHERIDAN ON THE VALLEY PIKE—NEW MARKET TO WOODSTOCK

The handsome brick home of Dunkard elder John Neff overlooked the North
Fork of the Shenandoah from the northern side of Rude's Hill, which had been
the scene of many actions during the war. Col. John Francis Neff of the
Thirty-third Virginia Infantry of the Stonewall Brigade, the elder's son, had been
killed at the second battle of Manassas; his body was interred just over the hill
from the house.[1]

Elder Neff had seen what was coming his way, and he rushed out to meet
Sheridan. "General," he implored, "I am a Southerner, of course, but I have no
slaves. I don't believe in slavery. Please don't burn my new house and barn."
Sheridan told him to have no fear for his buildings, but that he must move out
for a while, as his home would serve temporarily as the general's headquarters.

While at the Neff house Sheridan himself investigated a rumor that the
wounded partisan chief Hanse McNeill was nearby in the care of Addison
Weller, a Dunkard minister, and his wife. It was said that he had been brought
to them by several Southern horsemen on October 3. When Sheridan entered
the room where the patient lay, he found a newly shaven, middle-aged man.
The general asked him straightforwardly, "Are you not McNeill himself?" and
the man in the bed replied, "I am." It was obvious that the wound was mortal,
and Sheridan left one of the most effective partisan leaders undisturbed. McNeill
was later moved to Harrisonburg, where he died.[2]

1.   (Wine 1985, 53-54)

Capt. John Hanson McNeill,
Confederate partisan ranger leader.
(Library of Congress)

Band member George Sargent was lagging behind his general on this march. He wrote in his diary the night of the 6th, "Camped at night in a barnyard five miles south of New Market, four of us sleeping on the top of a stack of wheat." It is almost certain that their bed was a blazing mound when the troops pulled out the following morning.[3]

As the leaden sky began to lighten and the pike ahead was cleared out for a distance, the men of Colonel Macauley's infantry brigade finished breakfast and once again spread out to resume their assignment. To their south they could see Colonel Kidd's cavalry skirmishers in a long line to either side of the pike peering into the murky haze hanging low over Rockingham County.

The town of New Market was a major farm trade center in 1864. The North Fork of the Shenandoah flowed to the northwest, with steep bluffs rising high above the water on the east or town side. The residents thought they had seen the very worst of war already that year, when the Confederates under John C. Breckinridge bested Franz Sigel in a battle fought across their doorsteps on May 15. The town had become one large hospital after the battle, although townsfolk had been so riled up at the Yankees that most refused to open their homes to wounded Northern soldiers. Mrs. Jesse Rupert, a Northerner living in the place, had to seek out Confederate general John D. Imboden and secure an order from him that any empty building she chose was to be turned over to her for the care of Union wounded.

Now the men in blue were back again, in far greater numbers, and they were not wounded prisoners this time—they were on a mission. The abundant crop of wheat that had been harvested in August was said to have been the largest

2.   (Wayland 1927, 329-30)
3.   (Morgan and Michaelson 1994, 179)

in many years. The grain from that reaping, and another bountiful one in September, disappeared in flame and smoke.[4] Every barn in the fields around the town was set on fire but one; its owner became suspect in the minds of his neighbors, and relations were strained for years to come.[5]

A couple of miles north of New Market and just to the west of the North Fork was Edge Hill, the extensive country home farm of Samuel and Amanda Moore, whose mill complex at Willow Grove in Page County had been destroyed by Powell's men a few days earlier. Mrs. Moore and her two young sons were not there; they had sought the relative safety of their townhouse in Mount Jackson. Infantrymen from Sheridan's main body swarmed over Edge Hill farm. Although they might have been impressed with the private race track, they were not distracted from their primary duty, and "the barn and saw Mill and the stacks in the fields were burnt up."[6]

Other infantry squads crossed Rude's Hill, passing the home where the commanding general had spent the night. All came out onto a magnificent river plain known as Meem's Bottom. Nearly surrounded by water, with the North Fork to the west and north and Smith's Creek coursing in from the east, this was perhaps the finest wheat-growing estate in the Valley. In a time when real estate valued at ten thousand dollars made a family part of the landed gentry, the Meem family holdings in Shenandoah County were valued at more than one hundred thousand dollars. The estate had been established by others in colonial times.

Three of the Meem brothers—who owned the land with their father—lived in the area. Dr. Russell Meem lived on the Mount Airy farm in the bottom. In addition to husbanding the verdant wheat and grazing lands, Dr. Meem was known for the introduction of new varieties of apples in his orchards on the lower slopes of the Massanutten. He was a gentleman farmer of the old school, but since the beginning of the war he had spent a good amount of his time in Mount Jackson as chief surgeon of the Confederate hospitals there.

While Dr. Meem was at his post in the town, still tending to the wounded from the battle of Fisher's Hill and the third battle of Winchester, the burners arrived at his lovely old estate. They spared the manor house, but every outbuilding and support structure on the place was a smouldering pile by the time the Confederates arrived on the scene late in the afternoon of the 7th.[7]

4.   (Wine 1985, 53-54)
5.   (Swartz 1946, 13)
6.   (Burruss 1993, 139)
7.   (Wayland 1927, 17; 1860 Census for Shenandoah County; Gilmor 1866, 265)

The Valley Pike looking north through Meem's Bottom toward Mount Jackson. (Estate of John W. Wayland)

Across the North Fork the burners entered the lands of Dr. Meem's brother, Gilbert Meem, a general in the state militia. The northern boundary of his property, Mill Creek, was the southern limit of the town of Mount Jackson, an important center for farmers and manufacturers of the region. To the west, along the course of Mill Creek, flour, woolens, and lumber had been produced in great quantities at Levi Rinker's enterprises. A branch of the Manassas Gap Railroad linked Strasburg in the north to its terminus at Mount Jackson. Farmers from lower Rockingham and upper Shenandoah counties hauled their produce to the freight depot and there picked up items that had been ordered from trading houses in Alexandria and Baltimore. The river ran east of the town, and its main street was the Valley Pike.

On many occasions during the past two years six-year-old Robert Hugh Martin had watched troops move through the town from an upper porch of his family's home. One day, when he happened to be wearing a suit of deep blue cloth that his mother had made for him, some Northern cavalrymen passed by. One spotted Robby and called out, "That's my boy!" The young rebel was highly insulted and ran off, the laughter of the horse soldiers following him.

On the morning of October 7 Robby found his family gathered on a back porch. The Martins were looking off to the south and west and were plainly worried about something. The boy could not tell what they were watching, and his questions fell on deaf ears, so after a few minutes he moved to the front porch. From there he saw a few small groups of women and old men standing in the middle of the roadway; they were also looking to the south. Robby returned to the back porch in time to hear an old man, a stranger, say that he had heard that an ammunition wagon had exploded. Someone pointed off into the distance and observed that "the explosion is spreading!" It then dawned on the group that what they were seeing was something even more ominous than a single explosion: "They're burning!"

Little Robby Martin, who witnessed the burning around Mount Jackson. (A Boy of Old Shenandoah)

William Sigler's farm, called Shenstone, was south of town. Robby thought he could see the Sigler barn burning,[8] but what he really saw was the destruction of a slave cabin. The soldiers had set the barn on fire, but a steady wind was blowing toward the house where Mrs. Sigler lay ill. The sight of her anxious children "screaming and wringing their hands" in fear that the fire would jump to the house and "burn up their mother" convinced an officer to order his men to put the fire out. Aunt Lucy, the slave whose cabin had been set ablaze, lost "everything she had in the world."[9]

From the upper portico of their townhouse in Mount Jackson, Amanda Moore and her two young sons watched the smoke pillars rise. Mrs. Moore probably sensed that the family's Edge Hill farm had not escaped the burners. She was later moved to write, "I shall never forget that day it looked to me like the day of judgement, our Father's old mill & barn and fulling Mill, [now owned by the Rinkers] and all the Mills and barns ten miles up [Mill] creek were burning at

8.   (Rutherford 1977, 34-36)
9.   (Burruss 1993, 139)

once and the flames seemed to reach the skies it was awful to behold."[10]

Some soldiers passing by looked up at Mrs. Moore, and seeing her distress they asked, "Do you remember *Chambersburg?*" The question, a reminder of the destruction of that Pennsylvania town, was enough to convince her that Mount Jackson was scheduled to be burned to the ground. She began to pack up trunks and tie up other belongings into bundles in anticipation of the order to vacate.[11]

An order to burn the town was never given, as Macauley's infantrymen were more interested in moving northward as quickly as possible than in setting more fires. Although General Sheridan did not seem too concerned, the men in the ranks wondered who or what might be coming on behind Lomax's cavalry.

This nervousness about the unknown was partly responsible for the survival of a mill on the southwestern edge of town. A party of burners set it afire, then walked away over a wooded hill. When the soldiers looked back and saw no smoke rising, they went back to check and found that a woman from a nearby house had extinguished the tinder piles. They reset the fires, admonished the lady not to interfere a second time, and again left. The woman ignored their warning and saved the building. The soldiers, if they looked back a second time, were not willing to invest any more time at the site; they felt a need to keep moving.[12]

Another mill was not so fortunate. Martin later described the scene as it was imprinted on his young mind:

> I have always carried ... a vivid picture of the mighty roaring, vari-colored flames that licked up the flour mill. The flames leaped upward in great pointed spirals like trogons that twisted as they rose, some five or six of them at a time. The vivid red that predominated had for contrast all shades of green and other colors as smoke clouds and possibly partly consumed gases from wheat and flour and meal mingled with the real flames.[13]

10.   (Ibid.)
11.   (Ibid.)
12.   (Shenandoah County Bicentennial Committee 1972, 26) One of the few mills in the vicinity
      to survive, it served the community until the general rebuilding could begin.
13.   (Rutherford 1977, 36) The war imprinted itself on Robby Martin's mind, and he was
      perceptive enough to understand the ramifications that affected his young life most severely.
      The death of his uncle, Capt. Hugh Ramsay Koontz (who was killed fighting the burners to
      the west of town), was traumatic for him, but he also mourned the fact that, during those
      closing moments of the Civil War, "Santa Claus forgot to come to the Shenandoah Valley."

He admitted that he "was terribly frightened," for he feared that they would now starve.[14]

The hospital complex at Mount Jackson had originally consisted of three two-story, barrack-style buildings by the railroad north of town on land donated by Levi Rinker. When Sheridan passed through after the battle of Fisher's Hill, one of the buildings was empty, and he had it burned. As his troops moved back north they passed by the ruin and the surviving buildings, in which their foes were still being attended by Dr. Meem.[15]

Less than a mile north of town the Lemuel Allen home, called Greenwood, was at this time occupied by nine women (six white and three black) and ten children (five white and five black). Mary Allen, Lemuel's wife, was the mother of four of the white children; the fifth was the child of a deceased sister whose husband was in the army. Mary's two younger sisters, who were in their twenties, were in residence at Greenwood with their cousin, Harriet Stribling, who was ill in bed. Two friends, Annie Samuels and Mary Bird, had chosen this inopportune time to visit the Allens for a week. The only adult male on the farm was Uncle Bob, an old slave.

It was cousin Harriet who, from her sickbed, heard the far-off sounds of many wagons moving toward them in the predawn hours of the 7th. She sat up in bed and said to her cousin Margaret Muse, who was taking a turn sitting with her, "The Yankees are coming! Don't you hear their wagons?" Margaret opened the window and trembled at what she heard. She roused the household as the refugee train rumbled by in the darkness. Mary later recalled that "by dawn the yard was blue with Yankees." When it was discovered that the soldiers were from Gen. George Getty's division of the VI Corps, the women appealed to him for protection. An eight-man guard assigned to the house sent the other soldiers on their way. Margaret was grateful for the protection and had their cook, Eveline, prepare a hot meal for the detail.

Two of the men, Ames and Moore, were posted to protect the house. The women remembered Ames as "a plain, good man, and we appreciated his kindness." The women told the two men that, if one would fetch water from the spring, which was some distance from the house, and the other keep the rest of the soldiers from the kitchen, their cook would prepare breakfast for them "with pleasure." This was agreed to and was done.[16]

The leader expressed the thanks of his men, yet warned the women that theirs

14. (Ibid.)
15. (Interview: Robert Allen Frye; Hanaburgh 1894, 157)
16. (Interview: Betty Burke)

was a retrograde movement—once they were called away, there was no guar-
antee that the next Northern troops to pass by would not loot and destroy. As
the last of the VI Corps moved down the road, "Mr. Ames came in and said the
Sixth Corps was passing and he would have to leave, that he would not be caught
for the Valley of Virginia. He supposed our men would not take any prisoners
today, and he would not blame them if they did not."[17]

Upon learning that one more infantry corps, the VIII Corps, would pass by,
Harriet and Mary were beside themselves with fear that the barn and house
would be destroyed. Margaret recalled that, a couple of weeks earlier, during
Sheridan's advance up the Valley, the women had met Dr. Joseph Webb, the
surgeon of the Twenty-third Ohio Infantry of the VIII Corps. Webb was the
brother-in-law of the regiment's colonel, Rutherford B. Hayes, and a cousin to
Harriet Stribling's mother, who lived in the Lower Valley. Margaret thought
that perhaps she could get him to look in on the distraught women and prevent
any burning on the Allen property.

She went out to the pike but was not sure she would be able to spot him, as
two columns passed behind the house and another one marched along the other
side of the pike. It was quite something to watch the army passing, sometimes
in six columns. The wagons and the artillery had the right of way on the pike
itself; the infantry corps marched along both sides of the road. Margaret
somehow decided that the best bet was to watch across the pike, and in this
endeavor she was joined by Lemuel, her twelve-year-old nephew. Once they
thought they had spotted Webb in the third column, which sent them dodging
across the road and wading into the solid mass of men on the other side, but
they were mistaken. Margaret later commented that the soldiers were "quiet
and polite" and had parted enough for her and Lemuel to pass through. They
heard one soldier say, "I guess she is looking for a Johnny Reb."

They inquired for Dr. Webb and were told that he was near the rear of the
column; they then knew that they were at least in the right place to make
contact. While they waited they noticed that the day was very clear, and the
mountains were lovely "with all their beautiful autumn hues." To the south
Margaret counted eighteen pillars of smoke rising at one time. She thought they
were like smoke coming from a train engine, "disappearing in the heavens
without affecting the atmosphere in the least."

For three hours they watched, and as the time passed they began to worry
that he might have taken another path. Their patience was rewarded, however,

17.   (Ibid.)

as finally Lemuel's sharp young eyes spotted their quarry. Dr. Webb was astride a fine bay charger that had once belonged to Confederate general John Hunt Morgan. He stopped when he recognized them and inquired after Cousin Harriet. Margaret asked if he would take the time to have a look at her, and he agreed.[18]

When the Northerner entered Harriet's room she cried out, "You will not let them burn the barn, Dr. Webb?" He reassured her that all would be well. Privately, he told Margaret that he thought Harriet would not survive a burning on the place as her nerves were so taut. He wrote a strong appeal that the property be spared and gave the safeguard to Margaret, but he told her that she had better keep a sharp eye on the barn, as burners might get around on the other side where she could not see them. She promised to go there directly.

As Dr. Webb took his leave he suggested that Harriet be given a mild stimulant, but the only stimulant they had was some "Confederate coffee" made from burnt rye. It was weak at its best.

Margaret, her friend Mary Bird, and another nephew, fourteen-year-old Rhesa Allen, sat on a pile of fence rails under an old oak tree, where they could see both entrances to the barn and the house, too. Hardly any time had elapsed when they saw two Federals ride up to the house and enter it. In a couple of minutes they came out, remounted their horses, and came on toward the barn.

The three watchers thought that the riders were just passing by, but Margaret noticed a box of matches in the hand of one. She jumped to her feet and cried, "The Burners!" She confronted one of the cavalrymen, telling him, "You must not burn this barn." She handed the soldiers the safeguard and explained the circumstances to the men. One of them said he would honor the paper, but the other one said, "This is a heap of wheat to leave." As their fate hung in the balance, Mary Bird tried to tip the scale. "Dr. Webb said if we met gentlemen, we would have no trouble in saving the barn, but I was so much afraid they would send rough men here." Her words must have appealed to the second man's vanity, as he, too, agreed to withhold the fire, but he warned them to keep watch, as the infantry was the main source of destruction.[19]

18.   (Burruss Private Collection, Pennybacker Memorial; 1860 Census for Shenandoah County; Hoogenboom 1995, 157-58; Ellis 1898, 31) The Twenty-third Ohio Infantry had earlier been part of a force in Kentucky trying to shut down raids by Gen. John Hunt Morgan's Confederate cavalry. The infantrymen caught the general and a number of his men on July 18, 1863, when they crossed into Ohio at New Lisbon. He was sent to the Ohio State Penitentiary.
19.   (Burruss Private Collection, Pennybacker Memorial)

When the two Northerners left, Margaret, Mary, and Rhesa went into the big barn and closed its doors. They watched through the cracks as the infantrymen passed in what seemed like endless lines. They heard soldiers say, "This will make a beautiful fire," and "This barn will go up in a few minutes," yet no one stopped to do the deed. The officers, with their swords drawn, were hurrying their men along now. The thought came to the three that this must be the tail end of the Union columns, anxious not to be overtaken by pursuing Confederates. They hoped Early's men were close.

Soon Lemuel called out to them to leave the barn and come to the house. From the house garden they saw but few Union horsemen passing, and those were soon out of sight. To the south, in the far distance and through a pall of smoky gauze, they saw more horsemen coming on. Eventually uniforms of gray and butternut could be discerned. The relieved civilians were thrilled to discover that some of the Confederates were Mount Jackson boys. One of the soldiers exclaimed, "If there isn't a barn! Lem Allen's barn is standing!" The novelty of a barn having escaped the mass destruction was definitely worthy of comment.

The three tired but grateful barn defenders finally went back into the house; they had been out for five hours. They imparted the good news to the other occupants and relaxed for the first time in what seemed an eternity. That evening Margaret complimented Mary Bird, crediting her flattery of the Union cavalryman in his moment of indecision with having saved the barn. [20]

• • •

From a hill north of town a trooper from Devin's brigade looked toward Mount Jackson and counted "one hundred and sixty-seven barns in flames at one time."[21]

• • •

North of Mount Jackson was historic Red Banks, a plantation with lands on both sides of the North Fork at a place where the river was close to the pike. The manor house faced the roadway, with the North Fork to its rear. The Pitman

---

20.   (Ibid.) Later, when nerves had settled, the Allens took stock of their prospects for the coming winter. Although the Yankees had dug up all of the vegetables with their bayonets, "even the salisfy and parsnips," they would get by, they thought. And indeed they did, even Cousin Harriet.

21.   (Bowen 1900, 243)

The Valley Pike near Red Banks, looking north. The North Fork of the Shenandoah flows to the right, with the Massanutten range beyond. (Estate of John W. Wayland)

family had built the house in the first few years of the nineteenth century and operated an inn and mill on the property. The second Pitman to own Red Banks was Philip, one of the most influential men in the Shenandoah Valley. At the age of sixteen he had served in the War of 1812, and in later life he was one of the prime movers in bringing the railroad to Mount Jackson. The railroad passed only a short distance to the west of the house and carried produce raised on Pitman's extensive holdings to the markets in the North. He sent other goods down the river to Harper's Ferry in an annual convoy of flatboats overseen by one of his slaves.

Red Banks had had its share of famous visitors during Philip Pitman's lifetime. Andrew Jackson once stopped when traveling between Washington City and his home in Tennessee and bounced the Pitman children on his knee. When Gen. Sam Houston spoke at a Democratic rally and barbecue nearby, he was entertained at Red Banks. Pitman's wife, Mary, was a cousin of the Texas hero.

Pitman was a state senator from 1846 until the outbreak of the Civil War, when at age sixty-four he enlisted in the Tenth Virginia Infantry with three of his sons. When his neighbors, in the last year of the war, urged him to come home and run for the state senate, he declined, saying that the ranks were thin and every man was needed.[22]

The thinned ranks of the Tenth Virginia were moving through the charred countryside somewhere to the south when the burners arrived at Red Banks. They immediately set the barn and mill ablaze and tossed nearby fence rails into the conflagrations. Pitman's daughter, Viola, wrote that the house was "pillaged from top to bottom," and that all of her treasures were "carried off." A daguerreotype belonging to a younger sister was stolen, as well as Viola's own needle book. The book of needles seems insignificant when compared to a pilfered set of ivory chessmen and "a *beautiful* sewing bird with which I had lately been presented." No matter how much the Pitman ladies pleaded, the looting and destruction continued. The soldiers broke into the locked parlor presses and forced every other lock in the house looking for valuables.[23] One Union soldier remarked in a letter home, "Sheridan allowed his boys to do about as they pleased. If they didn't live off the fat of the land, it was their own fault."[24]

Farther down the river, on the opposite bank, was another Pitman estate and house called Palmyra. The soldiers who went there did not loot the house, and they spared the barn because it was nearly empty. They did take away 193 sheep, which was all of the flock but seven. Viola later noted that it was far better to have lost the sheep than the barn. Seven horses were also taken from the Palmyra farm, including Nellie Boyd and Leather & Bones, who belonged to Pitman and his son Archibald, respectively.[25]

As squads of incendiaries approached Edinburg, they found many full barns in the hilly country south of town. One group of Federals, commanded by an officer, came to a farm where only an old woman was present. The officer asked her how many sons she had in the "Rebel army." She fixed on him a steely-eyed, defiant gaze and replied that she had only seven but wished she had seven more. Her courage so impressed the officer that he waved his men off, and the barn was still standing when the sons returned home.[26]

Edinburg, once known as Stony Creek, was a tidy town bordered on the south and east by its former namesake. It was near Edinburg that General Merritt's

22.   (Wayland 1927, 457, 719; Murphy 1989, 168; Frye 1988, 159)
23.   (Engle Private Collection, Pitman Letter)
24.   (Greenwood 1993, 25)
25.   (Engle Private Collection, Pitman Letter)
26.   (Wilson and Wilson 1982, 32)

The Grandstaff Mill in Edinburg was spared by General Sheridan, but there are conflicting stories as to how that came about. (Estate of John W. Wayland)

two brigades rejoined the main army on the pike from their own efforts along the Middle Road.

All along Stony Creek, from Lantz's Mill on the west to the creek's confluence with the North Fork east of town, mills of all descriptions were reduced to ashes. The big Grandstaff Mill and barn stood at the southern end of town, where the pike crossed the creek. Philip Grandstaff, an elderly miller and farmer, resided nearby in a house known as Fairfax Lodge. It was about noon when Sheridan stopped there to rest a while. The general made himself at home in the main house, and his officers did likewise in a building on the property known as the Wagoner's Shop, a former way station for stage drivers and teamsters.[27] The officers dusted themselves off and took refreshments as the foot soldiers went about their chores of destruction.

On the south bank of the creek a crowd of women and children watched in horror as the burners made ready to set fire to the mill and barn, both so vital

27. (VSL, WPA Historical Inventory of Shenandoah County)

to the townspeople's very survival. Among them were Melvina Grandstaff, the miller's granddaughter, and her friend Nellie Koontz.

There are a couple of tales as to how the mill escaped destruction on October 7. The first story says that Melvina and Nellie went to Fairfax Lodge and begged to see the general, and when ushered into his presence they pleaded that the mill be spared so that the women and children of the area would not starve that coming winter. Sheridan was supposedly distracted by a little dog that the women had with them and asked if they would name it "Phil" after him if he decided to grant their request. "Never!" cried Nellie Koontz. Sheridan laughed at her outburst, yet he wrote out the order to spare the mill anyway. With the reprieve in hand Nellie and Melvina ran the short distance to the building, which already had several fires going in it. The plucky women started a bucket brigade from the creek with the other women present and soon had the fires in the mill extinguished; the barn, however, was lost.[28]

According to another source, Melvina and Nellie went to the Wagoner's Shop and there pleaded with the officers, whose chivalry would not let them ignore a request from young ladies in such distress. One young officer ordered his men to quench the blaze, and this version also has the two heroines helping in the bucket brigade line. It is possible that the mill was twice set on fire and that the ladies applied for relief in both quarters to make sure it survived.[29]

A little farther down Stony Creek, where it curves around the town, the burners were having a difficult time getting close enough to the Wissen flour mill to inflict any damage due to heavy sniper fire from the bluffs and hills beyond. The Confederates who fired from concealment may have been soldiers who had fled from the field at the battle of Fisher's Hill on September 22. Whoever they were, their shooting was accurate enough to discourage the Federals from crossing the creek. The Northerners broke off the action and left the mill untouched.[30]

Earlier in the day, before the first infantry elements reached Edinburg, a convoy of eight Union ambulances had passed through the town with an escort of sixty cavalrymen of the Second West Virginia Cavalry Battalion under the command of Lt. James Hicks. Normally, the cavalrymen would have been riding with the rest of the Second Division of Cavalry in Page Valley, but they were also a unit of the Army of West Virginia and had been kept by General Crook as a mounted escort with the VIII Corps on the Valley Pike.

28. (Wilson and Wilson 1982, 32; Wayland 1927, 332)
29. (VSL, WPA Historical Inventory for Shenandoah County; Farrar and Hines 1976, 91)
30. (Wayland 1927, 333)

The ambulances did not carry wounded but were transporting dignitaries and officers to Martinsburg. Included in the entourage were two United States paymasters, a Michigan congressman, a newspaper correspondent, General Custer's adjutant general, and a few other military officers. Hicks was under orders to proceed as swiftly as possible with the ambulances and not to allow the convoy to be detoured for any reason. At Edinburg a citizen told Hicks that the Union supply and refugee trains were just ahead of him, when in reality they were already twelve miles ahead. Before they had cleared the other end of the town, one of Hicks's cavalrymen noticed an "old colored man," partially hidden behind a house, gesturing for him to come closer. The old fellow told the trooper that Confederate partisans were all around the area, and that after the main wagon train had passed through under heavy guard the rangers had burned a bridge a few miles north of town, so they would have to detour to the west to cross Narrow Passage Creek farther upstream. He also warned them to stay alert for ambushes.

Journeying on, the convoy arrived at Narrow Passage and found that the bridge had indeed been burned. Instead of fording near the ruined span, Hicks ignored his orders not to be detoured from the pike. He felt that he was being invited to cross through the water at this point because the Confederates, knowing the lay of the land better than he, were confident of having the advantage of terrain. He elected to look for another crossing upstream where he would have a clear field of vision when he brought his party to the other side.

They found a likely place to ford the stream in a short time, and Hicks had gotten everyone across safely and was heading back toward the pike when they were confronted by a line of mounted Confederates who looked to be almost twice the number of the escort. Hicks and his men, who were armed with fine carbines, formed in front of the vehicles in a solid line and began to exchange shots with the enemy horsemen. The Southerners, who could not answer to any degree the firepower of the Federals, were soon forced to retire, and Hicks and his small train of wagons moved briskly on. By early evening they had regained the pike and continued their journey. After dark they were again challenged, taking fire from attackers unseen in the gloom. Two horses were killed by the initial volley, but not a man was touched. The escorts fired their carbines in the direction of the muzzle flashes, but their fusillade was not answered. In the hush that followed, the West Virginia troopers broke the silence, calling out to their attackers that they were "bushwhackers and cowards." Later they learned that they had killed four Southerners, including the detail's officer. Following this encounter, Hicks's party continued on unmolested for the remainder of its journey.[31]

• • •

Between Edinburg and Woodstock, the seat of Shenandoah County, the ground along the pike is somewhat rugged in character, especially in the area where the Narrow Passage Creek courses into the North Fork from the west. Still, there were small farms in the hollows on both sides of the pike, including one that belonged to an elderly gentleman named John Koontz. He had read the signs in the south and devised a plan to save his barn and mill from the torch. He understood that the way to a soldier's heart was through his stomach, so he asked his wife and his tenant's wife to prepare a fine harvest-style meal.

A burning detachment under the command of a sergeant soon arrived, and Koontz went out to meet them. As the Northerners reined to a halt in the barnyard he greeted them in a friendly manner and invited them to come into the house for a meal. The sergeant resisted, telling him that they had orders to burn the barn, and if he accepted the hospitality it would bother him when he fired the structure. Koontz told the sergeant he understood perfectly well that a soldier had to obey orders and that he was not one to hold a grudge, but he still insisted the tired men take a few minutes to eat. He told them he had a son in the army and that he hoped someone would offer him a meal when he needed it most.

It took a little more persuasion, but the young men were obviously hungry, and the sergeant eventually relented. Everything that was good from the house garden and field was placed before men who had subsisted for the past thirty-six hours on the dubious government-issue items knocking about in their saddlebags or whatever they could grab in passing. They ate heartily and with much satisfaction, and as Mrs. Koontz began to clear the table she told them that now they could return to their duty.

Back in the barnyard, the sergeant looked over the substantial bank barn on its stone foundation with three log bays rising above it. He observed that their orders were to burn full barns and mills, and that this barn looked pretty empty to him. His men, their stomachs comfortably filled, agreed that it did indeed look empty, although in fact there were several hundred bushels of corn inside.

The sergeant asked if there was a mill close by, and the old man replied that there was a small one a couple of hills over, at the foot of a ravine. He said the ridges were heavily wooded and that bushwhackers were said to be in the vicinity. After weighing the difficulties for a minute or two the sergeant ordered

31.   (Sutton 1892, 65-67; *Army Register of the Volunteer Forces* 1987, 1105)

his men to mount up, and he led them back to the pike. Thus, by kindness and guile, John Koontz saved his barn and mill from destruction.

Within an hour or two of the scene at the Koontz farm, Capt. Hugh Ramsay Koontz, the son who was in the army, was mortally wounded fighting Custer's men along Mill Creek. Captain Koontz died in Mount Jackson the next day, probably at the home of his sister, who was little Robby Martin's mother.[32]

• • •

Near the end of the day on the 7th, the Union forces approached Woodstock. Capt. John DeForest of the Twelfth Connecticut Infantry remembered that by the time they got there, "the inhabitants were left so stropped of food that I cannot imagine how they escaped starvation. The valley was thus desolated, partly as punishment for the frequent bushwhacking of our trains and stragglers, but mainly to prevent Early from subsisting his army in it and marching once more to the Potomac. It was a woeful sight for civilized eyes; but as a warlike measure it was very effective."[33]

A correspondent traveling with the army recognized that some of the men exceeded orders when he wrote:

Such wholesale incendiarism could not have been pursued, however, without undue license being taken by the worst class of soldiers, and there have been frequent instances of rascality and pillage. . . . The poor, alike with the rich, have suffered. . . . The wholesale devastation of the valley from mountain to mountain, with the intent to render the entire region a desert, embittered the inhabitants to the last degree. Having lost all, and having no object in life but the destruction of their enemies by fair means or foul, they had no resort or occupation but to fight, in Early's ranks, or in connection with Mosby's bands, or solitary in the fearful guerrilla warfare everywhere raging.

The same correspondent also took notice of the refugees, writing, "Our teams are crowded with them. They crowd the wayside."[34]

During the march of the refugees Margaret Suter and her party of seven

32. (Rutherford, 37-38; Armstrong 1992, 178) Capt. Hugh Ramsay Koontz was credited with saving Col. Turner Ashby's life in an earlier action of the war.
33. (DeForest 1946, 197)
34. (Tomes undated, 492-93)

Engraving of Sheridan's position on the heights above Strasburg on the evening of October 8. (Author's collection)

watched some of the infantrymen gathering and driving livestock. On one farm close to the pike they observed several soldiers enter a hog pen preparatory to driving the swine away. The farm wife entered the sty armed with a broom and flailed at them with her humble but effective weapon. The men were startled and momentarily unsure how to respond. They finally retreated in confusion, leaving the victorious woman to her pigs.[35]

• • •

Earlier in the year a Lieutenant Pickett, a Union staff officer, had stayed in a house in Woodstock when General Hunter had used it briefly as his headquarters. William Supinger's brick house and blacksmith shop were at the northern end of Woodstock, on the west side of the pike. Supinger's daughter Sarah remembered that the lieutenant did a lot of writing and that "he was a nice man." Pickett returned to the Supinger house on October 7 and started in again

35.   (Suter 1959, 42-43; Hartman 1964, 26)

with his writing. Sarah looked up the street and saw fires in the southern part of the town. She asked the lieutenant if he could do anything, as she was worried that the whole town would be destroyed. He told her that he would "go up town and stop it all," and, she later reported, "he did."[36] What he probably found was that the troops had set fire to a building containing Confederate supplies and that the flames had leaped and caught the Presbyterian church on fire. The church was totally lost to the flames, an accidental casualty of the war.

Colonel Kidd, who was approaching Woodstock at this time, found that fires started in some small barns and haystacks on the outskirts had spread to adjoining buildings—part of the town was in flames. He dismounted two regiments, sent the horses beyond the village, and gave orders to put out the fires. The men went to work with a will but were interrupted in their laudable purpose by Lunsford Lomax's Confederates, who charged the rear guard and drove them into the town. There was some lively hustling by the dismounted men to get to the horses in time.[37]

The Union forces burned some barns north of the town before calling it a day.[38] Below the Supinger house and on the opposite side of the pike stood the first barn outside of the town boundaries, the property of P.W. Magruder. Sarah Supinger saw it reduced to ashes before the cavalrymen pulled back to their picket lines and encamped for the night.

On October 7 Sheridan halted the movement of the army for the night at Woodstock. At 9 P.M. he sent Grant a dispatch that read:

The whole country from the Blue Ridge to the North Mountain has been made untenable for a rebel army. I have destroyed over two thousand barns filled with wheat, hay, and farming implements, over seventy mills filled with wheat and flour. Four herds of cattle have been driven before the army, and not less than three thousand sheep have been killed and issued to the troops. This destruction embraces the Luray and Little Fork [Fort] valleys as well as the main valley. To-morrow I will continue the destruction of wheat, forage, etc., down to Fishers Hill. When this is completed, the Valley from Winchester up to Staunton, ninety-two miles, will have little in it for man or beast.[39]

36.   (VSL, WPA Historical Inventory for Shenandoah County)
37.   (Kidd 1969, 400)
38.   (Interview: Dr. Joseph Clower Jr.)
39.   (OR, Series I, Vol. XLIII, Pt. 1, 30) The reference to Winchester alludes to the burning that was carried out in southern Frederick County in August in response to area guerrilla activity.

The totals Sheridan enumerated may have included the outbuildings and personal property lost, as the county inventories do not support a total of two thousand barns. In any event, these totals were not final—there was still a day to go before this phase of the fall campaign would reach its end.

In Shenandoah County, from the Rockingham County line to Narrow Passage Creek just south of Woodstock, the Federals had destroyed 215 barns, 18 dwellings, 11 grist mills, 9 water sawmills, 2 steam sawmills, 1 furnace, 2 forges, 1 fulling mill, and 1 carding mill, plus a number of smaller buildings. The destruction of 18 dwelling houses is astonishing at first glance, but accounts point to the wind rising on October 7 and 8. Wind-borne sparks and hot ashes would account for the accidental loss of most of these.[40]

40.   (Staunton *Vindicator*, December 23, 1864)

Chapter Twenty

SHERIDAN ON THE VALLEY PIKE—WOODSTOCK TO STRASBURG

On the morning of October 8 the head of the army pushed on toward Strasburg. A detachment of cavalry reached the farm belonging to a young man, Abraham Rickard, a mile below Woodstock in one of the seven bends of the North Fork. Eleven-year-old William Spigle, who hired out to neighboring farms to help support his widowed mother and three sisters, was this day working for Rickard. They were using a two-horse team to haul corn from a field. Rickard knew there was war-related trouble approaching, but he needed to get his crops in. Not only was the weather ominous, but the next day was Sunday, and because of his religious beliefs he would not be able to work. As Rickard and Spigle loaded the fodder onto the wagon, a detachment of Union cavalrymen rode into the field and announced that they were following "General Sheridan's orders to take all of the horses." Despite Rickard's objections, the horses were taken out of harness and led "away toward the turnpike." Rickard and his young helper were left standing next to a pile of corn stalks.[1]

• • •

To the south, Devin's and Lowell's brigades, having completed their assignment on the Middle Road, arrived on the pike at Edinburg to reunite with the rest of Merritt's brigade. Their arrival signaled the end of the direct involvement

1.   (NA, Southern Claims Commission Files)

of Colonel Macauley's infantrymen in the burning of farm buildings. The infantry brigade cleared Edinburg with the rest of the foot soldiers in the early afternoon. From there Macauley's men hurried on toward Woodstock, four miles down the road, gathering cattle, horses, and sheep as they progressed. Although they were no longer directly involved, they were acutely aware of the "numberless conflagrations in our rear and on either flank, where the cavalry was at work carrying out the edict of destruction in the valley."[2]

Devin and Lowell continued to exercise the responsibilities for destroying the farm buildings, forage, and mills along the pike, and Colonel Kidd and his men continued to provide the skirmish line.

It was near Edinburg that Confederate brigade commander general Bradley Johnson decided to attack Kidd's skirmish line, although his Southerners were reluctant to move against the superior fire power of the Michiganders, who were armed with Spencer repeating rifles. Johnson was enraged with his men and damned their "cowardly souls." He grabbed the brigade battle flag and called to his men, "You may follow me or not, as you like." He moved forward with his staff, and in an instant his troopers sprang forward with a yell. The Michiganders retired "fighting stubbornly," yet the fighting soon lost momentum, and the two sides disengaged.

While Colonel Kidd's brigade was contending with Johnson's horsemen, Colonel Devin sent the Ninth New York Cavalry along the east side of the pike and the Nineteenth New York Cavalry down the west side with orders to consume everything in their paths deemed to be of importance to the enemy. As the Nineteenth New York neared Woodstock on a high shelf of land paralleling the pike, it came to the town's railroad depot, where an engine and three cars sat on the siding. Knowing that guerrillas had damaged the tracks farther on, they destroyed the rolling stock and everything else in the depot area.[3]

Two miles north of Woodstock, on Pugh's Run, was the farm of sixty-nine-year-old Joseph Hottel and his sixty-seven-year-old wife, Catherine. Hottel had served in the War of 1812 and by steady industry had built up an extensive farm where he and Catherine had raised fourteen children to maturity. When a burning squad arrived on their place the wind was up, driving specks of sleet across the landscape. The troopers, failing to consider which way the wind was blowing, set the barn on fire. The fire was carried to the Hottels' home, and it,

2.   (Stevens 1866, 410-11)
3.   (Lambert 1994, 82; OR, Series I, Vol. XLIII, Pt. 1, 477)

too, was destroyed, there being no way to battle both the flames and the wind. A small log cabin and corncrib were spared, and the old couple moved into the cabin, where at least they would have temporary shelter.

Adjacent to the Hottel home farm was the farm of a son, Abraham, a second lieutenant in the Thirty-third Virginia Infantry; his elder brother, Joseph Jr., served in the same regiment. When the burners arrived at Abraham's place, only his wife, Ann, and their four young daughters were at home.

At that time the brothers were with Early's forces, trudging down the pike. Like all of the Valley soldiers, they anxiously strained their eyes, looking ahead, hoping to find that their own farms and families had escaped harm. When Abraham crested a high hill, he saw the columns of smoke rising from his farm and from the home of his parents. There was nothing he could do but hope that family members were safe.[4]

As the Northern cavalrymen pressed northward, they reached the country-side around the village of Maurertown, and within sight of it they burned the barn of Jacob and Edith Pence. Not far from the Pence place one of the squads entered the Harman farm. Benjamin and Rebecca Harman had a fine brick home with a metal roof, but a large barn had been built close to a side portico of the house. When the barn was set ablaze, the portico and window frames closest to it were burnt away. The couple fought the fires and kept them from spreading to the rest of the structure. If it were not for the metal roof, all of their efforts would likely have led to nothing but further loss and sorrow.

In the same neighborhood George Shaver had a three-and-a-half-story, L-shaped brick house; it had been used as a hospital from time to time during the war. A fine bank barn stood nearby. When the Union cavalrymen set piles of tinder on fire inside the barn, Shaver's daughter Sallie pushed them out of the way and stamped the little blazes out before they got out of control. The Federals called her a brave woman, but some of the men grabbed and held her while others reset the fires. They succeeded in reducing the structure to ashes.[5]

In the big bend of the Shenandoah River east of Maurertown, Carrie and Henry Hockman had established their farm shortly before the war. By October 1864 they had four children six years of age and under. In the second year of the war, Hockman enlisted in the Twelfth Virginia Cavalry; he was wounded in June 1863 at the battle of Brandy Station. The wound was somewhat of a godsend for him, as he was able to come home, and after some time spent in

4.   (Huddle and Huddle 1930, 232-33)
5.   (VSL, WPA Historical Inventory for Shenandoah County)

recuperation, he was again able to see to the needs of his family.

On the morning of October 8 Hockman clamped his hat on his head, pulled his coat close around him because of the weather, haltered his horses, and led them out of the brick barn. Mounted on one of them, he led the string across the river and up into the Massanutten, where he hid them. He recrossed the river and was coming up through a belt of woods toward the farm when a unit of federal cavalrymen, thinking he was a scout or bushwhacker, shot and killed him. As the thirty-year-old father, farmer, and teacher lay lifeless on a blanket of damp autumn leaves, the cavalrymen picked up his hat and carried it to the nearest farm—his own.

When Carrie Hockman came to the porch, the men in blue showed her the hat and asked if she knew it. She replied that it was the hat her husband had been wearing when he had taken the horses to safety that morning. They told her what had happened and said they regretted their mistake. They also told her that they had orders to burn barns, but they would light only a small fire in hers and withdraw quickly, so she could put it out. The farm was saved, and the neighbors brought in Hockman's body to prepare it for burial.[6]

The army moved quickly down through the village of Tom's Brook and on through the Fisher's Hill battlefield with its fresh scars and detritus of battle. The proprietor of the thriving mill at the base of Fisher's Hill was eighty-four-year-old David Fisher. When the burners arrived and began to set fires in the middle floor of the mill, Fisher entered from the lower story, which was built into the beautiful, rocky bank of Tumbling Run. He climbed the stairs to the main floor, but a soldier clubbed him with the butt of his carbine, knocking him back down the stairs and into the basement. Fisher eventually roused himself, and as the troops moved on to Strasburg, he and one of his sons were able to extinguish the fires.

But the soldiers had broken up all they could inside the mill before they left. They had thrown the buhr stone down to the basement and cut the silk bolting reels into strips, some of which the soldiers took home "as souvenirs."[7]

Before much of the day went by sleet and a little snow began to fall intermittently. Along with the deteriorating weather, the skirmish units of Merritt's and Custer's divisions had also to contend with increasingly aggressive strikes by the Confederate cavalry. Merritt's forces laid their torches aside to skirmish with Lomax's cavalrymen; Custer, coming in from the Back Road, was still being

6.   (Interviews: John and Elizabeth Cottrell; Evans 1977, 103; Frye 1988, 137; Spratt 1992, 292; NA, CSR Henry M. Hockman)

7.   (Wayland 1927, 345)

hammered by Rosser, and at one point some of Merritt's men were sent to take some of the pressure off the Third Division.

• • •

With his arrival at Strasburg Sheridan considered the systematic destruction of the Valley to be concluded. Along the Valley Pike, Middle Road, and Broadway Road Merritt's regiments had destroyed 630 barns; 47 flouring mills; 4 sawmills; 1 woolen mill; 3,982 tons of hay, straw and fodder; more than 400,000 bushels of wheat; 3 furnaces; 515 acres of corn; 750 bushels of oats; more than 3,000 head of livestock; 560 barrels of flour; 2 tanneries; 1 railroad depot; 1 locomotive engine; and 3 boxcars.[8]

• • •

Before Sheridan released any troops to go to Grant at Petersburg, he ordered General Torbert to deal with the Confederate cavalry that had been a constant irritation since his departure from Harrisonburg on the 6th. In a meeting with Torbert on the evening of the 8th, Sheridan reputedly told him in no uncertain terms to "start out at daylight and whip the rebel cavalry or get whipped."[9]

On October 9 Merritt and Custer turned on the gray horsemen, and in a running battle at Tom's Brook they succeeded in destroying the effective fighting ability of the Confederate cavalry in the Valley for the remainder of the war. As a consequence of the defeat Rosser came under harsh criticism from Jubal Early, but he had done all that he was capable of doing under the circumstances. His vastly outnumbered men and horses had been campaigning hard with little or no sustenance for three days, and their nerves were raw. Trooper Whittle had written in his diary on the evening of the 8th: "I am fearfully hungry & no chance of anything. We have ridden very hard." He no doubt spoke for all of the men in Rosser's division and Lomax's as well.[10]

On October 17 a Pennsylvania cavalryman wrote home from his camp at Strasburg that "we burnt some sixty houses and all most all the barns hay grain and corn in the shock for fifty miles above strasburg . . . it was a hard looking sight to see the women and children turned out of doors at this season of the year but no worse than for those at chambersburg." In a letter the following day

8. (OR, Series I, Vol. XLIII, Pt. 1, 443; Richmond *Examiner*, October 24, 1864)
9. (Sheridan 1888, 57)
10. (UVAL, Whittle Diary)

he added that "starvation is staring the citisins in the face in the Valley."[11]

On October 19 Jubal Early summoned the last of his strength and at dawn attacked Sheridan's forces in their camps at Cedar Creek north of Strasburg. With the element of surprise on his side he experienced success early in the day, but the starving Confederates stopped to eat in the camps from which they had just driven the Union soldiers, and the momentum was lost. That pause to fill drawn and empty stomachs gave the Northerners time to get their wits about them and regroup; even without that fatal respite, the Confederates would have had little chance for a permanent success. Early's hungry and ill-supplied troops lacked staying power, and they were driven from the field later in the day.

Henry Frazier of the Fourteenth Pennsylvania Cavalry later wrote, "Once the enemy cheered for Gen'l [George B.] McClellan [commander in chief of the Union army] along the whole line our boys would then ask them where all their artilery was. Their answer was that they had traded it all to old Sheridan for hard tack."[12]

• • •

Sheridan's victory at Cedar Creek was seen as a major turning point in the war in the government and military circles of the North. Early was no longer considered a threat, and the evidence of daily desertions by disheartened Confederates into Grant's lines at Petersburg made it evident that Lee would never again be able to detach units to the Valley. Colonel Hayes of the Twenty-third Ohio Infantry wrote that there would be "no more supplies to rebels from this valley" and that "[n]o more invasions in great force by this route will be possible."[13]

What Sheridan accomplished in the Shenandoah Valley did a great deal toward helping Lincoln win re-election in November. His opponent, former army commander George McClellan, appealed to the large portion of the populace that had grown weary of the gruesome casualty lists, which for so long seemed to have been generated without any gain to the Union cause. Just before the election and following the victory at Cedar Creek, a Union cavalryman in Colonel Powell's division at Front Royal observed in a letter home that the Confederates, at least, still hoped the Lincoln administration would be turned

11.   (USAMHI, Martin Papers)
12.   (USAMHI, Frazier Papers) McClellan was running for president of the United States on a platform of negotiated peace, which was very appealing to the Confederates.
13.   (Hoogenboom 1995, 175)

out and a negotiated peace would result.[14]

The burning of the Valley, however, created conditions that could no longer support a mobile Confederate force in numbers that would be of more than a passing concern to the Union high command. Equally important, the flow of supplies to Lee's army would necessarily be reduced from a bountiful flood to a miserable trickle. And the Union troops in the field, exhilarated by their telling victories over the Confederates in the Valley, who were once perceived as invincible, could see the end of the war in sight. They would give to Lincoln the votes he needed to enable him to bring the conflict to a successful conclusion.[15]

Daniel Snyder of the Eleventh Virginia Cavalry wrote to his wife late in the fall:

Oh I do trust you have been spared the destruction and desolation of home that many others have been called upon to experience above [south of] Strasburg (the entire width of this Valley from mountain to mountain) to 12 miles above Harrisonburg is complete destruction as far as the necessary supplies to subsist man or beast are concerned. You recollect the many fine barns, mills, etc. that met the eye on your way through it last winter. Nothing remains now but a pile of ashes and rubbish to mark the spot."[16]

• • •

Confederate trooper and Rockingham County native W. H. Arehart noted in his diary entry for December 31, 1864, "The end of the year and cold as blazes."[17]

14.   (USAMHI, Frazier Papers)
15.   (Hoogenboom 1995, 175)
16.   (CCHA, Snyder Papers)
17.   (Alexander Private Collection, Arehart Diary)

Epilogue

OUT OF THE ASHES

The Rockingham *Register and Advertiser* of February 24, 1865, reported that "The present winter will stand out, in all coming time, as one of the hardest, one of the severest ever known in this latitude. It commenced very early, and has continued, with but a few days of intermission until the present period, within a week of the first Spring month—March."

Despite the report of harsh weather, the Valley farmers remembered the winter as severe or mild depending on the degree of their loss. The Mennonites and Dunkards who lived in southwestern Rockingham County south of Dry River remembered General Custer in a good light because he had spared their farms. His mercy toward them only embittered their neighbors, who were not so fortunate. The more vitriolic Confederate supporters referred to the anabaptists with scorn as those "nigger lovin' pacifists."[1]

A citizen of Woodstock pointed out to a Union soldier that the application of the torch was uneven at best. "You only seem[ed] to see the main pike, there are hundreds of folks living over in the bottoms, that you never see, the very richest part of the valley, where there are hundreds of acres of splendid corn untouched, while we that live on the pike are literally stripped of everything else."[2]

1. (Hess 1979, 134; Rockingham *Register and Advertiser*, April 5, 1867) An earlier issue of the same newspaper, that of February 3, 1865, took perverse pleasure in pointing out that "there are not less than thirty distilleries in Rockingham. Beautiful text books for the rising generation! It is a notable fact, that while Sheridan destroyed barns, mills and dwellings in this county; he did not touch a single distillery."

While some of the produce survived, most of the Valley's residents suffered from shortages as well as the cold that winter. Young Solomon Wenger of the Edom area of Rockingham County remembered that his father's horses "nearly starved." Many people sifted through the ashes of burned-out buildings in an attempt to salvage any hinges, bolts, or nails that might have survived the flames. At Fisher's Hill, one of David Fisher's grandsons crawled into the bolting chest at the mill and scraped up about a bushel of old flour dust. "We sifted the worms out of it and mother baked it into bread," he recalled.[3]

The presiding justice of Rockingham County wrote that many of his constituents were "without a pound of meat, bread, or anything to live on, to say nothing of fire-wood. It will require the daily and hourly exertions of the poor and those who have been burnt out to procure a scanty subsistence to sustain life during the winter."[4]

Emergency rations were made available by the very government that sanctioned Sheridan's campaign against the Valley. One day a week was set for the distribution of rations brought in by the Baltimore & Ohio and the Manassas Gap railroads, and the supplies could be drawn by anyone in need and able to make the trip to Winchester.[5]

Even while the United States authorities were trying to alleviate some of the suffering and privation, the editor of the Richmond *Examiner* wrote:

> The horror and crime of this devastation was remarkable even in Yankee warfare. They impoverished a whole population; they reduced women and children to beggary and starvation; they left the black monuments of Yankee atrocity all the way from the Blue Ridge to the North Mountain. It is remarkable that the worst of Yankee atrocities were always done in the intoxication of unexpected success, when no longer the fears of previous disasters held in check their cruel cowardice, and intimidated their native ferocity.[6]

A Confederate soldier journeying through the desolation in the Valley speculated in his diary that Sheridan was somebody who was "trying to crawl to fame through the ashes."[7] Gene Gordon, who had followed in Sheridan's wake

2.   (Starr 1981, 303)
3.   (Morgan 1962, 7; Wayland 1927, 345; Brown 1982, 31)
4.   (Pond 1892, 200)
5.   (Gause 1908, 351)
6.   (Pollard 1866, 405)

and had grappled with his forces at Cedar Creek, said that from what he had witnessed, there was "scarcely a family that was not struggling for subsistence."[8]

Margaret Caroline Kite, who lived on Elk Run near Conrad's Store in Rockingham County, had heard the stories of houses being burned when she wrote to her son, Sgt. William Edwin ("Ed") Kite, on November 20, 1864. He was with the county reserves in the fortifications around Richmond, and his mother wanted to prepare him for what he would see on his return. "The Yankees have burned the citizens out of their houses," she wrote. "I hope the Yankees do not get up here. This winter if you get a chance to come home it will not be like it was when you was at home the last time. It was bad enough to burn the barn but the houses would be a great deal worse."[9]

The Burning was over—and had been for more than a month—yet the fear of further destruction still gripped those who had already suffered so much. As the war continued, some who had yet to see the handwriting on the wall put on the best face they could manage under the circumstances. Ignoring the realities crowding in upon them, in February a "Grand Military Ball" was held by the soldiers of the Twelfth Virginia Cavalry at Harrisonburg's American Hotel. The event was described in glowing terms; the tables were said to have groaned under the weight of "turkies, ham, butter, bread, etc.," which made people think of the "stale and ridiculous threat of the Yankees" to "starve us into submission." The statement that the dance went "bravely on" until about ten o'clock has a bittersweet ring to it.[10]

Pvt. Norval Baker, of the Eighteenth Virginia Cavalry, was a Confederate soldier just trying to survive the winter. In later years he recalled, "My horse looked more like a fence rail with legs than a horse. All the feed in the Valley from Staunton north had been burnt by Sheridan's army and the [Confederate] cavalry in the Valley had to break up in small bunches and go into the little valleys and mountain coves in West Virginia to get feed for their horses."[11]

Mennonite and Dunkard families did not attend any galas. Except for those in the area spared by Custer, they had been hit pretty soundly. Those whose buildings were not burned had lost livestock, and their larders and granaries were stripped almost bare. Perhaps the hardest loss to bear was the loss of young

7. (Neese 1988, 321) George Neese refers to Sheridan as "the boss burner of this continent, so far as destroying barns is concerned."
8. (Gordon, 1903, 375)
9. (Kite Private Collection, Kite Letter)
10. (Rockingham *Register and Advertiser*, February 10, 1865; Frye 1988, 78)
11. (VMI, Baker Papers)

sons and other family members who had to leave—in many instances for unfamiliar parts.

In addition to the refugees who traveled with Sheridan's army when it pulled out of Harrisonburg on October 5 and those who joined the train along its route of march, other Valley residents left as the season progressed. Some of them never returned. Most of the earlier refugees had every intention of returning once the hostilities ended, and they spent the remaining months of the war with friends or relatives or working for strangers in Maryland, Pennsylvania, or Ohio.

John Coffman and Peter Hartman ended up near Harrisburg, Pennsylvania, where they worked on farms until the war was over. When the Lincoln funeral train brought the slain president to the state house in Harrisburg, the two young men were among the forty-five thousand mourners who stood in line to view the body.[12] Soon after that, they returned home.

Hartman's home farm on the northern edge of Harrisonburg had at one time been bounded on two sides by slaveholding neighbors. He came by stage up the Valley and asked the driver to drop him off a couple of miles short of his destination because he wanted to walk the rest of the way. As he crossed the meadow, his mother saw him and hurried to his side. He later recalled that it was the first time he had seen "anybody cry for joy."[13]

Coffman's family had prayed for his safe return every day since he had taken leave of them. Finally the moment came—his sister Mollie saw him walking up the lane and yelled to the other family members, all of whom rushed out to meet him. After he had had some time to settle in, he considered all that had transpired in his absence and determined to do something about it. He organized some other young men in the community into a carpenters' gang, and for the next few months they went from farm to farm, rebuilding that which had been destroyed.[14]

Margaret Suter and her family also returned. On June 10, 1865, they turned into their lane in central Rockingham County and were surprised to see the house and farm buildings standing. They found evidence in the barn that fires had been set, but someone had put them out; they never discovered who their benefactor had been. Before leaving they had stored their furniture with a neighbor who intended to ride the storm out, so they retrieved it and moved back into their own home.[15]

12.   (Hartman 1964, 29-30)
13.   (Ibid., 30)
14.   (Steiner 1903, 19) John Coffman married his sweetheart, Bettie Heatwole, and eventually became an evangelist for his faith.

The soldiers who left their Valley homes to fight for the South also returned—some from the field of conflict and others from Northern prisons. For one of them the war would go on for a while longer. Benjamin Franklin Shaver, the man who had killed Lieutenant Meigs, was not granted the amnesty accorded to other returning Confederates. General Meigs chose to believe that his son had been murdered in cold blood. On the first anniversary of his death, Meigs' father wrote to his own father, "The murderer is not yet certainly known. Various stories have reached my ear. More than one person is self accused & in time it may be that justice will yet have its course."[16]

One day during the summer after the war a stranger entered a barbershop in Harrisonburg and inquired about the location of the Shaver farm. A customer slipped out the back door and rode at a gallop to the farm, where he warned Levi Shaver, Frank's father, who in turn hurried to the field where his son was working and told him to make himself scarce for a while. When the stranger and a couple of companions arrived at the farm they were told that Frank would be home from the fields soon and that they might as well come in and have a bite to eat while they waited. Mrs. Shaver treated them to Virginia hospitality, serving them cider and coffee and pie. They finally tired of waiting and left.

Young Meigs was at first interred in a cemetery in the District of Columbia, but his father had his body moved across the Potomac to the national cemetery he created at Arlington, Robert E. Lee's estate. Maj. John Rodgers Meigs was laid to rest in Mrs. Lee's rose garden, at grave number one, plot number one. Later the general commissioned a recumbent bronze statue to surmount the tomb; it depicts his son as his body was found lying in the old Swift Run Gap Road, a revolver beside his outstretched hand. Eventually General Meigs let Shaver and the two scouts who had accompanied him on that tragic day live in peace.

Shaver married Elizabeth Byerly, a Dunkard cousin of Martha Jane Byerly, who had played "Dixie" on her concertina for the burners. Martha Jane married Lt. St. Clair Lewis of the First Missouri Confederate Cavalry soon after the war and moved with him to Missouri. His family had emigrated there from the Valley before the war.[17]

Elizabeth ("Lizzie") Coffman, who wrote about the occupation of Dayton, married Benjamin Franklin Ruffner, a veteran of the Twelfth Virginia Cavalry,

15. (Suter 1959, 46-47)
16. (LCMD, Meigs Papers)
17. (Southern Historical Society Papers 1881, Vol. IX, 78; Byerly 1994, 75, 79) Martha Jane and St. Clair reared eight children.

after the war. Soon after their marriage they moved to Illinois, where Lizzie had one child who died at birth.[18]

Andrew Long of the Stonewall Brigade walked back to his boyhood home beside the Valley Pike in Augusta County after an eight-month confinement in a federal prison. "I had been gone for two years," he wrote. "Everything had been burned by the Yankees in the meantime. Houses, barns, fences had been burned. The livestock had been stolen, cattle, sheep, horses, all were gone—everything but the old house built in 1796. [They] burned our barns which were much larger and better than the old story and a half log house. I do not know why they did not burn it." Before the war his father had told him they would one day replace the old log home, but since Andrew's brothers, Henry and Frank, had both died during the war from wounds received in battle, there was no longer a compelling reason to build a new house.[19]

Sgt. Henry A. Heatwole returned home from his days as a Woodson guerrilla to pick up the pieces and start over again. His standing crops and barn had been destroyed by Custer's men on October 6. Although he rebuilt and continued to farm, he also went into another business—he became the secretary and treasurer of the West Rockingham Mutual Fire Insurance Company.[20]

Newton Burkholder, the telegrapher who closed his office to ride with Winfield's guerrillas for two weeks, rode out several times to scout for General Rosser and was wounded in the spring of 1865 in a cavalry action at Melrose in Rockingham County. After the war he was graduated from the Baltimore College of Dental Surgery, and he received a Master of Arts degree from the New Market Polytechnic Institute in 1876. He was a contributor of accounts of the war to publications in Virginia. He died in December 1900 and is buried in the Cook's Creek Presbyterian Church cemetery in Rockingham County.[21]

Samuel Hockman, who saved his mill at Forestville in Shenandoah County by displaying the United States flag, fell on hard times, but it was his own fault. Mr. Hockman was in truth a Union man, not just a clever manipulator, and he grew very arrogant about his success in saving the only mill over a wide area. Residents along Holman's Creek who had a little money or goods to trade were able to procure some flour from Hockman that winter, but when destitute families asked for credit until better times he sneered at them. One of these people asked him, "How are we going to feed our families?" He thought a

18.   (Kauffman 1940, 575)
19.   (Long 1965, 32, 35)
20.   (Heatwole 1970, 79)
21.   (Bridgewater *Herald*, December 14, 1900)

moment and, shrugging his shoulders, answered, "You will have to bake cakes." When the war ended and nearby mills were rebuilt, the custom at Hockman's fell off dramatically; his neighbors' memories were long. Once he approached a group of farmers and asked, "What am I going to do?" One of the farmers answered, "You will have to bake cakes."[22]

Solomon Rothgeb served in the Tenth Virginia Infantry through most of the war. Following the surrender of Lee at Appomattox, he, like all of his comrades-in-arms who were lucky enough to have survived, laid down his weapon and made the long walk home, to Page County. He had been a millwright before the war, and along the South Fork of the Shenandoah and the Hawksbills he saw the ruins of many structures that he had helped to build. He did not have the nature to remain defeated long, and he began to line up lumber and work crews. In the first year of peace he supervised the erection of seventeen mills; many replaced ones that had been burned by Powell's men.[23]

Robert Hugh Martin, young Robby who had watched the Burning from his porch in Mount Jackson, attended Washington and Lee College in the mid-1870s and then taught school in Shenandoah County. His interests soon led him to newspaper work, and for the remainder of his long and eventful life he was a respected newspaper publisher and editor in Virginia and West Virginia.

The Presbyterian Church in Woodstock that was destroyed by accident was rebuilt by 1867. The church's minister, the Reverend J. M. Clymer, solicited friends in the North for funds, and they responded generously.[24]

Nonmilitary property destroyed in the war was of great interest to speculators. Lawyers and agents advertised in Valley newspapers that they would handle applications for restitution of property taken or destroyed by United States troops during the conflict. The Southern Claims Commission was formed in Washington to hear cases and empowered to decide who would be compensated. The applicants had to be able to prove that they were loyal to the United States at the time when the confiscation or destruction of their property occurred.

Only a minority of Mennonites and Dunkards applied for the restitution funds, and those who did found it hard going to have their claims honored. Even people who had voiced opposition to the war and had helped deserters and other

22.   (Wine 1985, 165)
23.   (White 1961, 16)
24.   (Interview: Dr. Joseph B. Clower Jr.) Help came to the people of the Shenandoah Valley from many areas. The people of Baltimore, Maryland, many of whom were sympathetic to the Confederacy, sent what supplies they could to help alleviate the suffering. Relief also came from West Virginia, from folks who had historical and family ties with the Shenandoah Valley.

dissenters to escape to Union lines found their claims rejected. If investigators found a record of even one sale by a claimant of livestock or cured meat or produce, no matter how small, to a Confederate quartermaster or commissary officer, the petition was disallowed. This decision seems harsh in light of what someone would have had to do in order for his family to survive in a wartime environment; it would have been a rare case in the Valley had someone not been compelled at one time or another to sell something to a representative of the Confederacy. Quartermasters at regimental level would occasionally show up on a farm, take what was needed, and hand the hapless owner a draft to be honored after total Confederate independence had been achieved.

In rejecting one Mennonite's claim the commission took another tack, stating, "We do not think him justified upon his own statement. He was obviously opposed to war on religious principle. It is rather to be inferred from his general conduct that he was opposed to the rebellion, but he acted rather according to the rules of his church to keep out of the war than from strong Union principle."[25]

Jacob Spitzer, who was from the Cherry Grove area, close to the Back Road in Rockingham County, applied for reimbursement for the loss of one sorrel horse, twenty-two years old, and forty pounds of butter. He testified that he was "loyal to the North" and that he always left his house at the approach of the "Rebel Army." He stated that he was "opposed to war entirely." The commission findings said, "A little old mare over 20 years of age would not make a very formidable Cavalry Charger." The request was denied without consideration of the lost butter.

Many Southern sympathizers and even former Confederate soldiers and offi-cers applied to the commission for redress; some of them lied outright about their participation in the war. To many the United States authorities would always be the enemy, and in their minds any type of deceit was justified. Other people, including those who might have been able to file legitimate claims, decided instead to put the past behind them and to get on with the rest of their lives.[26]

The outcry about the decision to make war on civilians was not limited to the South, and like some correspondents in the South who had not actually borne witness to the destruction, many Northerners resorted to hyperbole to fan the fires of hatred with wild assertions. A Youth's History of the Great Civil War, printed in New York in 1866, was very critical of U. S. Grant's conduct of the

25.   (Horst 1967, 114-15)
26.   (NA, Southern Claims Commission Files)

war and the policy that caused the Burning, almost labeling its designers demoniac:

> And now General Sheridan, with the instincts of savage warfare, determined to utterly devastate this beautiful valley. He therefore set his troops at work, and all the way from Staunton to Winchester was soon one scene of desolation. He burned every house, every barn, every mill, all the corn cribs, hay-stacks, and the entire food crops of all kinds for the year. Not only this, but he seized all the ploughs, harrows, spades, and every description of farm implement, and putting them into piles, made his soldiers burn them. He then drove off all the cows, horses, oxen, cattle, sheep, pigs, and every living animal for the use of man in all that wide valley. In fact nothing that devilish ingenuity could invent was left undone to transform the loveliest and most fertile valley in the world into a desolate and howling wilderness. Not less than ten thousand innocent women and children were by this savagery reduced to starvation, and thrown, in the fall of the year, out of comfortable homes, to perish in tents and caves by the cold of the winter.[27]

With lurid descriptions like this, is it any wonder that the true story of the campaign to make the Valley untenable has been cloaked in myth for so many years? Obviously, for whatever purposes, there were those who would labor to fan the flames of resentment between the sections of the country indefinitely. Most people wanted to leave the horror and bitterness behind them as they built new lives and institutions upon the ashes of the past.

• • •

In November 1886 Gen. Philip Sheridan, now commanding general of the entire United States Army, and Senator Don Cameron of Pennsylvania visited the Shenandoah Valley and stayed overnight at the Shenandoah House in Woodstock. One might think that Sheridan would have been greeted with torches, pitchforks, and rifles, yet Schaeffer's Coronet Band serenaded the pair.[28]

Perhaps the intervening years had softened the hard edge of war, and perhaps thoughtful individuals had come to realize that the Burning had, in its own way,

27.   (*A Youth's History of the Great Civil War* 1866, 338-39)
28.   (Interview: Dr. Joseph B. Clower Jr.; Shenandoah *Herald,* November 19, 1886)

helped to end the war and save the many lives that would have been lost had it continued into the summer of 1865. Capt. John Opie, a Confederate cavalry-man from Augusta County, supported that view when he wrote:

> This Valley, which once blossomed as a flower garden, was one scene of desolation and ruin. A great deal of abuse has been heaped on Sheridan for this barbarous mode of warfare, but he was no more responsible than the humblest private in his army. The records show that he was acting under orders from the War Department.[29]

Not everyone was in a mood to forgive Sheridan for his wartime actions in the Valley. On the occasion of the announcement of the general's death in 1888, the *Clarke Courier* wrote:

> It is not to be expected that any lamentations shall be heard in the Valley of Virginia over the death of this officer, even though the people thereof have accepted the results of the war in good faith, for they can never forget as long as they live that he resorted to the use of the torch in order to bring them into subjection.[30]

Another Valley newspaper referred to Sheridan during his lifetime as the "desolator of the fair, Valley of Virginia—barn burner and hen roost robber."[31]

Captain Opie, perhaps trying to settle the question in his own mind, ended his reflections with a query: "Which is the worst in war, to burn a barn, or kill a fellow-man?"[32]

29.   (Opie 1899, 254-55)
30.   (*Clarke Courier*, August 9, 1888)
31.   (Staunton *Spectator*, January 26, 1875)
32.   (Opie 1899, 255)

Appendix A

XIX INFANTRY CORPS

Second Division
 Third Brigade (Col. Daniel Macauley)
 38th Massachusetts; 128th New York; 156th New York; 175th New York (battalion);
 176th New York
 (Burned along the Valley Pike October 6 and 7.)

ARMY OF WEST VIRGINIA (VIII CORPS)

First Infantry Division
 First Brigade (Lt. Col. Thomas F. Wildes)
 116th Ohio
 (Ordered to burn Dayton on October 4; order rescinded by Sheridan.)

First Cavalry Division (Brig. Gen. Wesley Merritt)
 First Brigade (Col. James Kidd)
 1st Michigan; 5th Michigan; 6th Michigan; 7th Michigan
 (Burned in eastern Rockingham County and northern Augusta County September 26-30.
 Acted as rear guard for infantry along the Valley Pike October 6-8.)

 Second Brigade (Col. Thomas C. Devin)
 4th New York; 6th New York; 9th New York; 19th New York; 25th New York
 (Burned in eastern Rockingham County and northern Augusta County September 26-30;
 burned along Broadway Road, Middle Road, and Valley Pike October 6-8.)

 Third Brigade (Col. Charles Russell Lowell)
 2nd Massachusetts; 6th Pennsylvania; 1st U.S.; 2nd U.S.; 5th U.S.
 (Burned in Augusta County September 26-29; burned along Middle Road and Valley Pike
 October 6-8.)

Second Cavalry Division (Col. William H. Powell)
    First Brigade (Col. James M. Schoonmaker)
    8th Ohio (detachment); 14th Pennsylvania; 22nd Pennsylvania
    (Burned in eastern Rockingham County September 26-28. Burned along Valley Pike in
    Augusta County September 29, while under Custer's command. Burned along the South
    Fork of the Shenandoah River and in Page County October 1-7.)

    Second Brigade (Col. Henry Capehart)
    1st New York; 1st West Virginia; 2nd West Virginia; 3rd West Virginia
    (Same itinerary as First Brigade.)

Third Cavalry Division (Brig. Gen. George Armstrong Custer)
    First Brigade (Col. Alexander C. M. Pennington)
    1st Connecticut; 3rd New Jersey; 2nd New York; 5th New York; 2nd Ohio;
    18th Pennsylvania
    (Under command of General Wilson, the division burned in Augusta County September 26-
    30. On October 4-5 the Fifth New York was detailed to burn houses and barns within a
    three-mile radius of Dayton. The First Brigade burned along the Back Road October 6-8.)

    Second Brigade (Col. William Wells)
    3rd Indiana; 1st New Hampshire (battalion); 8th New York; 22nd New York; 1st Vermont
    (Wilson burned in Augusta County September 26-30; acted as division rear guard along the
    Back Road October 6-8.

Appenöix B

Chronology of the Burning

August

August 7: Sheridan arrives in Harper's Ferry to assume command of the new Middle Military Division and Army of the Shenandoah; confers with engineer officer Lt. John Meigs.

August 9: Sheridan assigns Meigs to the position of chief engineer of Gen. George Crook's Army of West Virginia. Crook's command is designated the VIII Corps while serving under Sheridan in the campaign against Early.

August 15: Meigs is reassigned to Sheridan's staff as aide-de-camp while retaining his status as chief engineer of the Army of West Virginia.

August 16-17: Sheridan's army skirmishes almost daily with Early's forces. In reaction to guerrilla raids, Sheridan orders crops and forage burned in a portion of southern Frederick County.

September

(For the first half of the month the sparring between Sheridan and Early continues.)

September 16: Grant visits Sheridan's headquarters at Charles Town, West Virginia; Sheridan assures Grant that he is about to bring Early to battle.

September 19: Sheridan defeats Early at the third battle of Winchester; Early withdraws to high ground above Strasburg.

September 22: Sheridan defeats Early at the battle of Fisher's Hill.

September 23: A skirmish at Front Royal between troopers of Lowell's Third Brigade and a contingent of Mosby's partisan rangers results in the execution of six of the rangers. Sheridan relieves Gen. William Averell from command of the Second Cavalry Division and replaces him temporarily with Col. William Powell.

September 24: Confederate partisan leader George Stump is severely wounded in a fight near Forestville in Shenandoah County by troopers under Powell's command.

September 25: Sheridan arrives in Harrisonburg, Rockingham County; Early has retreated to Brown's Gap in southeastern Rockingham. Grant requests that Sheridan send either Gen. Alfred Torbert or Gen. James Wilson to Sherman's Military Division of the Mississippi to act as chief of cavalry; Sheridan does not act immediately.

September 26: Sheridan orders Torbert, in command of Wilson's Third Division of Cavalry and Lowell's Third Brigade of the First Cavalry Division, south to Staunton and Waynesboro.

September 27: Custer is temporarily assigned to command the Second Division in Colonel Powell's place. Custer skirmishes with Wickham's Confederate cavalry at Mount Meridian in Augusta County. Maj. Gen. Joseph Kershaw's division reinforces Early in Brown's Gap.

September 27-28: Custer burns crops, barns, and mills across northeastern Augusta County. Torbert tears up Virginia Central Railroad between Staunton and Waynesboro and at the same time destroys Confederate government installations in both places. Merritt, with two brigades of his First Division, watches Brown's Gap for signs of movement by Early and begins to gather forage and livestock in east central Rockingham County.

September 28: Early sends out a portion of his command to challenge Federals in Waynesboro and succeeds in saving a railroad bridge and the tunnel running through the Blue Ridge.

September 29: Torbert withdraws across east central Augusta County, burning barns and mills. Custer burns along the Valley Pike in Augusta County from Mount Sidney back toward Mount Crawford in Rockingham. Sheridan sends Wilson to Sherman. Custer is given command of the Third Division of Cavalry; Powell regains command of the Second Division.

September 30: Merritt, with the First Division, burns eastern Rockingham County between Harrisonburg and the South Fork of the Shenandoah River.

October

October 1: Powell and the Second Cavalry Division leave Port Republic and start north toward Luray in Page County, burning along the base of the Blue Ridge Mountains as they move. Early has moved over to the Valley Pike north of Mount Sidney. If he can find food and forage for his men and animals he plans to strike Sheridan at Harrisonburg on October 6.

October 2: Cavalry skirmish at Mount Crawford and Bridgewater. In the evening Colonel Powell arrives in Luray, which he is to occupy until the 7th. Thomas Rosser's Confederate cavalry division arrives in the Valley.

October 3: Sheridan offers a wagon and a team to families wishing to leave the Upper Valley with his army. Confederate partisan chief John H. McNeill is mortally wounded just south of Mount Jackson. Meigs is killed by Confederate scouts near Dayton. Sheridan, believing that Meigs was killed by civilian bushwhackers, orders Dayton and every house within three miles burned. Lt. Col. Thomas Wildes asks Sheridan to reconsider the decision to burn Dayton.

October 4: Sheridan rescinds the order to destroy Dayton, but the order to burn homes in the immediate area remains intact. Davy Getz is shot by Custer's order at Dayton. Powell has two bushwhackers executed at Luray; his troops continue burning in Page County.

October 4-5: The Fifth New York Cavalry is detailed to burn houses and barns within a three mile radius of Dayton.

October 5: Sheridan starts the refugee wagons down the Valley Pike from Harrisonburg.

October 6: General mission of destruction begins. Sheridan pulls out of Harrisonburg with the infantry and artillery and Kidd's brigade of Michigan cavalry of the First Cavalry Division as a rear skirmish line. Col. Daniel Macauley's infantry brigade is assigned to burn and round up livestock along the pike. The other two First Cavalry Division brigades under colonels Lowell and Devin move down the Middle Road and the Broadway Road respectively. Custer's Third Division moves down the Back Road; that evening it fends off attacks by Rosser's division at Brock's Gap.

October 7: Custer fans out to the east from the Back Road. His rear is attacked again, and he loses part of the cattle herd and some mobile forges.

October 8: Custer, Lowell, and Devin enter the pike near Edinburg and are reunited with the rest of the army. They continue burning, relieving Macauley's infantrymen of that duty.

October 9: The Burning ends. The Union cavalry defeats the Confederate cavalry under Rosser and Lunsford Lomax at the battle of Tom's Brook in Shenandoah County. Jubal Early is still following the track of the Union forces down the pike.

October 19: Sheridan defeats Early at the battle of Cedar Creek.

November

November 8: Abraham Lincoln is reelected president of the United States.

BIBLIOGRAPHY

In citing works in the footnotes, the following abreviations have been used: ACL, Augusta County Library; BCA, Bridgewater College Archives; CCHA, Clarke County Historical Association; EMU, Eastern Mennonite University Historical Library and Archives; HRCHS, Harrisonburg-Rockingham County Historical Society; JMUSC, James Madison University Special Collections, Carrier Library; LCMD, Library of Congress Manuscripts Division; NA, National Archives; OR, U. S. War Department Official Records of the War of the Rebellion; PCPL, Page County Public Library; RPLGR, Rockingham Public Library Genealogy Room; SCPLHC, Shenandoah County Public Library Historical Collections; SVCWRT, Shenandoah Valley Civil War Round Table; SPRP, Society of Port Republic Preservationists; USAMHI, U. S. Army Military History Institute; UVAL, University of Virginia Alderman Library; VMI, Virginia Military Institute; VSL, Virginia State Library; WLU, Washington and Lee University; WPA, Works Progress Administration; WPL, Waynesboro Public Library.

UNPUBLISHED SOURCES

INSTITUTIONAL REPOSITORIES

Augusta County Library, Fishersville, Virginia
    Whitesel, J. Warren. "Stories That My Grandfather Told Me and Subsequent Events."
Bridgewater College Archives, Alexander Mack Library, Bridgewater, Virginia
    John W. Wayland Diaries.
Clarke County Historical Association, Berryville, Virginia
    Jacob Engle Letter.
    Ann R. McCormick Letter.
    Daniel Snyder Papers.
Eastern Mennonite Univ., Menno Simons Historical Library & Archives, Harrisonburg, Virginia
    Church Records for Augusta, Rockingham, Page and Shenandoah counties.
    L. J. Heatwole Scrapbook.
Harrisonburg-Rockingham County Historical Society, Dayton, Virginia
    Churchman, Patricia. "History of Trinity Presbyterian Church House."
    Civil War Files.
    James A. Congdon Letters.
    Fisher, Lewis F. "Port Republic and the Lewises: 1862."
    Garber, Beverly L. Timberville: The Early Years. Typed copy, 1993.
    Kaylor, C. "Sheridan's Headquarters in Harrisonburg."

Kyger, Ellsworth. "Jacob Kyger (1844-1909): Rockingham Unionist and Abolitionist."
Kyger Family File.
Kyle's Meadows/Homeland File.
Lynnwood Farm File.
Nair, Charles E. *History of Cedar Run Community*. Typed copy, 1948.
Stoneleigh House File.
Clara Strayer Diary. Typescript excerpts.
The Historical Society of Pennsylvania, Philadelphia, Pennsylvania
Clement H. Congdon Papers.
Library of Congress Manuscripts Division, Washington, D.C.
Jubal A. Early Papers.
Ulysses S. Grant Papers.
Jedediah Hotchkiss Papers.
Montgomery Meigs Papers.
Rodgers Family Papers.
Philip H. Sheridan Papers.
Hazard Stevens Papers.
James Madison Univ., Carrier Library, Special Collections, Harrisonburg, Virginia
May, G. E. "Port Republic."
National Archives, Washington, D.C.
Barred and Disallowed Case Files of the Southern Claims Commission, 1871-1880.
Compiled Service Records for the Union and Confederacy.
Maj. G. A. Forsyth Letter, October 4, 1864.
Works Progress Administration Historical Inventory for Page County, Virginia.
Rockingham Public Library Genealogy Room, Harrisonburg, Virginia
Lilly, Margaret Kemper. "The Strayers."
May, G. E. "Port Republic."
Nair, Charles E. "History of the Cedar Run Community."
Works Progress Administration Historical Inventory for Rockingham County, Virginia.
Shenandoah County Public Library, Edinburg, Virginia
Levi Pitman Diary, 1864.
Shenandoah Valley Civil War Round Table Collection, Harrisonburg, Virginia.
John W. Wayland undated manuscript.
Levi Pitman Diary, 1864.
Society of Port Republic Preservationists, Port Republic, Virginia
Mary Heidenreich Statement.
C. Kaylor Letter.
Spellman Family Papers.
Clara Strayer Scrapbook.
United States Army Military History Institute Archives, Carlisle Barracks, Pennsylvania
I. Norval Baker Diary.
Charles Farr Diary and Papers.
Henry D. Frazier Papers.
Augustus V. Hanly Diary.
Stewart Hanna Papers.

William H. Martin Papers.
Benedict Tarring Stevens Diary.
Charles H. Veil Memoir.
Univ. of Virginia, Alderman Library, Charlottesville, Virginia
Milton W. Humphrey Diary.
Alexander Neil Papers.
Beverly K. Whittle Papers.
Virginia Military Institute, Institute Archives, Lexington, Virginia
I. Norval Baker Papers.
Virginia State Library, Richmond, Virginia.
Virginia Works Progress Administration Historical Inventory for Augusta County, Virginia.
Works Progress Administration Historical Inventory for Bath County, Virginia.
Works Progress Administration Historical Inventory for Rockingham County, Virginia.
Works Progress Administration Historical Inventory for Shenandoah County, Virginia.
Washington and Lee Univ., James Graham Leyburn Library, Special Collections, Lexington, Virginia
Alexander Telford Barclay Papers.
Horace O. Dodge Papers.
Frank Smith Reader Diary.
Waynesboro Public Library, Historical Research Room, Waynesboro, Virginia
Jedediah Hotchkiss Journal Extract.
Miscellaneous Civil War Files.

PRIVATE COLLECTIONS

Alexander, Nelson, Rockingham County, Virginia
W.H. Arehart Diary.
Bly, Daniel W., Bridgewater, Virginia
Extracts from the Diary of Levi Pitman, 1845-1892, of Mount Olive, Virginia. Biographical information.
Burke, Betty, Mount Jackson, Virginia
Margaret Muse Pennybacker Diary.
Burruss, Daniel Warrick, II, Rinkerton, Shenandoah County, Virginia
Elon O. Henkel Letter.
Margaret Muse Pennybacker, War Memorial.
Diehl, Wayne, Cross Keys, Virginia
Jacob P. Diehl Recollections.
Elliott, John, Rockingham County, Virginia
G. A. Bucklin Letter.
John Rowe Letter.
Engle, Elizabeth, Mount Jackson, Shenandoah County, Virginia
Viola Pitman Letter.
Evans, Beverley and Jeffrey, Rockingham County, Virginia
Pleasant A. Kiser Diary from the estate of Farel Long.

Fechtmann, Dora, Ocala, Florida
    Cyrus H. Cline Sr. Memoir.
Garber, Nancy, Harrisonburg, Virginia
    Monthly Account of the Military Telegraph of the Confederate States of America.
    Samuel Sheets Farm Book.
Heatwole, John L., Rockingham County, Virginia
    Jackie Damiani Letter.
    Lena Fuller Letter.
    Mary Jo Miley Keller Letter.
    Harry E. Long Letter.
    Winfield Massie Letter.
Hedrick, George, Harrisonburg, Virginia
    George Sipe Memoir.
Hottinger, Dolores, Cross Keys, Virginia
    Jacob P. Diehl Recollections.
Hulvey, Velma June, Harrisonburg, Virginia
    Silas Good Letter.
Keller, Mary Jo, and Pauline Dudas, Fisher, West Virginia
    Bettie Robinette Miley Boyer Memoir.
Kite, Mary Elizabeth, Rockingham County, Virginia
    Margaret Caroline Kite Letter.
Kuhn, Maude Pinney, Waterford, Pennsylvania
    Katherine Fox Letter.
Leigh, Lewis, Jr., Leesburg, Virginia
    Lizzie Coffman Letter.
Roller, Robert, Winston-Salem, North Carolina
    J.S. Roller Memoir.
Shank, Randall, Broadway, Virginia
    Samuel Shank's Enumeration of Losses, April 17, 1865.
    Mollie Zigler Meyers Memoir.
Swanson, Richard C., Hamilton, Virginia
    Confederate Special Order 257, November 3, 1862.

PUBLISHED SOURCES

NEWSPAPERS

Berryville, Va. *Clarke Courier*
Bridgewater, Va. *Herald*
Harrisonburg, Va. *Daily News-Record*
Harrisonburg, Va. *Rockingham Register*
Harrisonburg, Va. *Rockingham Register and Advertiser*
New York, N.Y. *Frank Leslie's Illustrated Newspaper*
New York, N.Y. *Herald*

New York, N.Y. *Tribune*
Richmond, Va. *Richmond Dispatch*
Richmond, Va. *Richmond Examiner*
Staunton, Va. *Spectator*
Staunton, Va. *Vindicator*
Staunton, Va. *Yost's Weekly*
Washington, D.C. *The Washington Herald*
Woodstock, Va. *Shenandoah Herald*

BOOKS AND PERIODICALS

Alberts, Don E. 1980. *Brandy Station to Manila Bay: A Biography of General Wesley Merritt.* Austin, Tex.: Presidial Press.

Armstrong, Richard. 1989. *11th Virginia Cavalry.* Lynchburg, Va.: H. E. Howard, Inc.

_____. 1992. *7th Virginia Cavalry.* Lynchburg, Va.: H. E. Howard, Inc.

Army Register of the Volunteer Forces Vol. I. 1987. Reprint. Gaithersburg, Md.: Olde Soldier Books, Inc.

Arrington, Mary Marie Koontz. 1982. *Mountain Valley People: A Historical Sketch of a Section of Rockingham County Virginia and Its People.* Baltimore: Gateway Press, Inc.

Ashby, Thomas A. 1914. *The Valley Campaigns, Being the Reminiscences of a Non-Combatant While Between the Lines in the Shenandoah Valley During the War of the States.* New York: Neale Publishing Co.

Ashcraft, John M. Jr. 1988. *31st Virginia Infantry.* Lynchburg, Va.: H. E. Howard, Inc.

Ashley, Betty Miley. 1988. *My Miley Notebook.* Tollhouse, Calif.: privately printed.

Battles and Leaders of the Civil War. Volumes 1-6. [1887] 1956. New York and London: Thomas Yoseloff, Inc.

Beach, William H. 1902. *The First New York Lincoln Cavalry.* New York: The Lincoln Cavalry Assoc.

Beery, William, and Judith Beery Garber. 1957. *Beery Family History.* Elgin, Ill.: Brethren Publishing House.

Bonner, James C. 1956. "Sherman at Milledgesville in 1864." *Journal of Southern History,* no. 22.

Boudrye, Rev. Louis N. 1865. *Historic Records of the Fifth New York Cavalry, First Ira Harris Guard.* Albany, N.Y.: S. R. Gray.

Bowen, Rev. J. R. 1900. *Regimental History of the First New York Dragoons During Three Years of Active Service in the Great Civil War.* Privately printed.

Brice, Marshall. 1965. *Conquest of a Valley.* Verona, Va.: McClure Press.

Brown, Ann L. B. 1982. "Valley Mennonites in the Civil War." *Virginia Country.* July-August.

Brunk, Harry A. 1959. *History of Mennonites in Virginia.* Vol. 1. Staunton, Va: McClure Printing Co.

Buck, Capt. Samuel D. 1925. *With the Old Confeds: Actual Experiences of a Captain in the Line.* Baltimore: H. E. Houck & Co.

Bureau of the Census. 1850; 1860. Census records for various Shenandoah Valley counties.

_____. Slave schedules for various Shenandoah Valley counties.

Burruss, Daniel Warrick, II. 1993. *The Rinkers of Virginia, Their Neighbors and Kin and the Shenandoah Valley*. Stephens City, Va.: Commercial Press, Inc.

Byerly, John F., Jr. 1994. *The Byerly Family in the Valley of Virginia*. Richmond: The Dietz Press.

Cartmell, T.K. 1963. *Shenandoah Valley Pioneers and Their Descendants*. Berryville, Va.: Chesapeake Book Co.

Catton, Bruce. 1953. *A Stillness at Appomattox*. Garden City, N.Y.: Doubleday & Co., Inc.

_____. 1968. *Grant Takes Command*. Boston: Little, Brown & Co.

Cheney, Newel. 1901. *History of the Ninth Regiment, New York Volunteer Cavalry, War of 1861 to 1865*. Poland Center, N.Y.: Martin Merz & Son.

Civil War Times Illustrated. 1984a. Vol. 23, no. 5 (September).

Civil War Times Illustrated. 1984b. Vol. 23, no. 6 (October).

Civil War Times Illustrated. 1993. Vol 31, no. 6 (January-February).

Coffman, Barbara F. 1964. *His Name Was John*. Scottdale, Pa.: Herald Press.

Colt, Margaretta Barton. 1994. *Defend the Valley*. New York: Orion Books.

Confederate Veteran. 1909. Vol. 17, no. 12 (December).

Confederate Veteran. 1910. Vol. 18, no. 7 (July).

Confederate Veteran. 1912. Vol. 20, no. 4 (April).

Confederate Veteran. 1912. Vol. 20, no. 6 (June).

Confederate Veteran. 1921. Vol. 29, no. 4 (April).

Confederate Veteran. 1923. Vol. 31, no. 12 (December).

Confederate Veteran. 1925. Vol. 33, no.7 (July).

Couper, William. 1952. *History of the Shenandoah Valley*. 2 vols. New York: Lewis Historical Publishing Co., Inc.

Culpepper, Ruth Lynn Rodes. 1982. *My Heritage: The Ancestors and Descendants of Mary Alberta Coiner and Edward Thomas Rodes*. Harrisonburg, Va.: Park View Press.

Crute, Joseph H., Jr. 1982. *Confederate Staff Officers, 1861-1865*. Powhatan, Va.: Derwent Books.

Davis, Burke. 1980. *Sherman's March*. New York: Random House.

Davis, Julia. 1945. *The Shenandoah*. New York: J. J. Little & Ives Co.

Dean, Henry Clay. 1868. *Crimes of the Civil War and Curse of the Funding System*. Baltimore: Innes & Co.

DeForest, John William. 1946. *A Volunteer's Adventures: A Union Captain's Record of the Civil War*. New Haven, Conn.: Yale Univ. Press.

Delauter, Roger U., Jr. 1985. *18th Virginia Cavalry*. Lynchburg, Va.: H. E. Howard, Inc.

_____. 1986. *McNeill's Rangers*. Lynchburg, Va.: H. E. Howard, Inc.

_____. 1988. *62nd Virginia Infantry*. Lynchburg, Va.: H. E. Howard, Inc.

Delp, Emma Shank. 1990. *Six Little Orphans: My Story*. Waynesboro, Va.: privately printed.

Denison, Frederic. 1876. *Sabres and Spurs: The First Regiment Rhode Island Cavalry in the Civil War, 1861-1865*. Central Falls, R. I.: First Rhode Island Cavalry Veterans Association.

Devine, John E. 1985. *35th Battalion Virginia Cavalry*. Lynchburg, Va.: H. E. Howard, Inc.

Diehl, Jacob P. 1990. *Diehl Family*. Edited by Wayne Diehl. Richmond: privately printed.

Douglas, Henry Kyd. 1968. *I Rode with Stonewall*. Chapel Hill, N.C.: Univ. of North Carolina Press.

Downs, Janet Baugher, Earl J. Downs, and Pat Turner Ritchie, comps. 1997. *Mills of Rockingham County*. Dayton, Va.: Harrisonburg-Rockingham County Historical Society.

Driver, Carolyn Click, and Bertha Driver Gassett. 1990. *Descendants of Ludwig Treiber (Lewis Driver) and Barbara Sprenkle in the Shenandoah Valley of Virginia, the United States of America*. Waynesville, N.C.: Don Mills, Inc.

Driver, Robert J., Jr. 1988. *14th Virginia Cavalry*. Lynchburg, Va.: H. E. Howard, Inc.

_____. 1991. *1st Virginia Cavalry*. Lynchburg, Va.: H. E. Howard, Inc.

Duffey, Rev. J. W. 1944. *McNeill's Last Charge*. Moorefield, W. Va.: The Moorefield Examiner.

DuPont, H. A. 1925. *The Campaign of 1864 in the Valley of Virginia and the Expedition to Lynchburg*. New York: National Americana Society.

Early, Jubal Anderson. 1969. *War Memoirs: Autobiographical Sketch and Narrative of the War Between the States*. Bloomington, Ind.: Indiana Univ. Press.

Ellis, Edward S. 1898. *From Tent to White House*. New York: Street & Smith, Publishers.

Emerson, Edward W. 1971. *Life and Letters of Charles Russell Lowell*. Port Washington, N.Y.: Kennikat Press.

Evans, Robert Lee. 1977. *History of the Descendants of Jacob Gochenour*. Boyce, Va: Carr Publishing Co., Inc.

Farrar, Emmie Ferguson, and Emilee Hines. 1976. *Old Virginia Houses: Shenandoah*. Charlotte, N.C.: Delmar Publishing Co.

Farrar, Samuel Clarke. 1911. *The Twenty-Second Pennsylvania Cavalry and the Ringgold Battalion 1861-1865*. Pittsburgh: Ringgold Cavalry Association.

Faust, Patricia. 1986. *Historical Times Illustrated Encyclopedia of the Civil War*. New York: Harper & Row Publishers, Inc.

Firebaugh, Marshall A. 1984. *Rockingham County Personals*. Harrisonburg, Va.: Harrisonburg-Rockingham County Historical Society.

Fisk, Wilber. 1983. *Anti-Rebel: The Civil War Letters of Wilber Fisk*. Croton-on-Hudson, N. Y: Emil Rosenblatt.

Freeman, Douglas Southall. 1942-45. *Lee's Lieutenants: A Study in Command*. 3 vols. New York: Charles Scribner's Sons.

Frye, Dennis E. 1988. *12th Virginia Cavalry*. Lynchburg, Va: H. E. Howard, Inc.

Funkhouser, Jacob. 1902. *A Historical Sketch of the Funkhouser Family*. Harrisonburg, Va.: Rockingham Register Press.

Gates, Paul W. 1908. *Agriculture and the Civil War*. New York: Alfred A. Knopf.

Gause, Isaac. 1908. *Four Years with Five Armies: Army of the Frontier, Army of the Potomac, Army of the Missouri, Army of the Ohio, Army of the Shenandoah*. New York: The Neale Publishing Co.

Geier, Clarence R. 1993. The night they drove old Dixie down. Presented at Council of Virginia Archaeologists Symposium VII, 29-30 October, at Alexandria, Va.

Gerberich, Albert H. 1938. *The Brenneman History*. Scottdale, Pa.: Herald Press.

Gilmor, Col. Harry. 1866. *Four Years in the Saddle*. New York: Harper & Brothers Publishers.

The Joseph M. Glick Family Historical Committee. 1959. *Across the Years: The Glick Family in the Shenandoah Valley of Virginia*. Charlotte, N.C.: Delmar Printing Co.

Goldsborough, W. W. 1972. *The Maryland Line in the Confederate Army 1861-1865*. Port Washington, N.Y.: Kennikat Press.

Good, William Algernon. 1992. *Shadowed by the Massanutten: A History of Life Along Smith*

Creek, *The Good Family Genealogy and Civil War Notes*. Stephens City, Va.: Commercial Press, Inc.

Gordon, John B. 1903. *Reminiscences of the Civil War*. New York: Charles Scribner's Sons.

Grant, Maj. Gen. Ulysses S., III. 1969. *Ulysses S. Grant: Warrior and Statesman*. New York: William Morrow & Co.

Greenwood, Neil. 1993. "Devastation in the Valley: The Perspectives of Union and Confederate Soldiers in the Shenandoah Valley During the 1864 Campaign." Shenandoah Valley Regional Studies Seminar.

Grimsley, Mark. 1995. *The Hard Hand of War: Union Military Policy toward Southern Civilians 1861-1865*. New York: Cambridge Univ. Press.

Hale, Laura Virginia. 1968. *Four Valiant Years: In the Lower Shenandoah Valley, 1861-1865*. Front Royal, Va.: Hathaway Publishing.

Hardeman, Nicholas. 1981. *Shucks, Shocks and Hominy Blocks*. Baton Rouge: Louisiana State Univ. Press.

Hanaburgh, D. H. 1894. *History of the One Hundred and Twenty-Eighth Regiment, New York Volunteers in the Late Civil War*. Poughkeepsie, N.Y.: Regimental Association.

Hannaford, Ebenezer. 1868. *A History of the Campaigns, and Associations in the Field, of the Sixth Regiment Ohio Volunteer Infantry*. Cincinnati: privately printed.

Harrison, J. Houston. 1935. *Settlers by the Long Grey Trail*. Dayton, Va.: Joseph Ruebush Co.

Harrisonburg-Rockingham County Historical Society Newsletter. 1994. Volume 16, no. 4 (fall).

Hartman, Peter S. 1964. *Reminiscences of the Civil War*. Lancaster, Pa.: Eastern Mennonite Associated Libraries and Archives.

Heatwole, Cornelius J. 1970. *History of the Heatwole Family*. North Newton, Kans.: The Mennonite Press.

Heatwole, John L. 1995. *Shenandoah Voices: Folklore, Legends and Traditions of the Valley*. Berryville, Va.: Rockbridge Publishing Co.

Hergesheimer, Joseph. 1931. *Sheridan: A Military Narrative*. Boston: Houghton Mifflin Co.

Hess, Nancy B. 1976. *The Heartland*. Willard, Oh.: R.R. Donnelley and Sons.

_____. 1979. *By the Grace of God*. Harrisonburg, Va.: Park View Press.

Hildebrand, John R., ed. 1996. *A Mennonite Journal 1862-1865*. Shippensburg, Pa.: Burd Street Press.

Hoogenboom, Ari. 1995. *Rutherford B. Hayes: Warrior and President*. Lawrence, Kans.: Univ. Press of Kansas.

Horst, Samuel. 1967. *Mennonites in the Confederacy: A Study in Civil War Pacifism*. Scottdale, Pa.: Herald Press.

Hotchkiss, Jedediah, and Joseph Waddell. 1885. *Historical Atlas of Augusta County, Virginia*. Chicago: Waterman, Watkins & Co.

Huddle, Rev. W. D., and Lulu May Huddle. 1930. *History of the Descendants of John Hottel*. Strasburg, Va.: Shenandoah Publishing House, Inc.

Huffman, James. 1940. *Ups and Downs of a Confederate Soldier*. New York: William E. Rudge's Sons.

Hulvey, Velma June. 1996. *William Good Family*. Stephens City, Va.: Commercial Press, Inc.

Hutton, R.B. 1976. *The History of Elkton*. Elkton, Va.: Elkton Independence Bicentennial Committee.

Irwin, Richard B. 1892. *History of the Nineteenth Army Corps*. New York: G.P. Putnam's Sons.

Jaquette, Henrietta Stratton, ed. 1937. *South After Gettysburg: Letters of Cornelia Hancock from the Army of the Potomac 1863-1865*. Philadelphia: Univ. of Pennsylvania Press.
Jones, Virgil Carrington. [1944] 1972. *Ranger Mosby*. McLean, Va.: EPM Publications, Inc.
Judge, Joseph R. 1994. *Season of Fire*. Berryville, Va.: Rockbridge Publishing Co.
Kauffman, Charles Fahs. 1940. *A Genealogy and History of the Kauffman-Coffman Family*. Scottdale, Pa.: Mennonite Publishing House.
Keen, Hugh C., and Horace Mewborn. 1993. *43rd Battalion Virginia Cavalry, Mosby's Command*. Lynchburg, Va.: H. E. Howard, Inc.
Keister, E. E. 1972. *Strasburg, Virginia and the Keister Family*. Strasburg, Va.: Shenandoah Publishing House, Inc.
Kellogg, Sanford. 1903. *The Shenandoah Valley and Virginia 1861-1865: A War Study*. New York: The Neale Publishing Co.
Kennedy, Frances H., ed. 1990. *The Civil War Battlefield Guide*. Boston: Houghton Mifflin Co.
Kennett, Lee. 1995. *Marching Through Georgia*. New York: Harper Collins.
Kercheval, Samuel. 1981. *A History of the Valley of Virginia*. Harrisonburg, Va.: C.J. Carrier Co.
Kerkhoff, Jennie Ann. 1962. *Old Homes of Page County, Virginia*. Luray, Va.: Lauck and Co., Inc.
Kidd, J. H. 1969. *Personal Recollections of a Cavalryman with Custer's Michigan Brigade in the Civil War*. Grand Rapids, Mich.: Black Letter Press.
Kleese, Richard. 1996. *23rd Virginia Cavalry*. Lynchburg, Va.: H. E. Howard, Inc.
_____. 1992. *Shenandoah County in the Civil War*. Lynchburg, Va.: H. E. Howard, Inc.
Kline, Agnes. 1971. *Stone Houses on Linville Creek and Their Communities: Rockingham County, Virginia*. Harrisonburg, Va.: Park View Press.
Kline, Paul G. 1971. *Cline-Kline Family*. Dayton, Va.: Shenandoah Press.
Krick, Robert K. 1979. *Lee's Colonels*. Dayton, Oh.: Morningside Bookshop Press.
Lake, D. J. & Co. 1885a. *Atlas of Rockingham County, Virginia*. Philadelphia: D. J. Lake & Co.
_____. 1885b *Atlas of Shenandoah and Page Counties, Virginia*. Philadelphia: D. J. Lake & Co.
Lamb, Frank A. 1962. *The Henry Cowen Family of Virginia*. Waterford, Pa.: privately printed.
Lambert, Dobbie E. 1994. *25th Virginia Cavalry*. Lynchburg, Va.: H. E. Howard, Inc.
Lantz, Jacob W. 1931. *The Lantz Family Record: Being a Brief Account of the Lantz Family of the United States of America*. Cedar Springs, Va.: privately printed.
Lehman, James O. 1995. "Bishop Jacob Hildebrand Votes for Secession," Parts 1 and 2 *Shenandoah Mennonite Historian* (spring and summer).
Lewis, Thomas A. 1988. *The Guns of Cedar Creek*. New York: Harper & Row Publishers.
Leyburn, James G. 1962. *The Scotch-Irish: A Social History*. Chapel Hill, N.C.: Univ. of North Carolina Press.
Liskey, J. Nelson, and W. Cullen Sherwood. 1990. *Rockingham County Men in the Confederate Service*. Dayton, Va.: Harrisonburg-Rockingham Historical Society.
Long, Andrews Davidson. 1965. *Stonewall's "Foot Cavalryman."* Austin, Tex.: Steck-Vaughn Publishers.
Long, E. B., and Barbara Long. 1971. *The Civil War Day by Day: An Almanac 1861-1865*. Garden City, N.Y.: Doubleday & Co., Inc.
Madison College. 1949. *The Madison Quarterly*. Vol. 9, no. 2 (March).
Matter, William D. 1988. *If It Takes All Summer: The Battle of Spotsylvania*. Chapel Hill, N.C.: Univ. of North Carolina Press

Mauzy, Richard. 1911. *Genealogical Record of the Descendants of Henry Mauzy: A Huguenot Refugee and of Jacob Kisling*. Harrisonburg, Va.: Free Press of the Daily News.

May, C. E. 1976. *Life Under Four Flags in the North River Basin of Virginia*. Verona, Va.: McClure Press.

McDonald, Archie E. 1907. *Make Me a Map of the Valley: The Civil War Journal of Stonewall Jackson's Topographer*. Dallas: Southern Methodist Univ. Press.

McDonald, William N. 1907. *A History of the Laurel Brigade*. Baltimore: Sun Job Printing Office.

Meaney, Peter J. *The Civil War Engagement at Cool Spring: July 18, 1864*. Berryville, Va.: privately printed, 1980.

Memorials of Edward Herndon Scott, M. D. 1873. Singers Glen, Va.: Attached Friends.

Merritt, Wesley. [1887] 1956. "Sheridan in the Shenandoah Valley." *Battles and Leaders of the Civil War* Vol. 4. New York: Thomas Yoseloff.

Miller, Joyce DeBolt. 1994. *Until Separated by Death*. Bridgewater, Va.: Good Printers, Inc.

Miller, Lula Mae. 1982. *Johannes Friederick Kirshof: Early Settler and Patriarch of Northern Augusta County*. Bridgewater, Va.: privately printed.

Miller, William J. 1993. *Mapping for Stonewall: The Civil War Service of Jed Hotchkiss*. Washington, D. C.: Elliott & Clark Publishers.

Moon, William Arthur. 1937. *Historical Significance of Brown's Gap in the War Between the States*. Waynesboro, Va.: Waynesboro News-Virginian.

Moore, Edward A. 1907. *The Story of a Cannoneer under Stonewall Jackson*. New York: The Neale Publishing Co.

Moore, Mrs. John H. 1920. *Memories of a Long Life in Virginia*. Staunton, Va.: McClure Co.

Morgan, Edith Wenger. 1962. *Stories My Father Told Us*. Berryville, Va.: privately printed.

Morgan, Speer, and Greg Michaelson, eds. 1994. *For Our Beloved Country: American War Diaries from the Revolution to the Persian Gulf*. New York: The Atlantic Monthly Press.

Morris, Roy, Jr. 1992. *Sheridan*. New York: Crown Publishers, Inc.

Murphy, Terrence. 1989. *10th Virginia Infantry*. Lynchburg, Va.: H. E. Howard, Inc.

Musick, Michael B. 1990. *6th Virginia Cavalry*. Lynchburg, Va.: H. E. Howard, Inc.

Myers, Frank M. 1871. *The Comanches: A History of White's Battalion, Virginia Cavalry*. Baltimore: Kelly Piet & Co.

Neese, George M. 1911. *Three Years in the Confederate Horse Artillery*. New York: The Neale Publishing Co.

O'Ferrall, Charles T. 1904. *Forty Years of Active Service*. New York: The Neale Publishing Co.

Opie, John N. 1899. *A Rebel Cavalryman with Lee, Stuart and Jackson*. Chicago: W. B. Conkey Co.

Page County Bicentennial Commission. 1976. *Page: The County of Plenty*. Luray, Va.: Bicentennial Commission.

Painter, Fred, and Joseph B. Clower Jr., eds. 1981. *Yesterday in Woodstock*. Woodstock, Va.: Woodstock Museum.

Phillips, John. 1954. *Virginia Magazine of History and Biography Quarterly* Vol. 62.

Pollard, E. A. 1866. *Southern History of the War*. Richmond: The Fairfax Press.

Pond, G. E. 1892. *The Shenandoah Valley in 1864*. New York: Charles Scribner's Sons.

Powers, George W. 1866. *The Story of the Thirty-Eighth Regiment of Massachusetts Volunteers*. Cambridge, Mass.: Dakin & Metcalf.

Professional Memoirs, Corps of Engineers, United States Army. 1915. Vol. 6, no. 35 (September-October).

Rable, George. 1989. *Civil Wars: Women and the Crisis of Southern Nationalism*. Chicago: Univ. of Illinois Press.

Reader, Frank S. 1890. *History of the Fifth West Virginia Cavalry Formerly the Second Virginia Infantry and of Battery G, First West Virginia Light Artillery*. New Brighton, Pa.: Daily News.

Reidenbaugh, Lowell. 1987. *33rd Virginia Infantry*. Lynchburg, Va.: H. E. Howard, Inc.

Rhea, Gordon C. 1994. *The Battle of the Wilderness May 5-6, 1864*. Baton Rouge: Louisiana State Univ. Press.

Roberts, Allen E. 1961. *House Undivided: The Story of Freemasonry and the Civil War*. Richmond: Macoy Publishing & Masonic Supply Co., Inc.

Robertson, James I., Jr. 1961. *Virginia, 1861-1865: Iron Gate to the Confederacy*. Richmond: Va. Civil War Commission.

_____. 1963. *The Stonewall Brigade*. Baton Rouge: Louisiana State Univ. Press.

_____. 1971. Ed. *Four Years in the Stonewall Brigade*. Dayton, Oh.: Morningside Bookshop.

_____. 1988. *Soldiers Blue and Gray*. Columbia, S.C.: Univ. of South Carolina Press.

Rockingham Recorder. 1959. Vol. 2, no. 3 (October).

Rosenberry, Naomi, and Alta Showalter. 1989. *The Swift Years Come and Go: Life of Harry Showalter*. Harrisonburg, Va.: privately printed.

Rosenblatt, Emil, and Ruth Rosenblatt, eds. 1983. *Hard Marching Every Day: The Civil War Letters of Private Wilber Fiske*. Lawrence: Univ. Press of Kansas.

Ruh, Virginia, and James Fadely, eds. 1989. *A Fadely Family History and Genealogy: Descendants of Michael Fadely*. Shenandoah County, Va.: privately printed.

Rutherford, Carolyn Martin, ed. 1977. *A Boy of Old Shenandoah*. Parsons, W. Va.: McClain Printing Co.

Sappington, Roger E., ed. 1976. *The Brethren in the New Nation: A Source Book on the Development of the Church of the Brethren, 1785-1865*. Elgin, Ill.: The Brethren Press.

Scott, Robert Garth. 1985. *Into the Wilderness with the Army of the Potomac*. Bloomington, Ind.: Indiana Univ. Press.

Shea, William L., and Earl J. Hess. 1992. *Pea Ridge: Civil War Campaign in the West*. Chapel Hill: The Univ. of North Carolina Press.

Shenandoah County Bicentennial Committee. *Shenandoah County: Industry with Plenty*. Woodstock, Va.: Bicentennial Committee, 1972.

Shenandoah Mennonite Historian. 1995. Vol. 2, no. 3 (summer).

Sheridan, Philip H. 1888. *Personal Memoirs of Philip H. Sheridan, General United States Army*. New York: Charles L. Webster & Co.

Sifakis, Stewart. 1988. *Who Was Who in the Civil War*. New York: Facts on File Publications.

Sites, Carrie B., and Effie A. Hess, eds. 1962. *A History of the Town of Dayton, Virginia*. Dayton, Va.: Shenandoah Press.

Smith, Helda Neff. 1967. *From the Alps to the Appalachians*. Arlington, Va.: Beatty Publishing Co.

Sommers, Richard J. 1981. *Richmond Redeemed: The Siege at Petersburg*. Garden City, N.Y.: Doubleday & Co.

Southern Historical Society Papers. 1881.Vol. 9.

Southern Historical Society Papers. 1904. Vol. 32.

Spratt, Thomas A. 1992. *Shenandoah County Men in Gray*. Vol. 1. Athens, Ga.: Iberian Publishing Co.

Starr, Louis M. 1954. *Bohemian Brigade*. New York: Alfred A. Knopf, Inc.

Starr, Stephen Z. 1981. *The Union Cavalry in the Civil War*. Vol. 2. Baton Rouge: Louisiana State Univ. Press.

Steiner, M. S. 1903. *John S. Coffman, Mennonite Evangelist: His Life and Labor*. Scottdale, Pa.: Mennonite Book and Tract Society.

Stevens, George T. 1866. *Three Years in the Sixth Corps*. Albany, N.Y.: S. R. Gray, Publisher.

Stiles, Robert. 1903. *Four Years Under Marse Robert*. New York: The Neale Publishing Co.

Strickler, Harry M. 1977. *Forerunners: A History and Genealogy of the Strickler Families, Their Kith and Kin*. Harrisonburg, Va.: C. J. Carrier Co.

Surber, Edwin F. 1921. *Lest We Forget*. Richmond: Standard Printing Co.

Suter, Mary Eugenia. 1959. *Memories of Yesteryear: A History of the Suter Family*. Waynesboro, Va.: Charles F. McClung, Printer, Inc.

Sutton, J. J. 1892. *History of the Second Regiment West Virginia Cavalry Volunteers During the War of the Rebellion*. Portsmouth, Oh.: privately printed.

Swartz, M. Alberta. 1946. *Historical Reminiscences of Three Interesting Families of Shenandoah County, Virginia*. Privately printed.

Swope Family History Committee. 1977. *History of the Swope Family and Descendants of Rockingham County, Virginia*. Verona, Va.: McClure Press.

Tomes, Robert. Undated. *The War with the South: A History of the Late Rebellion*. Vol. 3. New York: Virtue & Yorston, Publishers.

Tompkins, Edmond Pendleton. 1952. *Rockbridge County, Virginia*. Richmond: Whittet & Shepperson.

Trudeau, Noah Andre. 1989. *Bloody Roads South*. Boston: Little, Brown & Co.

U. S. War Department. 1881-1901. *War of the Rebellion: A Compilation of the Official Records of the Union and Confederate Armies*. 128 vols. Washington, D.C.: U. S. Government Printing Office.

Viola, Herman J., ed. 1993. *The Memoirs of Charles Henry Veil: A Soldier's Recollections of the Civil War and the Arizona Territory*. New York: Orion Books.

Waddell, Joseph A. 1972. *Annals of Augusta County Virginia*. Harrisonburg, Va.: C. J. Carrier Co., Inc.

Walker, Aldace F. 1869. *The Vermont Brigade in the Shenandoah Valley 1864*. Burlington, Vt.: The Free Press Association.

Wallace, Lee A., Jr., comp. 1964. *A Guide to the Virginia Military Organizations 1861-1865*. Richmond: Va. Civil War Centennial Commission.

Warner, Ezra J. 1964. *Generals in Blue*. Baton Rouge: Louisiana State Univ. Press.

————. 1988. *5th Virginia Infantry*. Lynchburg, Va.: H. E. Howard, Inc.

Wayland, John W. See also SVCWRT undated manuscript.

————. 1912. *A History of Rockingham County, Virginia*. Dayton, Va.: Ruebush-Elkins Co.

————. 1927. *A History of Shenandoah County, Virginia*. Strasburg, Va.: Shenandoah Publishing House, Inc.

————. 1969. *Stonewall Jackson's Way*. Verona, Va.: McClure Press.

————. 1973a. *Historic Harrisonburg*. Harrisonburg, Va.: C. J. Carrier Co.

————. 1973b. *Virginia Valley Records*. Baltimore: Genealogical Publishing Co.

_____. 1987. *The Lincolns of Virginia*. Harrisonburg, Va.: C. J. Carrier Co.

Weaver, Jeffrey C. 1994. *45th Battalion Virginia Infantry: Smith and Count's Battalions of Partisan Rangers*. Lynchburg, Va.: H. E. Howard, Inc.

Weber, Richard R. 1993. *Stoner Brethren: A History of John Stoner and His Descendants*. Shenandoah County, Va.: privately printed.

Weigley, Russell F. 1959. *Quartermaster General of the Union Army: A Biography of M. C. Meigs*. New York: Columbia Univ. Press.

Wenger, John C., and Mary W. Kratz. *A. D. Wenger—Faithful Minister of Christ*. Harrisonburg, Va.: Park View Press.

Wenger, Jonas G., Martin D. Wenger, and Joseph H. Wenger. 1903. *History of the Descendants of Christian Wenger*. Elkhart, Ind.: Mennonite Publishing Co.

Wenger, Samuel S., ed. 1979. *The Wenger Book: A Foundation Book of American Wengers*. Lancaster, Pa.: Pennsylvania German Heritage History, Inc.

Wert, Jeffry D. 1987. *From Winchester to Cedar Creek: The Shenandoah Campaign of 1864*. Carlisle, Pa.: South Mountain Press, Inc.

Wertz, Mary Alice, and Marguerite Hutchinson. 1973. *History of the Halterman Families of the Shenandoah Valley, Virginia*. Privately printed.

White, Rita Rothgeb. 1961. *Papa's Diary*. Luray, Va.: privately printed.

Wildes, Thomas F. 1884. *Record of the One Hundred and Sixteenth Regiment Ohio Infantry Volunteers in the War of the Rebellion*. Sandusky, Ohio: I. F. Mack & Brother, Printers.

Wilson, James D., and Louise E. Wilson. 1982. *Edinburg 1861 to 1865: Civil War Incidents & Anecdotes*. Woodstock, Va.: American Speedy Printing Centers.

Winchester-Frederick County Historical Society. 1955. *Diaries, Letters and Recollections of the War Between the States*. Winchester, Va.: The Winchester-Frederick County Historical Society.

Wine, J. Floyd. 1985. *Life Along Holman's Creek*. Stephens City, Va.: Commercial Press.

Worsham, John H. 1912. *One of Jackson's Foot Cavalry*. New York: The Neale Publishing Co.

Yancey, Rebecca L. 1977. *Ancestors and Descendants of Capt. William Layton Yancey and His Wife Frances Lynn Lewis*. Baltimore: Gateway Press, Inc.

A Youth's History of the Great Civil War. 1866. New York: Van Evrie Horton & Co.

Zigler, D. H. 1914. *History of the Brethren in Virginia*. Elgin, Ill.: Brethren Publishing House.

INTERVIEWS

Marie Arrington. Broadway, Virginia. 9-20-95.

Nell Baugher. Rockingham County, Virginia. 7-21-78.

Elizabeth Barry Thrift Brown. Chester, New Jersey. 10-20-96.

Betty Burke. Mount Jackson, Virginia. 1-14-98.

Burner Family Members. Page County, Virginia. 6-4-96.

Daniel Warrick Burruss II. Shenandoah County, Virginia. 1-31-95.

John F. Byerly Jr. Richmond, Virginia. 6-14-95.

Nellie Cline. Rockingham County, Virginia. 8-12-93.

Dr. Joseph B. Clower Jr. Woodstock, Virginia. 4-18-95.

David Coffman. Rockingham County, Virginia. 2-12-95.

Dr. John and Elizabeth Cottrell. Maurertown, Virginia. 12-13-95; 12-15-95.
Alice D. Crider. Turleytown, Virginia. 9-8-95.
Anita Cummins. Port Republic, Virginia. 10-22-96.
Emma Shank Delp. Harrisonburg, Virginia. 5-21-97.
Wayne and I. W. Diehl. Broadway, Virginia. 5-14-97.
Janet Downs. Rockingham County, Virginia. 3-24-95.
William Eakle. Augusta County, Virginia. 10-1-79.
John Elliott. Cootes's Store, Virginia. 3-25-95.
Dora Fechtmann. Ocala, Florida. 5-14-97.
Nellie Flora. Piedmont, Virginia. 6-9-93.
Robert Allen Frye. Mount Jackson, Virginia. 6-7-95.
Bennie Getz. Rockingham County, Virginia. 4-12-97.
John A. Getz. Charlottesville, Virginia. 4-12-97.
Florence Gordon. Timberville, Virginia. 4-18-97.
Thomas M. Harrison. Melrose, Virginia. 10-21-76.
Paul V. Heatwole. Bridgewater, Virginia. 12-9-80.
Dr. George R. Hedrick. Harrisonburg, Virginia. 7-5-94.
Samuel Horst. Harrisonburg, Virginia. 8-14-94.
Dolores Hottinger. Cross Keys, Virginia. 5-14-97.
Mary Jo Miley Keller. Fisher, West Virginia. 9-16-94.
Mary Elizabeth Kite. Rockingham County, Virginia. 2-1-97; 2-11-98.
Dr. Ellsworth Kyger. Bridgewater, Virginia. 11-15-94.
Olen Landes. Cross Keys, Virginia. 7-8-95.
Allen Litten. Harrisonburg, Virginia. 4-18-97.
Houston Lynch. Harrisonburg, Virginia. 8-1-94.
Cheryl Lyon. Harrisonburg, Virginia. 2-12-94.
Arthur and Edith Martin. Shenandoah County, Virginia. 4-19-97.
Sarah Winters McCue. Massenetta Springs, Virginia. 10-11-95.
Joseph H. Meyerhoeffer. Dayton, Virginia. 6-3-94.
Jesse Thomas Modisett. Page County, Virginia. 4-27-98.
John H. Modisett. Page County, Virginia. 4-27-98.
Dr. James Patrick. Staunton, Virginia. 9-16-94.
Gray Pifer. Mount Crawford, Virginia. 9-13-77.
Frances Price. Shenandoah County, Virginia. 4-19-97.
Jon Ritenour. Rockingham County, Virginia. 2-10-94.
James H. Roadcap Jr. Rockingham County, Virginia. 4-27-98.
Kathleen Roller. Bridgewater, Virginia. 4-23-97.
Paul Roller. Endless Caverns, Virginia. 7-29-95.
Richard Roller. Dayton, Virginia. 6-15-95.
Robert Roller. Winston-Salem, North Carolina. 6-17-95.
Randall and Samuel S. Shank. Broadway, Virginia. 5-21-97 and 5-22-97.
William H. Sipe. McGaheysville, Virginia. 5-23-95.
Bill Sites. Augusta County, Virginia. 5-4-80.
Joan Sparks. Mount Crawford, Virginia. 8-14-95.
James O. Swope. Bridgewater, Virginia. 1-30-94.

Ruby Dunn Thacker. Harrisonburg, Virginia. 2-12-94.
Minnie Wagenschein. Bridgewater, Virginia. 7-1-95.
George L. Wenger. Edom, Virginia. 2-20-96.
John Wenger. Rockingham County, Virginia. 2-22-96.
Norman Wenger. Rockingham County, Virginia. 4-13-97.
Rachel White. Harrisonburg, Virginia. 7-2-95.
James Wilson. Mossy Creek, Virginia. 2-27-94.
Glenn Wine. Augusta County, Virginia. 9-5-93.
Louis Wood. Augusta County, Virginia. 11-12-94.
Sue Hamersly Yancey. Rockingham County, Virginia. 6-4-96.
Blair and Maxine Zirkle. Shenandoah County, Virginia. 4-29-98.

Acknowledgments

What follows is the most important part of this book. Without the generous help of the individuals mentioned here there would not be a history of the thirteen days of devastation in the Shenandoah Valley in the fall of 1864. The research required to construct a picture of an event which has heretofore been neglected and/or basically misunderstood for more than a century was daunting. Two people in particular were instrumental in bringing clarity to the subject. George Hansbrough of Page County has long been a friend and has a greater overall knowledge of the American Civil War than anyone else I know. Besides imparting unfailing encouragement, George gave assistance on some of the most productive searches for documents and sites pertaining to the subject. Dr. W. Cullen Sherwood of Harrisonburg, friend, private tutor, and Confederate artillery historian, helped me build a bridge from the nineteenth century to the dawn of the twenty-first. His counsel was invaluable and his patience boundless. My unending thanks to both of you.

In the bibliography there is a list of people who shared stories of the Civil War and photographs that have been passed down through the generations in their families. I thank them for trusting me to tell their stories.

A special thank you to Debbie Hansbrough and Phoebe Sherwood. Debbie was very helpful with the research, and Phoebe kept lines of communication running smoothly.

Jeff Mellott of Harrisonburg, who made the legislation for the Shenandoah Valley Battlefield Commission understandable and kept it before the public in his role as a member of the Bohemian Brigade, kept my spirits up, and offered many worthwhile suggestions.

Three historians who have been an inspiration to me through the years offered comments that smoothed out the rough edges and gave the pages a polish born of experience. The kindness and candor of Robert K. Krick and Jeffry Wert will always be remembered with appreciation. Thanks to Dr. James I. Robertson Jr. for his initial suggestions.

The staff of the Alexander Mack Library of Bridgewater College was the rock around which the tide of this book swirled. Along with Chief Librarian Ruth Greenawalt, Thelma Miller, Terry Barkley, Audrey Moats, Carin Teets, and Phyllis Ward all went the extra mile to contribute to this book.

Chris Bolgiano, head of Special Collections of the Carrier Library of James Madison University, never failed to answer my requests for information.

Dr. Richard Sommers of the U.S. Army Military History Institute at Carlisle Barracks,

Pennsylvania, lived up to his reputation as an historian and archivist of uncommon ability. He and staff members David Keough, James Baughman, and Pamela Cheney brought manuscripts to my attention that added considerably to the narrative. A special thank you is extended to Michael Winey and Randy Hackenburg of the Photographs Division for their help in searching the collections for needed images.

Gayle Cooper and Barb Fehse of the Manuscripts Division of the Alderman Library of the University of Virginia helped me to locate materials relating to the subject in their extensive collections.

Rodney Ross of the National Archives in Washington, D.C., will forever have my gratitude for supplying the key that allowed me to travel through the maze of the Southern Claims Commission papers. Mary Giunta gave freely of her time, both on and off the job, at the National Archives. Her knowledge of the life of Lt. John Rodgers Meigs is probably unparalleled and was generously shared with me. Also, I would like to thank Regina Davis of the National Archives Publications Office for her patience and efficiency in preparing materials for my inspection.

Paula Bowders Hogan, a dear friend and colleague from my days with the Library of Congress, was there when I needed her most. Her contribution to this book is beyond words. Also many thanks to Bill Hogan for his valuable assistance to a stranger.

Maj. Diane Jacob and Regenia Roethler of the Institute Archives of the Virginia Military Institute were very helpful in checking for materials pertaining to the latter part of the Civil War in the Valley.

Lisa McCown in the Special Collections section of the Leyburn Library of Washington and Lee University brought several obscure and interesting papers to my attention.

I would also like to acknowledge the help of the late Grace Showalter of the Menno Simons Historical Library of Eastern Mennonite University in Harrisonburg, Virginia. Her enthusiasm and talents will always be remembered. Lois Bowman, who is Grace's worthy successor, was generous with her time, and her assistance is appreciated.

The staff of the Rockingham County Public Library was always available; many of its members deserve individual recognition. Sincere thanks for being so helpful for so long to Linda Derrer, Sue Finn, Susan Huffman, Lois Jones, Pat Manley, Eileen Nelson, Sandra Shifflett, Anna Steele, and Nick Whitmer.

Marcelle Niday of the Waynesboro Public Library guided me through its admirable holdings, which opened several doors.

Dr. Owen Graves of Harrisonburg made me aware of the existence of a letter written by a witness to the burning around Dayton, and Lewis Leigh Jr. of Leesburg graciously gave me permission to quote from it. Owen also provided materials which pertained to Woodson's rangers.

A word of praise for my 'Yankee' friend, Fred Daniels of Bridgewater. Near the completion of the manuscript Fred acted as my rear guard and aided me with his superior firepower.

Many thanks to Larry Bowers of Bridgewater for first showing me the George Sipe memoir and to Dr. George Hedrick for allowing me further access to the document.

Joseph H. ("Jody") Meyerhoeffer of Dayton read the manuscript and gave me the benefit of his extensive knowledge of that area.

John Elliott, who straddles the line between Rockingham County and Shenandoah County, lent two important federal letters to the project early on and offered other encouragement as well.

Many thanks to Samuel Horst, author of *Mennonites in the Confederacy*, for offering valuable suggestions and materials.

Dr. Ellsworth Kyger of Bridgewater continues to be a mentor and has shared his wealth of knowledge in so many areas of common interest.

Lena Fuller of Maurertown in Shenandoah County took a stranger under her wing and opened the Levi Pitman diaries to him.

Ed Latham of Bridgewater opened the lines of communication with members of the Wenger family; much valuable information came from the contacts.

Besides relating accounts of the Rinker family of Shenandoah County, Daniel W. Burruss of Rinkerton provided leads to important manuscripts pertaining to the burning in that area.

Jim Britt of WSVA Radio in Harrisonburg has for the past six years allowed me to share my interest in the Civil War with the public. The program we do with George Hansbrough brought forth stories and manuscripts from the listeners that became valuable components of this book.

Mary Jo Keller of Fisher, West Virginia, responded to a call for family memories of the Burning with the memoir of Bettie Miley Robinette of Shenandoah County, which told how the Clover Hill Plantation fared at the hands of the Federals.

Robert Roller of Winston-Salem, North Carolina, contributed the brief, yet pithy, reminiscence of his ancestor J. S. Roller. This came to the author's attention through Robert's brother, Richard Roller of Dayton, who shared a wonderful story of the Roller family on the radio one morning a couple of years ago.

Harry E. Long of New Market provided information on the Moore family of Shenandoah County, as did Sarah Winters McCue for the McCue family of Augusta County.

Faye Witters and the late Maxine Early were constant, as always, with their help on my visits to the Harrisonburg-Rockingham County Historical Society Library in Dayton, Virginia.

Anita Cummins of the Society of Port Republic Preservationists went beyond the call of duty to help me sort through the society's holdings.

James Wilson of James Madison University and Mossy Creek helped with information on iron furnaces, and Janet and Earl Downs of Good's Mill were generous with advice on the mill operations in the Valley.

Dr. Clarence Geier of James Madison University helped me to go through manuscripts in the possession of the Clarke County Historical Association, while Mary Morris, the association's archivist, offered untiring and fruitful assistance.

Nancy Garber, Harrisonburg's most acclaimed archivist, has always kept her eyes open for materials on the subject of the devastation which occurred between the mountains so long ago. She is a kind and generous friend.

William Kyger of the Rockingham County Board of Supervisors shares an avid interest in this period of history in the Valley; he has been a constant source of encouragement.

I owe a debt to Nancy Hess of Harrisonburg for making available material from her extensive research for her own books on Valley families and institutions.

Randy Stover, as always, encouraged and prodded, and he eventually made me move forward on this project.

I would also like to thank the personnel of the Virginia State Library, the University of Vermont Library, the Augusta County Library, the Page County Library, the Shenandoah County Library, and the City of Staunton Public Library for help that they were probably not aware of rendering.

To my publisher, Katherine Tennery, and her editorial assistant, Tracey Barger: thank you both for all of your good work.

Richard C. Swanson of Hamilton, Virginia, has been involved with almost all of the creative endeavors of my adult life. As a patron, and more importantly as a friend, he has given unfailing support.

My son David shares with me the need to change thought into substance. I know he has an understanding of the tides that eat away at the sands of my time here on earth and thus overlooks my faults. The depth of his talent inspires me to do better work.

Lastly, though always first in my heart, Miriam, you have helped me to turn another corner, as you have from the beginning. You have made everything possible.

I sincerely hope that I have not overlooked anyone who has contributed to the creation of this book; I know what it can feel like. If I have, it was inadvertent, and I ask your pardon for any omissions caused by my weary memory.

Index